Riccardo Martinelli
Philosophy of Music

Riccardo Martinelli

Philosophy of Music

A History

Translated by Sarah De Sanctis

DE GRUYTER

The translation of this work has been funded by SEPS

Segretariato Europeo per le Pubblicazioni Scientifiche
Via Val d'Aposa 7 – 40123 Bologna – Italy
seps@seps.it – www.seps.it

This work has originally been published in Italian language: I filosofi e la musica
© Il Mulino, Bologna 2012. www.mulino.it

ISBN 978-3-11-062627-8
e-ISBN (PDF) 978-3-11-062741-1
e-ISBN (EPUB) 978-3-11-062472-4

Library of Congress Control Number: 2019949282

Bibliographic information published by the Deutsche Nationalbibliothek
The Deutsche Nationalbibliothek lists this publication in the Deutsche Nationalbibliografie;
detailed bibliographic data are available in the Internet at http://dnb.dnb.de.

© 2021 Walter de Gruyter GmbH, Berlin/Boston
This volume is text- and page-identical with the hardback published in 2019.
Printing and binding: CPI books GmbH, Leck

www.degruyter.com

Preface

Today, interest in the philosophy of music is stronger than in the past: publications are multiplying, international conferences are being organised and associations dedicated to the study of the subject are flourishing. In many cases, though, this is not matched by increased awareness of the historical foundations of philosophical thought about music. When I started working on the project that is presented here in the English translation, the ground was practically uncultivated, so to speak. Let me be clear: there were several excellent studies on many individual authors or periods, without which this book would not have been possible. What was missing, however, was a general historical reconstruction of the philosophy of music, from its origins to the contemporary world. I do not believe that this shortcoming is due to the fact that nobody has bothered to put together materials from different eras. What's at stake is a deeper problem, which concerns the precise definition of the subject matter of the work. Without claiming to exhaustively clarify a question of such magnitude, in this preface written for the English edition I would like to shed light on some issues that have emerged from discussions following the original publication of the volume in Italian. Further methodological aspects are dealt with more extensively in the Introduction.

The expression "philosophy of music", which appears in the title of the present book, is controversial, to the point that some prefer the more neutral expression "philosophy and music". From a historical point of view, it is especially relevant that contemporary reflection—however one wishes to label it—is the heir to a number of very ancient philosophical problems. Some of these have essentially remained unchanged over time, while others have lost their relevance, leaving room for new perspectives. The Italian title of the book (*I filosofi e la musica*) was intended to underline the open character of the investigation; the content of the book would perhaps be even more precisely defined in the ancient way, as *quid philosophi de musica senserint*. In all this, the emphasis must be firmly placed on philosophy: on the fact, that is, that I have investigated *philosophical* ideas and doctrines on music. Musicians, writers and intellectuals in general have written interesting and, in some cases, *very* interesting things about music, each from their own particular point of view. These works, however, are not covered here because they do not have a specifically philosophical orientation and relevance. The line of demarcation, of course, is not always easy to draw; however, this only concerns a minority of cases. Also, my focus on philosophy is not peremptory: by way of comparison, it may be worth extending the discourse to neighbouring fields of research. However, it seemed to me that philosophical arguments already offered a sufficiently broad and defined framework for the analysis.

Because of its acclaimed ability to affect the human soul, music has always received particular attention from philosophers, who often feared or condemned its sensual power, while however envying its persuasiveness. It is no coincidence, therefore, that already in Plato music and philosophy are combined in a relationship of attraction and repulsion that runs through much of the subsequent thought, at least up to Adorno. Seen from this perspective, music is by no means a marginal and accessory theme, but rather one of the most important objects of philosophical reflection. This thesis may seem exaggerated, yet one of the tasks of this book is to show that it is not so. In reflecting on music, philosophers are confronted with some pressing general problems of a metaphysical, ethical and anthropological (and not just aesthetic) nature; indeed, they are often led to reflect on philosophy itself. In contemporary terms, one could say that music raises issues that are not only philosophical but also meta-philosophical. Of course, it is impossible to generalize any further: to say more, it is necessary to go into the merits of philosophical thought in different epochs and thinkers. This requires lowering the curtain on this preface and moving on to the text. However, it is still possible, at a preliminary level, to identify general recurring ways of approaching the question. I will support the thesis that there are essentially three fundamental lines of philosophical thought on music, which I will provisionally indicate by the names of Pythagoreanism, Aristotelianism and scepticism.

1. *Pythagoreanism* is frequently presented as the main philosophical answer to the question about the nature of music. After all, even at the level of common sense, the idea that music is significantly related to mathematics is widespread. But Pythagoreanism is not only about underlining the role of numbers in relation to the musical phenomenon. Some speak of the Pythagorean-Platonic current: I chose to avoid this expression in the present volume because it is too general, but it nevertheless has a *raison d'être* in that it underlines the fundamental role of the psychological element, with its ethical-political implications, in this approach to the problem. Mathematical proportions, through the exercise of music, penetrate the soul almost getting hold of it, with two possible outcomes: the establishment of a virtuous harmony in the subject, or vice versa the latter's fearful and dangerous upheaval. This perspective already anticipates the twofold —celestial or demonic—character of music, destined to great popularity in the medieval and modern ages.

2. It is not always obvious in the literature that Aristotle was the first to show a clear alternative to the perspective illustrated so far. Rather, it is sometimes suggested that Aristotle, in substantial continuity with Plato, would simply

have given more space to an authentically aesthetic enjoyment of music. On closer inspection, however, Aristotle made the first clear formulation of the fact that the key to the problem lies in the analogy between music and verbal discourse. Hence his focus on the voice (*phoné*), i.e. the element within which both spheres are defined. On a theoretical level, Aristotle's student Aristoxenus would be the one to formalize the double articulation of voice into word and song; but it was Aristotle who developed the consequences of this shift of attention. Unlike in tragedy, action is represented in music only in an analogical way, so that the specifically musical catharsis appears weaker and is rendered somewhat virtual by the presence of infinite possibilities to fill it with meaning. However, musical catharsis is no less important or effective for this reason: on the contrary, it would be possible to argue for the opposite thesis.

3. On the basis of arguments found in the tradition of the rhetors and probably of the sophists, a third fundamental philosophical option was established in the Hellenistic age, which it would be short-sighted to label as minor. I have defined this option as *scepticism* also in view of the common meaning of the term, even if it is not typical of scepticism alone in the strict sense. According to these authors, the reflection on music must first be brought back to reasonably circumscribed terms: it makes no sense to deal with it in a context that is full of metaphysical or ethical references. The traditional relationship between music and ethos is here under attack: music cannot express, or instil in listeners, any "character", no more than, for example, culinary art can. The controversy is not pretentious and one would be wrong to disregard such arguments. Traditional anecdotes and myths (think of Orpheus, who proved capable of convincing the underworld gods to return to him his bride Eurydice) have in fact a metaphorical value, while sceptics constantly remind us of the actual daily fruition of music, in which—like it or not—there are no wonders.

Taking a further step forward, it is not difficult to translate the above tripartition into dehistoricized terms, starting from the basic elements that are underlined in each current: the physical-mathematical order, the analogy with language, the call to direct experience. In this sense, we could therefore speak of naturalism, phenomenology and empiricism.

1. In today's philosophical debate it is common to indicate as "naturalistic" all those theories which, in the different fields, leave the solution of some problem to science. From this point of view, one could easily argue that, as regards the philosophy of music, Pythagoras was the first of a long series of naturalists. It goes without saying that the historical forms of naturalism changed with the evolution of thought and scientific knowledge (even if there have been decidedly anti-Pythagorean scientists), so that the explanations provided e.g. by Mers-

enne, Leibniz or Helmholtz are quite different, even though they are all referable to a naturalistic perspective.

2. Leaving aside its specific historical use, the term "phenomenology" should be understood here in its broadest sense, which is also widespread in the contemporary philosophical debate. What characterizes this position is the idea that there is a phenomenal field, which can be defined primarily in relation to intentionality. In this case, the reference is to the sound that becomes *musical* (Aristoxenus's *phthongos*) when it is the object of a secondary or reflective intentionality, so to speak. In other words, it no longer counts as an object of the world: it is de-naturalized. Once any sign-function has been eliminated, the sound no longer stands for the source that emits it but begins to only signify itself within a given system of musical references.

3. In this context, the term "empiricism" should be referred to the views that strongly emphasize what happens concretely when you hear a piece of music. If you have the intellectual honesty to approach the issue in an unscrupulous way, you have to recognize that what emerges subjectively is quite little. Of course you could argue that the problem is methodological: when, as an empiricist, I stop *playing along* with music and try to observe what happens to me when I listen to it, I do the same thing as someone who tries to catch the moment when he falls asleep—clearly I can't find anything and end up embracing a sceptical perspective. In defence of the empiricists, one can, however, object that their position is a valid antidote against the ethical-metaphysical excesses of which the debate is saturated, and which sometimes prevent the immediate and genuine fruition of music.

Like any generalisation, the proposed tripartition does not aim to capture every single aspect and every nuance of the philosophers who have dealt with music. It can however suggest a transversal reading path, alternative to the chronological order that is adopted here for obvious reasons. Yet, my work is completely independent from the proposed threefold division, which does not refer to the articulation underlying the structure of the present book. The distinction between the naturalistic, phenomenological and empirical currents in the philosophy of music, if anything, should be understood as a result of the research work in the history of the philosophy of music. This also allows me to emphasize that historical research should not be understood as a mere doxographic repertoire, but as something that can influence our theoretical beliefs, sometimes enriching them in a virtuous feedback mechanism.

Leaving it to the reader to verify the adequacy of this reading proposal, I will limit myself to mentioning one example, that of Kant's philosophy. Despite the great amount of critical work on the topic, it cannot be said that there is full clarity about the position on music expressed in the *Critique of the Power of*

Judgement, an issue that could derive at least in part from the lack of an adequate overall historical reference framework. As far as I'm concerned, I think that Kant's reflection on music is part of the "phenomenological" strand (in the sense specified above, and within those very precise limits) because it focuses on the analogy between verbal and musical language, the latter characterized by the disappearance of the semantic aspect and by the persistence of the only affective accents that distinguish the musical "modulation". For Kant, the mathematical component is only the precondition for music to be intelligible: we could add that it is somewhat like the laws of statics, which make it possible for a building not to be reduced to a heap of rubble, but are not enough to determine its architectural value.

Finally, one last problem deserves mention due to the rapid progress of studies in the philosophy of music, which I mentioned at the beginning of this preface. One might think that the concluding section of this book, dedicated to the philosophy of music in the contemporary age and in particular to analytical philosophy, needs to be updated. In fact, it would be difficult to deny that many interesting studies have appeared in the years following the original publication of the volume in 2012. However the final paragraph, which ideally ends with the twenty-first century, was already largely incomplete at the time of the first draft. Like other parts of the book (I am thinking in particular of medieval philosophy) it did not and does not claim to be exhaustive. Rather, it should be considered as an orientation and an invitation to further study, both for the readers and for the researchers who want to devote themselves to a subject that, in itself, deserves much more than a single volume.

Trieste, July 2019

Contents

Introduction —— 1

First Chapter: The Art of the Muses —— 5
1   Pythagoras's Hammers —— 5
2   Plato and Supreme Music —— 10
3   The voice of Aristotle —— 15
4   Aristoxenus: the Harmonic Science —— 20
5   The End of the Ancient World. Augustine —— 24
6   The Middle Ages —— 33

Second Chapter: Harmony and Disenchantment —— 40
1   Humanists and Scientists —— 40
2   From Descartes to Leibniz —— 50
3   Sounds and the Light of Reason: Rousseau —— 56
4   Music and Play in Kant —— 63

Third Chapter: The Century of Music —— 71
1   Romantic Acoustics —— 71
2   From the Romantics to Schopenhauer —— 79
3   Hegel and Trembling —— 87
4   Musical Science and Aesthetics —— 92
5   The Case of Nietzsche —— 99

Fourth Chapter: Dissonances —— 106
1   Bloch and the Art of Utopia —— 106
2   Adorno: Philosophy of Music —— 110
3   Phenomenologies of Listening —— 118
4   Logic and the Symbol: Wittgenstein and Susanne Langer —— 125
5   Music and Analytic Philosophy —— 131

References —— 143

Index of Names —— 160

Subject Index —— 165

Introduction

This book is about music in the history of philosophy. In more traditional terms, one could say it is a history of the philosophy of music. However, it is important to note that this is no subdiscipline aimed at applying philosophical theories to the subject under discussion (music). Rather, the philosophical discourse relates to music through most of its facets: metaphysics, ethics, logic, aesthetics, psychology, anthropology, philosophy of nature, philosophy of language. This is why the present work does not assign a hegemonic role to aesthetics, as many aspects of the philosophical reflection on music fall outside of its domain. Moreover, while the history of musical aesthetics traditionally draws on heterogeneous sources, here I chose to mainly focus on the philosophical discourse and its typical argumentative modes. It goes without saying that this approach doesn't underestimate in any way musical aesthetics or other disciplines like the history of science, which often goes hand in hand with the history I'm reconstructing in this book.

At first glance, music and philosophy seem to be two very different human activities, as far apart as the soft sensuality of singing and the silent rigor of rational thought. Yet, since antiquity, philosophers have posited a secret affinity between music and philosophy, which irreversibly intertwined their destinies. If philosophy is not ashamed to qualify as "supreme music", music seems to be the bearer of a truth inaccessible to logos, which echoes from supreme celestial heights or from the most hidden depths of the human soul. Music is therefore not a philosophical topic like any other. While being different from philosophy, music challenges it, forcing it to address questions of capital importance and ultimately its very *raison d'être*.

Let me give an overview of the most recurring themes, to illustrate what this work is about. As mentioned, I often discuss the issue of the relationship between music and philosophy, noting how in some cases they tend to coincide while in others they don't. One has to keep in mind the ethical tension that runs through much of what has been said on the subject, in different forms depending on the historical period. The strong impact of music on human beings is a peculiarity that makes it akin to, and yet different from, philosophy, in a dynamic of attraction and repulsion. Occasionally philosophers have acted based on the wish to regulate the uses of music in the context of social life. More frequently a music genre, an aspect (sacred or profane music, vocal or instrumental music), a style, a single composer or even a specific piece have been invested with particular significance, shedding light on the meaning of music as a whole.

Such considerations have usually been supported by an explanation of the effect of music. In this regard, special attention must go to scientific perspectives. As a first approximation, mathematical sciences characterize the ancient and medieval times, while physical, physiological and psychological ones prevail in the modern age. However, it is pointless to attempt to draw sharp distinctions, because the ancients also focused on physical acoustics and auditory physiology, and arithmetical models or the link between music and astronomy did not disappear with the scientific revolution. From a different perspective, the analogy between music and language marked many discussions as well. The human voice, in its double form of speech and song, often takes a paradigmatic role for the conceptual clarification of musical experience. This trend unfolds along several lines, which involve either the analysis of the links (rhythm and intonation) between music and poetic language, or more formalized investigations like those of logic and philosophy of language.

Another important branch is that of philosophical psychology: how we perceive sound has often been deemed decisive to fully understand the phenomenon of music. Philosophers have tried to shed light on the meaning of *listening* as a specific form of intentionality, opposed to simple *hearing*. Thinkers have also developed the idea of a secret deep bond between music and history. The enemy of fate, according to Adorno's famous definition ("*Musik ist der Feind des Schicksals*"), music conveys the hope (or utopia) of a humankind at peace with itself: nothing like its elusive expressiveness manages to give voice to the deepest authentic human needs, often denied in society. Furthermore, the modern age specifically discusses the value and meaning of Greek music. Then, a real musical controversy between the ancients and the moderns starts in the Renaissance: while arguing for the superiority of the Ancients, many philosophers express some of the most interesting topics related to music—musicians, instead, generally defend the Moderns.

At times, this reconstruction naturally intertwines with parallel issues that border on cultural anthropology, such as the relation between music and myth. It is in this complex texture of references that arise the perennial aesthetic issues about music: the role of feelings and emotions; genres and ways in which music interacts with poetry, theatre and dance; the "formalistic" side of music as opposed to the expression (or "representation") of human action or emotional experiences, not to mention the systematic comparison between music and the other arts as well as the special ontological status of the musical artwork.

It is easy to see how vast this material is. My choice has been to mainly privilege what refers to the *musical experience:* that is, to "real" music, made of sounds and voices, which can be heard, sung or performed. Regardless of the extreme historical variability of musical practice, this extraordinary experience—

which unites ancients and moderns, philosophers and ordinary people—provides a benchmark that no historian can ignore. However, this choice is far from obvious, first of all because it does not cover the entire semantic range of the word *music* in the history of thought. Even though I haven't failed to refer to a somewhat "intellectual" music, which cannot be heard because it is made of numbers rather than sounds, there are at least two reasons—in terms of subject and methodology—why I didn't overestimate it. First of all, the relation between concrete experience and intelligible music is much stronger than one would think. The reference to the musical experience therefore doesn't equal an underestimation of the metaphysical elements of the debate, but rather highlights some of its deepest motivational roots. Furthermore, it must be acknowledged that it is simply more interesting to focus on a concept of music akin to the one we are accustomed to today.

The fact that this perspective cannot encompass everything is not a bad thing as such, in that I had to make conscious choices within the vast universe of the available sources. This selection aims to keep within reasonable length reflections on a timespan that goes from Pythagoras to our age. I have given relatively small space to topics like the philosophers' individual competences, participation in music activities, personal relationships with musicians, and work as composers or performers. When necessary, for instance in the case of Rousseau, Nietzsche, Adorno or Jankélévitch, I have of course considered these factors, but only in view of understanding their philosophical positions. I have given little or no space to the thoughts on music expressed by those who are not part of the history of philosophy: musicians, but also musicologists, literates, and essayists.

It is worth mentioning that my methodology is thematic and not axiological: that is, it doesn't presume that philosophy has some privileged access to music. However, the opposite thesis seems unconvincing as well: embracing the image of philosophers trying to annex the peaceful reign of sounds to the authoritarian empire of reason, means giving up one of the most fascinating adventures of human thought on the basis of an unfounded prejudice. I have also left outside of my investigation "music theory" in the strict sense, e.g. the ancient and modern construction of scales and modes, or musical temperament, etc. These issues, the importance of which is not in question, do not identify the essence of what music offers to philosophical reflection. Similarly, the short space I dedicated to the evolution of musical forms is not due to a lack of appreciation for their role, but rather to the need to delegate any further analysis in the field to another work.

As much as possible, I have tried to spare the reader any technical jargon related to music theory and grammar or to the physical-mathematical aspects involved. Of course, basic knowledge in both fields will facilitate the understanding of the topics I am dealing with. As for critical literature, I have tried to privilege accessible texts in English language. Starting from the works mentioned in the footnotes it will be easy to find further sources of information.

Partly trusting in the easy access to these kinds of resources in the web, I have chosen not to include an extensive iconography even when it would have been more than merely decorative, as in Chladni's acoustic figures. Finally, for reasons related not only to lack of space, I have chosen not to take a stance in relation to the ideas presented. I have rather decided to expose the lines of reasoning, and sometimes the polemics, between the philosophers in question, letting them speak for themselves.

First Chapter
The Art of the Muses

1 Pythagoras's Hammers

By the term *music* (*mousikè techne:* art of the Muses) the Greeks referred to the profound unity between music, poetry, dance and theatre. However, this fascinating conception, unparalleled in modernity, didn't fail to distinguish between different areas. If Plato states that harmony and rhythm must adapt to the lyrics it is precisely because he grasps the specificity of music proper, which for him is subordinate to the higher forms of poetry. Compared to the traditional tripartition in harmonics, rhythmic and metric, it is harmony that identifies the specifically musical element, whereas rhythm and meter are also characteristic of poetry and the latter of dance as well.

Harmony shouldn't be intended as a polyphonic composition of different simultaneous sounds, as opposed to "melody". This conception, typically modern, was unthinkable for the Greeks, as simultaneity had no bearing at all for their music practice: even the late custom of associating different instruments didn't lead to polyphonic or harmonic forms. *Harmonia* comes from a verb (*harmozo*) which means to accommodate, to adapt, in the sense in which a carpenter fits two pieces together. In music, the term refers to the organization of two coherent sound elements, mostly intended as the acute and the grave. The plural "harmonies" (*harmoniai*) stands for the forms of sound organization described by ethnic terms (Dorian, Phrygian, Ionian, Lydian, etc.) and endowed with an ethical connotation; these should be distinguished from the scales (*systemata*) and the "genera" or "tunings" (diatonic, chromatic, enharmonic).[1] These musical uses, however, are far from exhausting the semantic scope of the term "harmony", which refers to the entire order of the cosmos and the human microcosm—ideas of the utmost importance in Western culture.[2] Harmony is then the soul of *mousiké*; but on the other hand the term widely exceeds the field of music. In Heraclitus the "most beautiful harmony" is independent from music; however, there are also musical references: "harmony consists of opposite tension, like that of the bow and the lyre".[3] In order to go into further depth, one cannot but start with Pythagoras and his followers.

---

1 A thoroughgoing treatment of these questions is given by Barker (2007, p. 6–18). An in-depth lexical analysis is offered by Rocconi (2003, *passim*). See also Lippman (1964).
2 Cf. Spitzer (1963, *passim*) and the essays collected in Wallace/MacLachlan (1991).
3 Cf. Diels/Kranz (1952, 22 B8 and B51).

Paradoxically, there aren't many ancient sources on Pythagoras, but much information comes from late antiquity—especially thanks to the neo-Pythagorean Iamblichus. However, by then some legends that had spread soon after the philosopher's death had fully blended with the truth: hence the idea of Pythagoras being able to hear the music of the spheres, a ubiquitous thaumaturge with a golden thigh, whose soul reincarnated several times.[4] In the Pythagorean doctrine, reality consists of opposites whose unity is called *harmony*, a concept that applies primarily to the celestial motions and the soul.[5] Like any movement, the rotation of the heavenly spheres generates sound, producing a harmony that humans cannot hear as they are accustomed to it from their birth. Likewise, the soul is the harmony of the body, of which it is the motor principle. This outlines a homogeneity between macrocosm and microcosm, both governed by harmony. These more rationalistic views must not make us forget that the Pythagorean circle was in other respects similar to a sect, to the point that it was often confused with Orphism for its adoption of the doctrine of the transmigration of souls.

Similarly, the central concept of the number—so important to Pythagoreanism—mustn't be understood in a solely rationalistic sense. The series of numbers 1, 2, 3 and 4 is the sacred *tetraktys:* number 10 (1 + 2 + 3 + 4), considered the "mathematical formula" of harmony. This brings us to the fundamental question of the relation between arithmetic ratios and musical consonances. For the Greeks, consonances (*symphoniai*) were only the intervals that we would now define octave, fifth and fourth. By using a monochord of his invention (a string-splitting bridge that slides over a notched board, thus allowing for an exact measurement of the proportions corresponding to different sounds), Pythagoras allegedly discovered that these intervals correspond to lengths of the string: the ratios are 2:1 for the octave, 3:2 for the fifth and 4:3 for the fourth.[6] Therefore, as can be seen, the numbers of the *tetraktys* make it possible to express all consonances. Also in regards to this discovery, though, there are no sources prior to late antiquity. Given the tendency of Pythagoreans and neo-Pythagoreans to attribute any innovation to their founder, one should be careful. This does not mean that the story is unfounded, but in the absence of reliable evidence the

---

[4] Iamblichus (1991, par. 15.66). For a comprehensive introduction to Pythagoreanism, cf. Huffman (2014, *passim*). In fact, after travelling in Egypt and the East, Pythagoras moved from Samos to Crotone, where he attracted a politically influential community. However, he died in exile in Metapontum and his followers were killed: the few survivors recreated communities in Taranto and Thebes.

[5] Lloyd (1966, p. 94).

[6] The attribution to Pythagoras of the invention of the "monochord" is controversial, as is the time of its discovery. See Burkert (1962, p. 353).

critics are divided. To reconstruct it in a plausible way I will therefore subvert the historical order of the protagonists in order to respect that of sources: I'll start from the Pythagoreans, continue with historical Pythagoras and conclude with some observations on the legendary Pythagoras.

Hippasus from Metapontum has been credited with witty experiments aimed at showing the correspondence between consonances and numerical ratios. It seems that he melted bronze discs to identify different levels of thickness such that the respective sounds would have rendered the octave, fifth and fourth.[7] With second generation Pythagoreans the word "harmony" acquired a new meaning, when Philolaus (or perhaps Archytas) referred to the mathematical ratio previously called "subcontrary" as "harmonic". Given four terms a, b, c, d, the latter is the mean expressed by the $(a-b):a = (c-d):c$ formula, which is distinct from the arithmetic mean $(a-b = c-d)$ and the geometric one $(a:b = c:d)$. The smallest numbers that satisfy the requirements of the harmonic proportion are 12, 9, 8 and 6.

Plato's friend, the philosopher and politician Archytas, posited that only one sound is perceived in consonance.[8] This is a very important principle: simultaneity, unknown in practice, is revealed as what distinguishes *symphoniai*. According to Aristotle, Pythagoreans also referred to some letters (ξ, ψ and ζ: *xi, psi* and *zeta*) as consonances corresponding to the three musical consonances: here, too, two sounds become one, in the same sense.[9] Note that the criterion in question has nothing to do with numbers; after all, to claim that consonances are defined by some numerical ratios one needs to know what consonances are—Archytas, indeed, wasn't satisfied with the empirical reference to musical practice. In terms of physics, it seems that Archytas linked the pitch of the sound to the greater or smaller speed of the movement. He makes the example of a rod shaken slowly or quickly, which leaves it unclear whether he thought of the speed of the body or of the air; but whichever interpretation one chooses, there is still an objective criterion at play, because the speed is doubled in the octave.[10] It seems

---

[7] See Diels/Kranz (1952, 18 A12). Perhaps the "art of Glaucus" in Plato (1938a, p. 373 [*Phaed.* 108d]) refers to studies of this kind, carried out by Glaucus of Rhegium. Following Theon of Smyrna, Lasus of Hermione and the school of Hippasus allegedly have carried out a similar procedure, using two vases, one filled with water to different degrees and one left empty: Diels/Kranz (1952, 18 A13).
[8] See Diels/Kranz (1952, 44 A24; 47 B2; 18 A15; 47 A18). Archytas also codified the diatonic, chromatic and enharmonic tunings. Cf. Barker (2007, p. 292).
[9] Aristotle (1935, p. 299 [*Metaph.* 1093a 20]). For the English translation of Aristotle's and Plato's works I will resort to the book series The Loeb Classical Library.
[10] Diels/Kranz (1952, 47 B1; 47 A19a). Cf. Barker (2007, p. 28).

that Archytas also invented the so-called "rattle" (a handle provided with a sprocket around which a stacked body rotates): not only a toy to entertain children, but also a model to investigate the relationship between speed and frequency.[11]

All these arguments presuppose that numbers can be applied to musical consonances. Even if it cannot be demonstrated, it is therefore plausible that this discovery was made by Pythagoras. Other sources suggest that Pythagoras might have anticipated another keystone of the ancient conception of music: the doctrine of the *ethos* of music genres, later codified by Damon of Athens, who can at least partly be connected to Pythagoreanism (see below, par. 2). Indeed, Pythagoras is one of the many people mentioned in the ancient anecdotes about the power of music over the soul. Iamblichus wrote that Pythagoras once calmed down a young drunk lad who was about to commit some wicked acts, by starting to play appropriate music; a similar episode is attributed by others to Empedocles or Damon. It is more likely that music played a part in the purificatory practices adopted by the Pythagoreans, given its supposed ability to create order and harmony in the soul.[12] But literature is full of episodes attributed to Arion, Orpheus, Amphion and others, who used music to enchant animals, people and objects. This trait is common to other ancient civilizations, including the Jewish one, as attested by the famous passage *Samuel* 16:23 (David calms Saul with the harp) and many others. In this area, special attention must go to the myth of Eurydice, which inspired across the ages not only poets and musicians but also, as we shall see, philosophers. Accompanying a sublime prayer with his lyre, Orpheus was given the opportunity to redeem his beloved from Hades; but he turned back for fear that she was not following him and to see her again, thereby violating the pacts with the infernal deities and condemning Eurydice.[13]

To conclude, one shouldn't neglect the legendary Pythagoras, the mythical inventor credited with a number of discoveries on sounds, numbers and music. Indeed, *this* Pythagoras has been one of the most important reference points for music ever since antiquity. The achievements traditionally attributed to the philosopher therefore deserve attention, regardless of the historical veridicity of the facts narrated. The discovery of arithmetic ratios related to consonance, shrouded in darkness as far as historians are concerned, has been passed

---

[11] Aristotle (1932, p. 661 [*Pol.* 1340b 26]). Cf. also Diels/Kranz (1952, 47 A2).
[12] Iamblichus (1991, par. 25.112); cf. also Diels/Kranz (1952, 58 D1).
[13] Ovid (1951b, p. 65–69 [10, 17–59]). On the ancient Orphic tradition see Colli (1977, p. 118–289).

down in an anecdote of great beauty and persuasive power.[14] Reflecting on musical consonances, Pythagoras allegedly recognized them by divine inspiration in the sounds made by the hammers in the forge of a blacksmith, which he happened to be passing by. At first he assumed that the different sounds depended on the power with which the hammers were being hit. But after asking the blacksmith to exchange hammers Pythagoras understood that the pitch of the sound depended on the hammers, not the men's vigor. Discarding a hammer that was "out of tune" (immeasurable),[15] Pythagoras found that the weight of the hammers was in a proportion of 12:9:8:6. Combined together, the hammers reproduced the consonant intervals of octave for 2:1 (12:6), fifth for 3:2 (12:8 or 9:6) and fourth for 4:3 (12:9 or 8:6), in addition to the tone (9:8), the foundation of the Pythagorean scale. Come home, Pythagoras would have verified that these affinities could also be obtained by putting in traction ropes with different weights, by blowing reeds of corresponding lengths and even by striking fluid-filled vessels at various levels. In all these cases the application of the same arithmetic proportions found for the weight of the hammers gave rise to the corresponding harmonies. At this point Pythagoras moved on to the monochord, where again he found the consonances by dividing the length of the string according to the identified proportions. By analyzing the narrative we can distinguish a first "observational" phase in the forge, when the intervals are identified in the blows of hammers on the anvils; then an "experimental" stage, with weights affixed to the strings, reeds and water-filled vases; finally, a third phase of "theoretical" reconstruction and geometric formalization with the monochord.

However, the fact remains that none of the above-mentioned experiments has the desired outcome, except for the monochord. The chords whose length are in a ratio of 2:1, 3:2, 4:3 actually reproduce the intervals of octave, fifth and fourth, but everything else is physically false. Moreover, ancient sources do not attest strings pulled by weights, nor reeds or vases. It isn't too hard to imagine Archytas laughing at this ingenuity, if he had heard about it. Later additions have therefore introduced false elements into the discoveries attributed to Pythagoras—and unnecessarily so. This makes one wonder why such a thing happened. In this specific case, regardless of historical and physical reliability, the purpose of the tale seems to be to extend harmony to the whole of matter. In other words, the myth of Pythagoras' hammers—as I will call it from

---

[14] The episode can be found already in Nicomachus of Gerasa and Gaudentius, later in Iamblichus. We will refer to Boethius' version (Boethius 1867b, p. 196–198).
[15] For a wide-ranging interpretation of this, cf. Heller-Roazen (2011, *passim*).

now on—must be read backwards, starting from the monochord, where the proportions are actually valid. The latter are then extended to the ordered musical cosmos arising from the acoustic chaos of the forge, a place with a very special role in the "phonosphere" of antiquity.[16] Insofar as it expresses this need, the myth is somewhat similar to Plato's *Timaeus* (see below, par. 2), which is also focused on the metallurgical art.[17] In the late ancient world, music embraced the whole domain of reality and could be integrated in philosophical speculation, even at the cost of physical truth and (often) of a departure from musical practice. Would Pythagoras have appreciated that this view were attached to his name? We will never know.

2 Plato and Supreme Music

Just before taking the poison that will kill him, Socrates talks about a strange recurring dream he's been having in which he is told to "make music and work at it".[18] Surprisingly, though, the philosopher takes this injunction as an encouragement—like a runner being encouraged by bystanders—rather than an order to do something new. The reason for this is that Socrates is already "making" the greatest music (*megiste mousiké*): philosophy. This close relationship between music and philosophy can be also found elsewhere in Plato's works, for instance in the *Phaedrus*. In it, it is said that cicadas used to be human, but they got so lost in music that they died of starvation; they were then given the gift of being able to sing all life without worrying about food. In exchange for this, they were asked to tell the Muses about the ways in which humans tribute them: they report to Calliope and Urania about "those who pass lives in philosophy and who worship these Muses who are most concerned with heaven and with thought divine and human and whose music is the sweetest".[19] Diogenes Laertius talks about another of Socrates's dreams: in this one, he had a swan on his lap, "which all at once [...] put forth plumage, and flew away uttering a

---

16 Aristotle (1938, p. 195 [*De cael.* 290b]): "an experience like that of the coppersmith, who becomes by long habit indifferent to the din around him".
17 Brisson (1974, p. 36 ff.).
18 Plato (1938a, p. 211 [*Phaed.* 61a])
19 Plato (1938b, p. 513 [*Phaedr.* 259d]).

sweet note". The next day Socrates was introduced to Plato, and "thereupon he recognised in him the swan of his dream".[20]

These passages testify to how important music was in ancient thinking—so much so that Plato compares it to philosophy itself. However, it is important to note that the relationship between music and philosophy wasn't balanced: philosophy is the highest music, whereas music is not philosophy. The subordinate position of music is also confirmed by Plato's rigid distinction between licit and despicable music forms: indeed, the philosopher's ethical-musical conservatism can be summed up in his undisguised admiration for the aesthetic stasis of the Egyptians, who have been able to maintain for ten thousand years the sacred chants originally set up by Isis.[21] And yet Plato's position on music—as well as on other arts—is a bit more complicated than that. Upon closer inspection, the very starting point of this chapter—Socrates' recurring dream—suggests a different line of interpretation. In fact, Socrates states that he has previously interpreted his dream as an exhortation to practice philosophy, adding:

> But now, after the trial and while the festival of the god delayed my execution, I thought, in case the repeated dream really meant to tell me to make this which is ordinarily called music, I ought to do so and not to disobey. For I thought it was safer not to go hence before making sure that I had done what I ought, by obeying the dream and composing verses.[22]

As he is getting ready to die, Socrates now finds it best to follow the order *to the letter* and compose music in the most ordinary sense of the term (in ancient Greece). It is ironic indeed that Socrates, who never wrote about philosophy, should have left behind some musical poetry, including a hymn to Apollo of which one verse seems to have come down to us. One might take this passage as Plato's answer to *The Frogs*, where Aristophanes blames Socrates for despising music and the foundations of tragedy; and yet, elsewhere Plato reports that Socrates learned to play the cithara in his old days from someone named Connus.[23] Therefore, it seems that Socrates genuinely engaged with music at some point, even in the current sense of the word, as a votive offer.

---

20 Diogenes (1972a, p. 281 [3.5]). In the myth of Er in Plato (1937b, p. 513f. [*Resp.* 620a]), Orpheus' soul chooses to reincarnate in a swan (although the provided explanation has nothing to do with music).
21 Plato (1926, p. 103 [*Leg.* 656d–675]); elsewhere, Plato (1926, p. 113f. [*Leg.* 660 b–c]) also expresses admiration for the Cretans and Spartans.
22 Plato (1938a, p. 213 [*Phaed.* 61a–b]).
23 Brancacci (2008, p. 37f.). Connus is mentioned in Plato (1924b, p. 383 and 463 [*Euthyd.* 272c, 295d]) and in Plato (1929b, p. 337 [*Menex.* 235e]).

In the light of these different possible readings, it is worth clarifying what music was for Plato. The widest kind is that of "choreutics", which includes gymnastics and music because it affects both the body and the soul. Gymnastics is about rhythm (like music) and the movements of the *body*. As for music, Plato's starting point is the *voice* (*phoné*), endowed with a rhythm (like the moving body) and harmony understood as the balance of the acute and the grave.[24] Music also encompasses something akin to movement: melody (*melos*), which embraces rhythm and harmony as well as words (*logos*). In this very broad sense, gymnastics as a discipline of the body has its counterpart in music, which is the set of "the vocal actions which pertain to the training of the soul in excellence".[25] So, music is a melodic form involving metrical composition, rhythm and harmony, which plays an important part in the wider context of choreutics. In this respect, one should note that Plato's position on music changed over time: in the Socratic dialogues he seems to accept music as wisdom (*sophia*), but in later works this view is rejected.[26] This evolution of Plato's thought was mainly influenced by the Pythagoreans and Damon of Athens, who endorsed musical traditionalism because he thought different music genres could affect the character (ethos) and therefore have political consequences.[27]

In order to understand the meaning of music in Plato, one must first of all acknowledge that the sense of sight is by far the most prominent in his work. *Timaeus* is particularly relevant in this respect, claiming that eyesight is a gift the gods gave us mortals so that we could "behold the revolutions of Reason in the heavens and use them for the revolvings of reasoning that is within us"[28] and correct the natural disharmony of our souls. One should keep this in mind: in Plato's myth, the Demiurge fashions the world according to mathemat-

---

[24] Rhythm and harmony (order of movement and voice) together give life to the choral dance (*choreia*): Plato (1926a, p. 157 and 129 [*Leg.* 672e, 665a]). In Plato (1926a, p. 93 [*Leg.* 654a–b]) the origin of "chorus" is derived from joy (*chará*), and the choreia is given by the unity of dance and singing. See also Plato (1925, p. 223 [*Phileb.* 17c–d]) and, on the harmony of the acute and the grave, Plato (1921, p. 399 [*Soph.* 253b]) and (1938b, p. 543 [*Phaedr.* 268d–e]).
[25] Plato (1926a, p. 157 [*Leg.* 673a]).
[26] Moutsopoulos (1989, p. 404). According to Moutsopoulos, the evolution of Plato's position is marked by the "artistic", "magic" and "philosophical" aspects of music respectively, although the three elements sometimes blend together and cannot be easily distinguished.
[27] On music and ethos, the work of Hermann Abert is still valid (Abert 1899). On Damon of Athens (Damon of Oia) see Brancacci (2008, p. 7–34). Plato quotes Damon as a musical expert in Plato (1937a, p. 253 [*Resp.* 400b–c]) and, with some reservations, in Plato (1924a, p. 13, 71 and 79 [*Lach.* 180c–d, 197d, 200a–c]). On Plato and the Pythagoreans, see Pelosi (2010, p. 140).
[28] Plato (1929a, p. 107 [*Tim.* 47b]).

ical ratios traditionally related to music (think of Chalcidius' *Commentary*).[29] However, in *Timaeus* there is no reference to music, not even to the sound of celestial spheres, which instead appears in book ten of *Republic:* back from Hades, the warrior Er explains that Ananke (Necessity) holds the spindle of the heavens. The eight orbits revolve around it, each with a Siren singing a different note: the eight sounds together form "the concord of a single harmony".[30]

For Plato, therefore, the harmony of the world is best grasped by the *eyes of the soul* of the philosopher, educated to dialectics. The higher "chant" (*nomos*) of dialectics and its counterpart in seeing can be found in the sensible world: "[...] the strain which [the chant] executes, of which, though it belongs to the intelligible, we may see an imitation in the progress of the faculty of vision".[31] This statement is the key to understanding the effective function of music in Plato. Indeed, music is a further means to introduce harmony in the soul, which is particularly important especially in some stages of human life. After clarifying the function of sight, in *Timaeus* Plato shows that hearing, voice and rhythm serve the same purpose. Those who make "intelligent use" of it, do not derive "irrational pleasure" from musical harmony: rather, the latter serves "as an auxiliary to the inner revolution of the Soul, when it has lost its harmony, to assist in restoring it to order and concord with itself".[32] Hence the ethical-pedagogical importance of music to the ideal city and especially to the education of its "guardians".[33]

So, the effects of music must be strictly kept under control. There is a musical therapy for any trouble of the soul, and the remedy is not homeopathic but allopathic: one has to choose musical modes that are opposite to the pathological state of the soul.[34] Harmonic chants soothe newborns and children, who are very energetic by nature, as well as any grown-up prey to Bacchic frenzy, which makes the soul akin to incandescent metal—as ductile as a child's.[35] Something similar is said in the *Symposium*, more specifically in the words of Eryximachus: just like medicine brings harmony to the contrasts in the body (hot/cold, dry/

---

29 Chalcidius (2016, par. 1.40) on Plato (1929a, p. 67 [*Tim.* 35b–36b]). Brisson (1974, p. 332) convincingly argues against musical interpretations of Plato's text.
30 Plato (1937b, p. 503f. [*Resp.* 617b]).
31 Plato (1937b, p. 197 [*Resp.* 532a]).
32 Plato (1929a, p. 109 [*Tim.* 47d]).
33 Thaler (2015, p. 412).
34 Moutsopoulos (1898, p. 135).
35 Plato (1926b, p. 11 [*Leg.* 790e]) and Plato (1926a, p. 135 [*Leg.* 666c]). Any young living creature, human or animal, is stirred by an inner fire that makes them move continuously: Plato (1926a, p. 91, 129 and 155 [*Leg.* 653d–e, 664e, 672c]).

damp), music harmonizes the soul.[36] In conclusion, music should be part of any child's education, even earlier than gymnastics (because the beauty of the soul affects the body, but not the other way around).[37]

And yet, music must be dealt with great discipline, keeping in mind its role in the *kallipolis:* failure to do so could result in the musical therapy causing even more damage. The chants—called *nomoi*, that is, laws—have to be preselected by a council of fifty-years-olds, because only those familiar with virtue and vice can be regarded as music experts.[38] Of all harmonies, only the Dorian and the Phrygian should be used, as they imitate respectively the sounds of brave men at war and those of just men at peace. Very few instruments can be admitted into the city (the cithara and the lyre, but not the aulos) and in the fields (the Pan flute, also called syrinx).[39] Indeed, instrumental music is rejected as artistically unworthy, because harmony and rhythm ought to come with lyrics, which play a prominent role.[40] This doesn't mean that pleasure shouldn't be a part of music. However, for Plato one cannot set music standards based on the pleasure it gives to just anyone, but rather on the taste of those who are virtuous and highly educated.[41] This is the best way to prevent musicians from going along with the lascivious taste of the audience, which can lead to so-called "theatrocracy", where every citizen feels entitled to give his opinion about anything—which would also affect politics.[42]

The ability of music to harmonize the soul also emerges in a different aspect, testified by the etymological proximity of "chant" (*odé*) and "enchantment" (*epodé*), also preserved in the Latin word *carmen*. In book two of *Laws*, Plato explains why the role of music isn't to educate just the young but people of all ages. The philosopher envisions three different choirs: that of the Muses, that of Apollo, and that of Dionysus, respectively made up of boys, men up to thirty, and men between thirty and sixty (after sixty, citizens no longer sing but tell myths). However, age tends to weaken the liveliness of youth, which can only be revived by convivial enthusiasm. Older men are hesitant about singing, feeling more ashamed than joyful about it. Children, as we have seen, have the op-

---

36 Plato (1953, p. 127 [*Symp.* 187a]).
37 Plato (1937a, p. 175 [*Resp.* 376e]). See Brancacci (2008, p. 83).
38 Plato (1926b, p. 49 [*Leg.* 802b]); see also Plato (1937a, p. 261 [*Resp.* 402c]).
39 Plato (1937a, p. 249 [*Resp.* 399d]). The *aulós* was a wind instrument similar to an oboe, often consisting of two pipes fitted together at the mouthpiece.
40 Plato (1926a, p. 147 [*Leg.* 669d – e]).
41 Plato (1926a, p. 109 [*Leg.* 658e]). However, pure sounds are beautiful as such, and produce natural pleasure in their melody: Plato (1925, p. 343 [*Phileb.* 51d]).
42 Plato (1926a, p. 247 [*Leg.* 701a]).

posite problem: their inner fire must be moderated and disciplined, whereas in old people it needs to be reignited. Once again, music is the remedy: "it is the duty of the every man and child –bond and free, male and female,– and the duty of the whole State, to charm themselves unceasingly with the chants we have described [...]", in order to make music and singing pleasurable.⁴³

Going back to the primacy of sight in Plato, as well as to Socrates' musical compositions in *Phaedo*, one can conclude that the famous identification between music and philosophy with which I opened this chapter is no proof of Plato's overestimation of music. While attributing great importance to it in the above-mentioned passages, especially in relation to particular stages of the soul, Plato doesn't grant it any special privilege within his dialectics. I am not trying to undermine the worth of music in Plato, but to challenge the traditional image of Plato as the philosopher who divided music into two separate non-communicating branches, the higher and superior "abstract" music, philosophical but inaudible, and the inferior "real" music, rejected as too sensible. This hierarchical, "vertical" articulation is due to a neoplatonic misinterpretation (see below, par. 5) of Plato's position on music. On the contrary, his work frequently makes a "horizontal" distinction between *good* and *bad* music, where good and bad are aesthetic as well as ethical opposites. The analysis of the philosophical value of music should follow this second line of interpretation: as Socrates knew all too well in his last hours, music is the best means to connect the human world to the divine.

3 The voice of Aristotle

In Aristotle's thought, physics, biology and psychology cooperate, paving the way to the idea of music developed in the eighth book of *Politics*. At the centre of this conceptual constellation lies the concept of "voice" (*phoné*), which in general means the sound of a living being. The sounds of the voice, for Aristotle, "are symbols or signs of affections or impressions of the soul".⁴⁴ As it conveys the elementary emotions of pleasure and pain, the voice is common to human beings and many animals, unlike speech (*logos*).⁴⁵ Aristotle then distinguishes the articulated voice from the non-articulated. The first is typically human, but things are not that simple: the voice of many birds is articulated as well, despite

---

43 Plato (1926a, p. 131 [*Leg*. 665c]).
44 Aristotle (1955, p. 114 [*De int*. 16a 3–4]).
45 Aristotle (1932, p. 11 [*Pol*. 1253a 9]).

being non-linguistic, while several human emissions such as coughing or clicking one's tongue are not articulated.⁴⁶ Finally, the voice plays a cognitive role as the correlate of hearing, which together with memory is irreplaceable to convey the learning skill of a given species.⁴⁷

Leaving aside the zoological aspects, here I will focus on the specifically musical use of the voice, whose theoretical foundations are found mainly in *De anima*. Aristotle starts from sound in general (*psophos*): the "proper sensible" of the auditory sense. Sound is generated when a body, which is potentially able to resonate, passes from potentiality to actuality due to a shock or percussion.⁴⁸ Even the subject's potential ability to hear must pass to actuality, which happens when an unbroken and compact portion of air is interposed between the resonant body and the ear. Based on direct anatomical observations, Aristotle then locates in the inner ear a certain amount of air, which resonates completing the hearing process.⁴⁹ The voice is a sound "produced by a creature possessing a soul", for "inanimate things never have a voice". In an analogous sense, Aristotle admits, the aulos, the lyre and other instruments have a voice as well, as they have "a musical compass, and tune, and modulation (*diálektos*)".⁵⁰ This is a fairly important point: the analogy with the voice elevates, so to speak, the music produced by instruments, which thus turn out to be capable of a pure and articulated melodic expression.

In the third book of *De anima*, when introducing the fundamental principle that sense is a proportion, Aristotle starts from the voice: this being a kind of "chord" (*symphonia*), and any chord being a proportion (*logos*), it follows that hearing is a kind of proportion, because voice and hearing in actuality are one and the same thing.⁵¹ Terms like *symphonia* and *logos* would normally refer to the mathematics of sound relationships. In Aristotle, though, their interaction happens in the realm of vocalism. It is the voice that carries an element of order, which then it donates to music. But this order has nothing to do with the cosmic harmony of the Pythagoreans, which is explicitly rejected in the second

---

46 Aristotle (1957, p. 119 [*De an.* 420b 30]).
47 Aristotle (1933, p. 3 [*Metaph.* 980b 23]). Intelligence without hearing makes learning impossible, as in the case of bees.
48 Aristotle (1957, p. 109 [*De an.* 419b 5]). See also Aristotle (1957 [420a 30]), where Aristotle possibly argues against Architas' theory, further developed by Plato (1929a, p. 173 [*Tim.* 67b]).
49 Aristotle (1957, p. 113 [*De an.* 420a 10]).
50 Aristotle (1957, p. 115 f. [*De an.* 420b 5–10]). The term for "modulation" (*dialektos*) is used to indicate the different types of human language and even the vocal articulations of animals of the same species, even when living in different areas. Aristotle (1965, p. 83 [*Hist. an.* 536b 8 f]).
51 Aristotle (1957 [*De an.* 426a 27–30]).

book of *De caelo*.⁵² The idea that the heavens resonate is very poetic, recognizes Aristotle, but impossible. Even assuming that due to habit we no longer hear the sound of celestial spheres, it should be noted that very loud noises have a physical effect that can even crush bodies. Given that planets are very large, their sound should be extraordinarily intense and therefore have devastating effects. However, planets rotate together with the correspondent heavens and therefore cannot produce sounds, as there is no friction.

Aristotle doesn't abandon any reference to mathematical ratios between sounds altogether.⁵³ Rather, he gives them less importance in relation to the effect of music. Once the relation of music with psychology and cosmology has been clarified, what remains is the issue of the link between music and ethos. Some information in this sense can be found in *Problems*, only partly attributable to Aristotle but still coming from the Peripatetic School: "even if wordless, melody still has an ethos, which colour or taste or smell do not have".⁵⁴ This happens due to the "perception of movement" that accompanies the sound, that is, the "similarity in the rhythms and in the order (*taxis*) of the acute and grave sounds, but not in their mixing (*mixis*): the consonance does not have ethos".⁵⁵ The theory of consonance as mixing is a fundamental point of the Aristotelian musical doctrine, which dismisses Pythagorean theories.⁵⁶ Most of all, it is the rhythmic-prosodic taxonomy of the melodic voice that gives music its ethical value. The reference to the "order" of acute and grave sounds in the melodic succession refers to the temporal flow of melody—something very similar to the articulated expression of the human voice. Music makes use of some specific intervals and harmonies, but the main thing that emerges in the process is the movement of a "voice", be it human or comparable to it by analogy, like that of instruments.

With this in mind, it is possible to look at the analysis of the conception of music illustrated by Aristotle in his *Politics*. Music is linked to human activity in three ways: "education, or amusement, or entertainment".⁵⁷ Aristotle's thesis is that all these dimensions contribute to defining the purpose for which one makes music. First, it has an educational value. To judge music, in fact, one must know it, to some degree. Those who practiced music in their youth may per-

---

52 Aristotle (1938, p. 193–195 [*De cael.* 290b 30–291a 25]).
53 Aristotle (1933, p. 71 [*Metaph.* 991b 14, 1092b 14]).
54 Aristotle (2011, p. 395 [*Probl.* 19.27]).
55 Aristotle (2011, p. 395 [*Probl.* 19.27]).
56 Cf. Stumpf (1896, p. 22ff.). Though it obviously reflects the state of the art of its times, this old essay still represents a valid contribution.
57 Aristotle (1932, p. 653 [*Pol.* 1339b 15]).

haps abandon this practice in adulthood, but will still remain music experts, whose judgment will not be misdirected. This is an important point, because it implies that the rules of good music (also in an ethical-political sense) have to be interiorized by everyone, not imposed by a legislator. Of course Aristotle does not hesitate to provide prescriptions: the aulos must be banished from childhood education, as it prevents the exercise of speech during learning, and the same goes for any instrument that leads to virtuosity, because in that case "the adolescent who practices music with these instruments aims not at his own excellence, but rather at the audience's pleasure" in a way that is not worthy of a free man. Therefore Aristotle only sets out the rules to prevent anything that can lower music to a mechanical exercise, contradicting the spirit in which it is practiced.

This tolerance is justified on the basis of an innovative approach. Aristotle affirms a fundamental principle: while other sensibles can at most count as indications or "signs" (*semeia*) of a character, the melodies allow for the "imitations" (*mimemata*) of characters.[58] This peculiarity derives from the combined effect, in them, of harmonies (in the technical sense of scale organizations) and rhythms. According to this principle, one can see why the ethical value of music should rest on the *melos* understood as movement in time. The imitation of human action makes music akin to tragedy, in which it plays an important role, briefly outlined by Aristotle in *Poetics*.[59] In addition, Aristotle ascribes an imitative function to music also in its autonomous execution, which is to be studied carefully.

Partly drawing on the tripartite division outlined above, Aristotle says that music should be cultivated in view of three purposes: education, catharsis and entertainment or relaxation.[60] It is a very famous passage, because Aristotle promises here to better explain what catharsis is in "our treatise on poetry", but the brief notes he devotes to it in the first book of the *Poetics* suggest that the topic was treated more extensively in a second one, now lost. According to Aristotle, however, no kind of melody—ethical, action-oriented and enthusiastic—should be banned. One should rather admit all kinds, directing them to their most appropriate purposes. Education goes hand in hand with the ethical modes that were already dear to Plato, but others also find adequate justification in catharsis or fun.[61]

---

[58] Aristotle (1932, p. 659 [*Pol.* 1340a 33, 40]). Cf. Sörbom (1994, *passim*), whose interpretation differs from mine.
[59] Aristotle (1995, p. 23 [*Poet.* 1449b]).
[60] Aristotle (1932, p. 667f. [*Pol.* 1341b 30ff.]).
[61] On the whole question see Lear (1988, *passim*).

The theme of catharsis of course has a special importance. On the one hand, as the above passage shows, it is one of the three specific purposes of music. On the other, it can be claimed that music as a whole has a cathartic function, albeit peculiar. Next to the "medical" meaning of purification from passions, Aristotle hints at a more "universalist" understanding of catharsis, which sees the latter as an identification with the human condition and its ordeals.[62] Rather than purification, this latter case signifies a "soft" rebalancing of the emotional sphere —something that fits well with music in general, where human action is represented indirectly, contrary to tragedy. This specific form of catharsis intervenes in the forms of enjoyment that characterize the most refined public, while musical catharsis in the first sense is typical of a simpler audience.[63] In any case, the function of music is never psychagogic: it doesn't condition and it doesn't affect, but rather it educates, relaxes and elevates. Aristotle doesn't dwell on the thaumaturgic power of music to calm one down or exalt one's spirit, but he underlines the value of its imitative ability, which is artificial but controlled: the "habituation in feeling pain and delight at representations of reality is close to feeling them towards actual reality".[64] It is therefore excluded that music might act on one's character in a mechanic or coercive way.[65] If that were the case, after all, one would simply not practice it and rather rely on professionals: the passive enjoyment of their art would be enough to achieve the desired effects. However, in addition to the fact that this would generate much competition, Aristotle's idea of music is very different.

Far from being accessory, the discourse on music fits perfectly well with Aristotle's view on politics. In fact, it illustrates the ultimate purpose of the legislator: war is for peace, activity is for idleness, and necessary things are pursued in view of beautiful ones. Those who admire Sparta and its primarily martial virtues are wrong: often such communities collapse in times of peace. Bellic and economic action must always be functional to support the industrious *otium* to come (*scholé*), which is the real reason why people organize their lives in a social form. It is not difficult here to notice profound differences between this view and Plato's. According to Aristotle, music has unheard-of functions: far from being instrumentally useful, it is close to the very purpose of social life. Aristotle doesn't appreciate music because it shapes the human spirit to allow for social cohesion, but because it befits the free man who has actualized this condition of

---

62 Cf. Golden (1976, p. 446).
63 Cf. Sorgner/Schramm (2010, p. 178).
64 Aristotle (1932, p. 657 [*Pol.* 1340a 25]).
65 Brüllmann (2013, *passim*).

freedom. If anything, music proves that disciplines that are only taken to have value due to their usefulness—like drawing—always have a further component endowed with its own meaning, regardless of a determined goal.[66] Music subjugates nobody: its disinterested character is the sign of a contagious freedom.

Overall, Aristotle introduces great elements of novelty by detaching music from the harmony of the macro- and microcosm. The heavens do not make any sound and music has no extraordinary medical or magical powers. This approach favours a sober philosophical consideration *of* music rather than the convergence between music and philosophy. The melodic voice, articulated but asemantic, imitates the movement of human actions without, however, signifying them. *Ethe* are therefore neither represented nor absent: they are, in a way, latent in music. While maintaining a pedagogic role, music has lesser normative pressure in this view, which benefits its aesthetic autonomy. Different musical harmonies can easily satisfy different kinds of people, who will find in them the type of edification they find more appropriate. Being educated to music in his youth, a noble person will autonomously make the best choice in the aesthetic-musical scale.

4 Aristoxenus: the Harmonic Science

Often in literature it is said that ancient music theory was characterized by two opposite schools of thought: the Pythagoreans and Aristoxenus's followers. The difference allegedly was a matter of methodology: the former explained everything by reference to numbers, while Aristoxenus elevated hearing to the status of sole judge of musical issues. Further research, though, has been showing more and more convincingly that this view is inaccurate and doesn't stand the test of a closer analysis of the source texts.[67] Understanding Aristoxenus has therefore a special significance: the point is not only to rehabilitate the honour of the scientist from Tarentum, but to call into question some prejudices concerning the historical development lines of the philosophy of music. By separating math and perception, in fact, this hypothesis makes the critics' classifications all too easy, sacrificing truthfulness to reality—which, in the ancient world as in the

---

66 Aristotle (1932, p. 639 ff. [*Pol.* 1337b 25–1338a 25]); see also Aristotle (1932, p. 607 and 611 f. [*Pol.* 1333a 30–35, 1334a 5–10]).
67 See Brancacci (1989, p. 101). Confusion as to Aristoxenus' methodology possibly arose from a text by Didymus quoted (and altered) by Porphyry: see Barker (1984, p. 242). On Aristoxenus' scientific (and musical) programme, see Barker (2007, p. 229 ff.).

modern, usually turns out to be much more complex than what our *a priori* constructs reflect.

Influenced by the Pythagoreans, Aristoxenus took from Aristotle the conceptual tools for something unprecedented: the formalization of the "harmonic science" as part of the tripartition of music into harmonics, rhythmic and metric—which Aristoxenus was the first to codify explicitly.[68] This epistemological setup is enough to make the image of Aristoxenus as a naive phenomenist rather implausible. Indeed, in *Elementa Harmonica* he doesn't polemicize with the Pythagoreans, despite distancing himself from them, but rather with the empiricist school (already criticized by Plato) of the so-called *harmonikoi*. These were his adversaries, and yet due to a misunderstanding dating back to late antiquity, Aristoxenus was mistaken for one of them.

The object of "harmonic science" is melody. In defining its scientific method, Aristoxenus follows Aristotle: one has to grasp the phenomena, distinguish what comes first and what comes later, and recognize the essential properties.[69] One also needs fundamental principles, chosen based on two criteria: each has to be "true and evident" and recognized "by sensation" as pertaining to the harmonic science.[70] Introducing an unprecedented level of formalization, Aristoxenus enumerates the principles of harmonic science: definitions, theorems and principles give rise to rigorous lexical and conceptual clarifications, which flow into real demonstrations. It should not be surprising, then, to read the following formulation:

> Taken as a whole, our science is concerned with all musical melody, both vocal and instrumental. Its pursuit depends ultimately on two things, hearing and reason. Through hearing we assess the magnitudes of intervals, and through reason we apprehend their functions.[71]

As Aristotle's follower, Aristoxenus starts from the voice to define melody. Here *phoné* is not the sound of music in general: Aristoxenus ascribes a decisive role for the whole musical universe precisely to the human voice, in its concrete ability to speak or sing. For this purpose Aristoxenus first of all considers the "movement of the voice, its movement, that is, with respect to place", a definition that can only be understood in the light of Aristotelian physics.[72] In fact, Aristotle dis-

---

[68] The picture of "music" is further completed by organology. In the present paragraph I will deal only with harmonics. On rhythmic see Aristoxenus (1990, *passim*).
[69] See Gibson (2005, p. 31). On the structure and the aim of the work see Barker (1984, p. 113 ff.).
[70] Aristoxenus (1984, p. 159 and 149).
[71] Aristoxenus (1984, p. 150).
[72] Aristoxenus (1984, p. 127). Cf. Aristotle (1934, p. 217 [*Phys.* 243a 35]).

tinguishes three kinds of "movements": with respect to place, with respect to quality (eg. an alteration) and with respect to quantity (i.e. a decrease or an increase). For Aristoxenus melody is a movement, which is not related to quality or quantity: therefore, it can only be a local movement. Clearly, Aristoxenus is not thinking of the local movement of those who sing while, say, crossing a room, but rather of the voice's movement between those two special "places" represented by the acute and the grave—which should not be confused with the modern "high" and "low", suggesting a kind of spatial representation absent from the ancient world.[73] In other words, the local movement of the melody does not occur in real physical space, but in a "sound space" that is entirely autonomous. But how can such a space be defined? It is inscribed within sensation (*aisthesis*) and lasts for the execution and hearing of the given musical fact. On the other hand, there are precise correspondences between the movement of the voice and movement in the physical sense, as illustrated by Archytas (see above, par. 1). If the physical body oscillates at a constant speed, its sound will always have the same pitch; if it changes speed, there will be movement from one pitch to another, in the sense that I will now show.[74]

Hence Aristoxenus's groundbreaking distinction between two different kinds of local movement of the voice: continuous and discontinuous. The continuous voice moves incessantly back and forth in the "space" of sound, pausing only when, so to speak, it ceases to exist, in silence. This, observes Aristoxenus, is the case with speaking, that is not of musical relevance.[75] The discontinuous voice (or "diastematic", that is, "intervalled") instead moves in jumps, by discrete sections, focusing on different "places":

> During its course it [*scil*. the voice] brings itself to rest at one pitch and then at another: it does this continuously (I mean continuously in respect of time), passing over the spaces bounded by the pitches, but coming to rest on the pitches themselves and sounding them alone, and is described as singing, and as moving in intervallic motion.[76]

The discontinuous voice does not stop moving only in silence (as speech does), but focuses on sustained notes, which individuates the "grades" (see below) in

---

[73] Barker (2007, p. 21). Aristotle highlights that the "acute" of the lyre's string is such only in relation to another string, and not—say—to that of the stylus: Aristotle (1934, p. 245 [*Phys*. 248b 5–10]).
[74] Aristoxenus (1984, p. 134 f.).
[75] The modern mind may find it difficult to understand in which sense the voice of the speaker can move between acute and grave, but we must keep in mind the more musical character of language by the ancient Greeks. Cf. Georgiades (1958, p. 42).
[76] Aristoxenus (1984, p. 132).

which the sound space is organized—or, to phrase it better in relation to this specific meaning, the *musical space*. The origin of this momentous distinction can perhaps be traced back to Plato's *Philebus:* in it, it is said that the voice is originally one and infinite and then concretizes itself (according to quantity and quality) on the one hand in the letters of the alphabet, on the other in sound intervals (that is, in the acute and the grave).[77] Nevertheless, Aristoxenus develops those ideas in his own original way.

Therefore melody, the object of the harmonic science, exists within a paradox: it is defined by something lingering (the voice sustaining a note), where this something is movement by nature. Indeed, when singing we try to hold the voice on a certain pitch: the more the emission is fixed and uniform, the more the melody will sound clear. The phenomena and rules of harmony can be traced back to this fact. The harmonic science then has to explain "how the voice naturally places intervals as it is tensed and relaxed. For we assert that the voice has a natural way of moving, and does not place intervals haphazardly".[78] Like any form of movement, the discontinuous voice follows an immanent order that defines and create music intervals. It is a precise and rigorous order: "none of the objects of perception displays so great or so fine an order".[79]

In this respect, Aristoxenus distinguishes five elements: the acute, the grave, the tension, the relaxation, and the grade. So he proceeds to the definition of "sound" (*phthongos*) in this specific musical meaning: "the incidence of the voice on one pitch".[80] To identify the different "grades", Aristoxenus starts from the minimum consonant interval, one traditionally known as "fourth". But this designation only makes sense within a reference system: one counts *to four* in the context of a certain tuning (e.g. of a lyre), a scale, or a previously defined system. On the contrary, Aristoxenus aims to define the reference system starting from the pitches that the voice, so to speak, *encounters* in its natural movement. This must be done starting from consonances, which are the best determined intervals. The voice fits them naturally, whereas it cannot pander to the whims of the constructors of abstract systems.

One has to start from the smallest consonance (fourth), find the next one (fifth), and therefore define "tone" their difference and "octave" their sum: then one can say that "according to the phenomenon" the smallest consonance has an extension of two and a half tones, and then construct every other interval.

---

77 Plato (1925, p. 223 [*Phileb*. 17a – d]).
78 Aristoxenus (1984, p. 149).
79 Aristoxenus (1984, 130).
80 Aristoxenus (1984, 136).

Adding up consonant intervals to the octave one obtains other consonant intervals, which distinguishes the octave from the other consonances.[81] This result, which is almost obvious if one's analysis starts from the voice, is a highly innovative argument. Aristoxenus introduces quite naturally the principle of the cyclical nature of the octaves, which poses major difficulties to the arithmetical view of the Pythagoreans. Thus he describes the contours of the "harmonically attuned melody",[82] that is, the melody responsive to the natural laws of the harmonic science. But I must stop here: going into the detail of the construction of musical systems is beyond the scope of this work.

To conclude, it is clear that Aristoxenus adopts different methods and gets different results from those of the Pythagoreans, but this doesn't mean that he acritically privileges sensation. What he does is rather try to scientifically formalize (in an Aristotelian sense) the generation of melody starting from the properties of the voice, whence it originates. What is left to clarify is his position in relation to the ethos.[83] Even though he doesn't deny that music has some ethical influence, Aristoxenus thinks it is wrong to seek in the harmonic science the means to improve the human character. More specifically, one's preferences for music genres shouldn't be supported by ethical-pedagogical reasons. Rather, Aristoxenus adopts an interesting scheme of the historical development of the music forms. The first tuning was the diatonic one, which is structurally simpler. Then came the chromatic and finally the enharmonic, which Aristoxenus considers nobler and higher—even though the ear struggles to get used to it.[84] The history of music thus generates an evolution of the forms: this idea of progress[85] is the opposite of Damon's and Plato's postulation that archaic music forms were excellent, as opposed to the modern degradation.

5 The End of the Ancient World. Augustine

Philodemus of Gadara's *De musica* (first century BC), found among the *Papyri* in Herculaneum, is our main source on the controversy about music between Epicureans and Stoics.[86] Based on a "scientific" sensation, more qualified than the

---

[81] Aristoxenus (1984, p. 142–143 and 160).
[82] Aristoxenus (1984, p. 136).
[83] See Rocconi (2012, *passim*).
[84] Aristoxenus (1984, p. 139).
[85] With due caution: see Meriani (2003, p. 15).
[86] See Rispoli (1974, *passim*) and Laurand (2014, *passim*).

"natural", the Stoics believed that music had a divine origin, was able to educate people to virtue and was appropriate for all occasions of human life, both public and private. Philodemus responded by showing the absurdity of these arguments, polemically referring to a piece—today lost—written by the Stoic philosopher Diogenes of Babylon. According to Philodemus, there is no special sensation able to grasp harmony. As for the supposedly divine origin of music, Philodemus cites Democritus, who believed that music was a recent art, due to idleness rather than necessity.[87] Indeed, Philodemus' criticisms addresses most commonplaces about music: from its alleged extraordinary power over the soul illustrated e.g. by the myth of Orpheus, to the doctrine of cosmic harmony.

Also, Philodemus takes great care to deny any relationship between music and ethos.[88] In his view, music aims exclusively at relaxation or entertainment, and can imitate virtues no better than cooking can. Philodemus does not despise music, but believes it has no interference in the intellectual and ethical spheres. These contexts, in fact, only belong to philosophy, because only the logos can really remove all pain from the soul. After all, there had been serious doubts about the relationship between music and ethos for quite some time, ever since the sophists.[89] So, Philodemus' book is the presumably the main surviving evidence of a whole important tradition of ancient thought, which one may generally define as "scepticism".[90] His argument also influenced Sextus's neophyrronian criticism of musicians.[91] No wonder these trends were met favorably in Rome in the first century BC, in a context where the public role of music and the theoretical interest in it had now profoundly changed.[92]

The loosening of the link between music and ethos, though, did not entail the end of speculations on cosmic harmony. With his *Somnium Scipionis* from *De re publica*, it was Marcus Tullius Cicero who left to posterity one of the most famous versions of the cosmological-music legend. In a dream, Scipio Ae-

---

[87] Philodemus' line of thought probably originated with Democritus: see (Tatarkiewicz 1980, p. 87). Regrettably, little is left of his writings on aesthetics and on music. For a comprehensive reconstruction, see Brancacci (2007, *passim*).
[88] Philodemus (2007, p. 216 and *passim*). Philodemus refutes not only the musical imitation of *ethe*, but also the Aristotelian version: see Wilkinson (1938, p. 177).
[89] As posited by Abert (1899, p. 38 ff.). Another important document is the papyrus *Hibeh*, traced back by Brancacci (2008, p. 57 f.) to the rhetoric of the third century BC.
[90] Abert (1899, p. 27 ff.) defines this trend "formalistic"; others call it "utilitarian" or "anti-musical" (Delattre 2007, ccxxxiii).
[91] Sextus (1986); cf. Greaves (1986, p. 24 f.).
[92] Cf. Abert (1905, p. 9).

milianus finds himself in a place full of stars, in the presence of his illustrious ancestor Scipio the African, who tells him about his fate and shows him that the souls of the blessed are welcomed in heaven. After contemplating the dazzling splendour of the Milky Way, home to the blessed souls, and the luminous brilliance of all the stars, Scipio notices the "deep and sweet" sound (*tantus et tam dulcis sonus*) that fills his ears, produced by the rotation of the spheres. Just as the eye cannot stand the sight of the sun, the human ear yields to the music of the spheres: this is why the celestial sound is not heard by us mortals, as happens to the people who live next to the Nile falls and no longer hear their roar.[93]

It is not surprising that neo-Platonism tends to highlight the separation between sensible and supersensible harmony. In the *Enneads*, Plotinus claims that Plato divided music in two areas, in reference to its sensible or intelligible nature.[94] Remarkably, the other imitative arts, such as painting, sculpture, dance and mime, belong entirely to the sensible sphere. Music, instead, "since the ideas which it has are concerned with rhythm and melody", falls within a different category: it is of the "same kind of the art which is concerned with intelligible numbers", and thus "considers and contemplates universal proportion in the intelligible".[95] But even here, one shouldn't acritically overestimate the importance of intelligible music, because after all, for who "sees the melody in the intelligible world and will not be stirred when he hears the melody in sensible sounds?"[96]

The theme of the harmony of the celestial spheres is found in Greek musical treatises, including those written by Nicomachus of Gerasa (first-second century A.D.) and Aristides Quintilian (second century A.D.). Neither author is entirely attributable to the line joining neo-Pythagoreanism and neo-Platonism, but both were also partially influenced by the peripatetic school. In his *De Musica* Aristides Quintilian interprets music, among other things, in an innovative way, in the light of the principle of male-female duality. His doctrine revolves around the concept of imitation (*mimesis*), which music fulfils in the most perfect way by imitating not static objects, but human activity in all its dynamics, which include will, word and action.[97] In his *Enchiridion*, Nicomachus instead looks at harmony through the "discontinuous voice", but specifying that it naturally

---

[93] Cicero (2017, p. 99 [6.18]). In the *Commentary on the Dream of Scipio* by Macrobius (1990), celestial music is traced back to the work of the demiurge that shapes the soul of the world.
[94] Plotinus (2014c, p. 227 [*Enn.* 6 3.16]).
[95] Plotinus (2014b, p. 313 [*Enn.* 5 9.11]). Cf. Panaiotidi (2014, *passim*). Its greater degree of dependence on bodiliness thus separates dance from music for Plotinus.
[96] Plotinus (2014a, p. 211 [*Enn.* 2 9.16]).
[97] Aristides Quintilian (1984, p. 470). Cf. Zanoncelli (1977, p. 62f.) and Mathiesen (1984, p. 273).

sings precisely the intervals regulated by the mathematical ratios in the Pythagorean sense. Interestingly, Nicomachus attributes Aristoxenus's distinction between continuous and discontinuous voice to the "Pythagoreans".[98] The typical outcome is that neo-Pythagoreanism ends up encompassing views of different origin, which then change and partly loose some of their potential in the new context. This isn't just a historical notion, because—as we shall see—Nicomachus is one of the main sources of an immensely influential author: Boethius.

In his *Harmonica*, Claudius Ptolemy (second century A.D.) criticizes both Pythagoreanism, despite remaining close to it, and Aristoxenus. Ptolemy accepts Aristoxenus's principle that by adding an octave to another consonance one gets consonant intervals.[99] Ptolemy believes that the Pythagoreans failed to make this point not because of the inappropriateness of the mathematical method as such, but rather because his predecessors didn't make good use of it. Aristoxenus, in Ptolemy's view, was wrong too: from the rational point of view, because the intervals of the discontinuous voice still depend on mathematical ratios and, from the practical point of view, because calculations show that the fourth isn't made up of two and a half tones.[100]

The most important thing about Ptolemy in this respect, though, is that he is aware of the false myth of Pythagoras's hammers. Conscious of the inaccuracy of part of the tale, Ptolemy believes that one could get no reliable result by using blow instruments, or in "the case of weights attached to strings", as such methods affect the accuracy of the pitch[101]. Ptolemy instead stakes his all on the monochord, from which one can and must deduce the entire "harmony", similarly to what was suggested by the treatise on the *Sectio canonis* traditionally (but probably wrongly) attributed to Euclid.[102] It is worth noting that the approach to the issue in Macrobius's later commentary (fifth century A.D.) to Cicero's *Dream of Scipio* is diametrically opposed to it. In this version of the story, the monochord is not even mentioned: Macrobius speaks instead of the sympathetic resonance between strings that make consonant intervals, assuming that the weights affixed to those strings are identical to those of the hammers.[103]

---

98 Nicomachus of Gerasa (1984, p. 248).
99 Ptolemy (1984, p. 284 and 287). The problem primarily concerns the interval of fourth. The eleventh—that is, fourth plus octave—wasn't indeed considered a consonance by the Pythagoreans, because it corresponds to the 8:3 ratio. Cf. Barker (2014, *passim*).
100 Ptolemy (1984, p. 293 and 295).
101 Ptolemy (1984, p. 291).
102 Euclid [Ps.] (1984, p. 194). Cf. Barbera (1984, *passim*).
103 Macrobius (1990, p. 12f.).

In the *Marriage of Philology and Mercury*, Martianus Capella (fifth century A.D.) presents a vast allegory of the rise of knowledge (Philology) to the divine dimension (Mercury). The liberal arts are here personified by female figures who parade as a wedding homage. Probably borrowed with some modifications from Varro, the encyclopaedic composition includes here (in order of appearance): Grammar, Dialectic, Rhetoric, Geometry, Arithmetic, Astronomy, and Harmony. Remarkably, the reference here is not to *music*, but to one of its parts according to the traditional division: *harmony*, which also absorbs rhythm.[104] Martianus places Harmony at the peak of his work, investing it with special dignity. In fact, she follows after Astronomy and descends from heaven, of which she regulates the motion, to "be the governess" of the souls of us mortals.[105] Indeed, she plays her role extremely well: she incites to war and celebrates peace, heals the troubles of body and soul, affects infants no less than terrestrial and aquatic animals of all species. The allegorical and neo-Platonic setting does not prevent Martianus from developing in detail the more specific theoretical and musical aspects of harmony and rhythm. Relying largely on Aristides Quintilian, Martianus incorporates the essential theorems of Pythagoreanism, but including some elements of Aristoxenus's thought such as the distinction between continuous and "divided" voice and his definition of sound.[106]

The life and work of Boethius are marked by the atmosphere of a world now politically and culturally transformed. Music, for Boethius, is one of the four mathematical sciences: arithmetic and music deal with multiplicity (in itself and in relation to other things), geometry and astronomy deal with magnitude (at rest and in motion).[107] However, music is distinctive in that it is the only discipline of this *quadrivium* that has a relationship not only with speculation but also with morality.[108] Referring to Plato and the usual anecdotes on the powerful influence of music on character, Boethius reaffirms the profound and indissoluble bond between music and man, whose body moves spontaneously listening to it, and whose mind automatically goes back to melodies heard in the past. To explain all these phenomena, Boethius introduces the distinction of three kinds of music: cosmic music (*musica mundana*), human music (*musica humana*) and instrumental music.[109] Cosmic music is that which is observed in

---

104 It is harder to locate metric, as it is not part of the trivium: Martianus Capella (1977, p. 105).
105 Martianus Capella (1977, p. 357).
106 Martianus Capella (1977, p. 361 and 363).
107 Boethius (1867a, p. 9).
108 Boethius (1989, p. 2). Boethius's main sources are Nicomachus and Ptolemy: cf. Chadwick (1981).
109 Boethius (1989, p. 9).

the heavens, in the combination of elements and in changing seasons; human music is what we grasp by focusing on ourselves and on the particular "consonance" that binds body and soul. With this seminal tripartition Boethius affirms the profound unity of different forms of music, as the only way to understand its "power" and explain its ethical effects.

The third kind, so-called "instrumental" music—but in a wider sense, as it includes singing—is the only one discussed in the surviving part of Boethius's piece.[110] His theory is filled with definitions and observations of sound physics, including considerations on melopoeia (the art of forming melodies) and on taste. *De institutione musica* has outstanding historic importance, as it was the only way by which the Greek music theory could reach the Latin Middle Ages. In addition to inserting music into the framework of the *quadrivium*, Boethius's treatise makes several other interesting points. For example, Boethius affirms that consonance cannot have place without sound (which isn't an obvious thesis in this context), understood as *pulsus* or "percussion of air remaining undissolved all the way to the hearing".[111] The nature of this pulsation and the hearing mechanism are explained with two famous examples: a spinning top bearing a diagonal red line, so when it spins it appears entirely coloured, and a stone thrown in a pond. But Boethius uses *sonus* in two ways: in the general sense and in the specifically music sense of *phthongos*. His definition is essentially the same as Aristoxenus's but influenced by Nicomachus: sound is "a melodic instance of pitch; it is 'melodic' in that it functions within a composition in a given tuning".[112] Boethius thus delivered to posterity a complex and layered discussion of music: the musical ethics, cosmic metaphysics, mathematics, music theory, but also other trends are all dealt with at the highest level.

Instead, Augustine of Hippo presents theses on music that are based on completely different intentions and views.[113] His work is so innovative that it justifies the inversion of the actual chronology, so as to place him after Boethius. In a series of early dialogues, Augustine deals with the liberal arts, considered useful to the contemplation of the order that reigns there and that leads to the "supreme measure" (*summum modum*).[114] It should be noticed that there is a signif-

---

[110] Mundane music is hinted at in the odes with which Lady Philosophy consoles the dying Boethius in *De consolatione philosophiae* (Boethius 1968). Cf. Chamberlain (1970, p. 85 ff).
[111] Boethius (1989, p. 11).
[112] Boethius (1989, p. 16).
[113] On the topics tackled here and in the next paragraph, see the insightful essays in Cristiani/Panti/Perillo 2007.
[114] Augustine (2007, p. 69). In his later *Retractationes* Augustine changed his position on liberal arts, admitting he had given them too much importance. Augustine (1999, p. 14).

icant semantic shift here, as the concept of *measure* dismisses that of *harmony*. Beside the neo-Platonic influences, the Augustinian concept of order rests on *Wisdom* 11.20: God has "arranged all things by measure and number and weight".[115] Of course, this is not to say that this reference would be obvious for any Christian author. On the contrary, Augustine's was a precise theoretical choice that differentiates his position. For Augustine there is properly no "harmony" in the world: rather, there is divine order, which gives every event and creature a rhythm that man can enjoy in moderation (a word stemming from measure, *modus*) insofar as it helps him rationally understand his first cause.[116] Even the opening lines of *De ordine* seem to express a "continuist" alternative to the discrete sound of Pythagoras's hammers: Augustine stops to listen to the water running in a discharge channel and wonders why its sound goes up and down in intensity.[117] In other words, the rationality of music goes through meter and rhythm, which most of *De Musica* (books 2–5) deals with, and only secondarily through the relation between grave and acute.

To understand Augustine's definition of music as *scientia bene modulandi* ("the science of mensurating well"),[118] one has to move away from any reference to the modern musical concept of modulation. For Augustine, the point is to implement measure (*modus*, whence *modulandi*) in whatever moves, as it is in danger of excessiveness and disorder: therefore music is also defined *scientia bene movendi*. However, it is not enough to move "with measure": one has to do it "well" (*bene*), in a moral sense.[119] Regardless of their skill, a singer or dancer who expressed themselves with lasciviousness would not be modulating well. To prevent this from happening, the *scientia* allows one to distinguish the human fruition of music from that of animals like bears or elephants, who also move to the sound of music. Something similar happens to ordinary folk, too, but great men must enjoy music in moderation, only when at rest and without any preoccupations.[120]

Adopting a rational understanding of music means abandoning the bodily level and considering the numerical one, but not in a Pythagorean sense: numbers here refer mainly to the above-mentioned Biblical verse. Numbers exist in

---

115 Cf. Beierwaltes (1969, p. 52).
116 Cf. Bettetini (2001, p. 110).
117 Augustine (2007, p. 9).
118 Augustine (2002a, p. 172).
119 Augustine (2002a, p. 175).
120 Augustine (2002a, p. 177).

music on several levels: in sound, in hearing, in performance (for example, in singing), in memory and in sensible pleasure.[121]

This last point deserves particular attention. Sensibility, as by "natural law", has the right to make a judgment "by accepting or rejecting" the rhythms in all aspects of music. One must therefore distinguish two aspects in perception: receptivity (the rhythms of hearing), which is passive and akin to the momentary shape of a body immersed in water, and judgment, which is decidedly active. The whole doctrine is inserted in a sophisticated doctrine of perception, based on the principle that the soul continually activates the senses, even in the absence of external stimuli. When the latter act, their rhythms are commensurate with the previous action of the soul, resulting pleasant or unpleasant. Aesthetic pleasure is no surrender to a pleasant feeling, but an *activity* that consists in affirming the phenomenal datum. This activity has full supremacy over all others so far examined.

Despite its complete aesthetic autonomy, sensibility cannot say anything on good modulation, as that is the realm of reason alone.

> It is one thing to approve or disapprove of these motions, either when they are first set in motion or when they are revived by remembrance, which occurs in the pleasure of that which is convenient and in the dismay of that which is inappropriate in such motions or reactions, and another thing to evaluate whether it is right or not to enjoy these things, which is done by reasoning.[122]

Judging everything that is submitted to it, reason wonders: what do we like about sensible rhythms? The answer must be sought in the philosophical concept of sameness: the tracing back of metrical and rhythmic multiplicity of the movements of music to the rational appreciation of the one.[123] Therefore, reason "investigates and questions the carnal pleasure of the soul, which claimed for itself the judicial role", noting some cases in which it might enjoy inappropriate (ill-modulated, or even "immoral") rhythms and inviting us to refrain from them.[124] Note that this doesn't take away any aesthetic value from music. The

---

121 Accordingly, in this context it is appropriate to translate *numerus* with "rhythm". I do not report here the rather difficult lexicon used by Augustine for the different species of "rhythms". The discussion is wide and complex: Augustine (2002b, p. 17). The lower rhythms, in descending order, are those of the act, of memory, of hearing, and finally those of the sound, or better the so-called "material" ones, so as to include dance.
122 Augustine (2002b, p. 59).
123 Augustine (2007, p. 113).
124 Augustine (2002b, p. 65).

rhythms that reason is weary of are "beautiful in their own kind", but "the love of inferior beauty [...] spoils the soul".[125]

Therefore, Augustine shows a rather ambivalent attitude, aiming to mitigate the ethical supremacy of reason. The latter is unquestioned, but doesn't exceed its sphere of competence: inferior rhythms must not attract and distract the soul, but ignoring them isn't the point. The soul has to become so "so good and righteous that [these numbers] can neither lie hidden nor take possession of it".[126] This explains Augustine's approach to music forms. On the one hand, the Ambrosian hymn *Deus creator omnium* ultimately pleases not the ear but the soul, because of its lyrical content. On the other, one shouldn't forget how moved Augustine was, short after his baptism, by listening to music.[127] This way one can understand Augustine's later appreciation for the *jubilus*, the song expressing the state of mind "poured forth in joy, expressing, as far as it is able, the affection, but not compassing the feeling".[128] Like the cries of exultation that the harvesters, happy for the fruitfulness of the earth, mingle with their singing, joy is praise of the inexpressible:

> A person who is shouting with gladness does not bother to articulate words. The shout is a wordless sound of joy; it is the cry of a mind expanded with gladness, expressing its feelings as best it can rather than comprehending the sense. When someone is exulting and happy he passes beyond words that can be spoken and understood, and bursts forth into a wordless cry of exultation. Such a person is clearly rejoicing vocally, but he is so full of intense joy that he is unable to explain what makes him happy.[129]

Christian singing has to be such that it expresses a spiritual joy accumulated in the silent inner process of deep meditation.[130] This, of course, recalls the thirty-year-old Augustine and how strongly impressed he was by Ambrose who, instead of reading out loud as was then customary, used to read silently.[131] Indeed,

---

125 Augustine (2002b, p. 95).
126 Augustine (1999, p. 46).
127 Augustine (1991, p. 304): "How I wept during your hymns and songs! I was deeply moved by the music of the sweet chants of your Church. The sounds flowed into my ears and the truth was distilled into my heart. This caused the feelings of devotion to overflow. Tears ran, and it was good for me to have that experience".
128 For a contextual discussion, cf. Cattin (1991, p. 13); Werner (1942, *passim*); Poirier (2010, p. 135 ff.).
129 Augustine (2003, p. 14).
130 Cf. Hornby (2007, p. 141 ff.) and Folli (2001, p. 182).
131 Augustine (1991, p. 192). "When he was reading, his eyes ran over the page and his heart perceived the sense, but his voice and tongue were silent".

to use the words of his *Exposition on Psalms*, "[i]n bad people the whole earth grumbles, but in the good the whole earth shouts with joy".¹³²

6 The Middle Ages

This paragraph is of course too short to deal with its topic extensively. Let me start with a short premise on the sources that were available to medieval thinkers. For the early Middle Ages there are Augustine, Boethius, Martianus and the commentaries of Chalcidius on *Timaeus* and of Macrobius on the *Dream of Scipio*. Only in the twelfth century do Euclid and Ptolemy penetrate in the West thanks to the Arab mediation. Most of all, at that point philosophers started engaging with Aristotle (along with his commentators), which accentuated the interest in the physical sciences. This dynamic interacted with the special requirements of the new liturgical function of music, which was the centre of a complex evolution. Over time, the monodic chant was replaced by polyphonic forms, and profane music eventually reached such levels that it could no longer be ignored. This is the unprecedented situation that medieval theoreticians had to deal with. For a long time they had a theory—the one handed down by Boethius—that spoke of a musical universe that simply did not exist anymore, while music developed according to its own modalities and demanding new solutions.

The very meaning of the term *musica* must be understood in the light of these considerations. In the middle ages, music mainly referred to the speculative science of the *quadrivium*. Music practice, which was mainly vocal, was instead defined with terms like *cantus* or singsong (*melodia*). Accordingly, a *musicus* was a theoretician, as opposed to a *cantor*, who had a subordinate role. Popular instrumental music was placed hierarchically even lower. Nevertheless, there were several attempts to insert the *cantus* into the definition of music—as well as to teach cantors its theory—, which shows that speculation wasn't the only concern. After all, music was also conceived of as *ars:* not in the modern sense of "fine art", but as a discipline whose aim lies in practice. Even though its quadrivial collocation was never seriously threatened, music has always been related also to the *trivium*, by whose disciplines it was strongly influenced. So, in addition to its bond with rhythms, philosophers investigated the relation of music with language. Given the complexity of the matter at hand, what follows only aims to offer the reader one of the many possible paths across the medieval

---

132 Augustine (2003, p. 14): "In malis murmurat omnis terra, in bonis iubilat omnis terra".

outlook on music.¹³³ In order to do this, I will outline a general periodization, distinguishing three phases: the first starts with Boethius (fifth century), the second with Carolingian musical manuals (ninth century) and the third with the arrival of new sources (twelfth century).

In his *Institutiones musicae*, Cassiodorus accepts Augustine's definition of music as *scientia bene modulandi:* all that in heaven and earth follows divine will is musical, whereas "injustice" is not.¹³⁴ In addressing the subdivisions of music in the classical tripartite division of harmonics, rhythmic and metric, Cassiodorus instead refers to the "numbers in relation to sounds".¹³⁵ Also in line with Augustine, in his *Etymologies* Isidore of Seville (sixth-seventh centuries) defines music as competence in measure (*peritia modulationis*) founded in sound and song. Isidore recognizes that without music "no other discipline can be perfected"; indeed, "nothing is without music" because the world was created with "a certain harmony of sounds" and the heavens revolve according to a harmonic modulation.¹³⁶ The perspective angle of the *Etymologies*, however, is far from the *quadrivium*. Isidore traces the etymology of music back to the Muses, daughters of Zeus and Memory: outside of human memory, in fact, sounds perish because "they cannot be written down".

This aspect must be assessed contextually. The absence of music writing, at the time, should not be attributed to backwardness but to the fact that *qualitas* was considered more important than *quantitas*, which is what allows for the notation of music "values".¹³⁷ Far from being the result of composition in the modern sense, liturgic chant was commonly believed to be of divine origin, often traced back to the imitation of the angelic choir that was allegedly heard by many. It was the Holy Spirit itself, represented in the traditional iconography of Gregory the Great by the inevitable dove (or robin) that dictated to the pope the founded liturgic chant. This idea of music would survive even in later times in musical reflection linked to mysticism, like in Hildegard of Bingen (eleventh-twelfth centuries) or in the doctrine of "spiritual hearing" related by Bonaventure to the cardinal virtue of faith.

The spread of music textbooks in the Carolingian period marks the beginning of a new phase. The most important works are those of Aurelian of Rêome (mid-ninth century), Regino of Prüm and the treatise on *Musica Enchiria-*

---

133 I will often refer to the following anthologies: Gerbert (1784), Coussemaker (1864–1877) and *Thesaurus Musicarum Latinarum*.
134 "[Q]uando vero iniquitates gerimus, musicam non habemus": Cassiodorus (1784, par. 5.2).
135 Cassiodorus (1784, par. 5, 2–4).
136 Isidore of Seville (2006, p. 95 [16.1]).
137 Cf. Mainoldi (2001, p. 39).

dis. These were important reforms to the Boethian tripartition, which was updated by means of the distinction between *musica naturalis* and *artificialis*. "Artificial" music included instrumental music in the strict sense, while "natural" music encompassed cosmic and human music, but this time also including songs. So, the speculative part also includes chant (as *musica humana*), guaranteeing it far superior dignity compared to secular music performed with instruments.[138] Ignoring the ancient references, useless for practical purposes, the basic working terms of such handbooks (tone, accent, note) are defined based on the categories of grammarians.[139] The anonymous *Musica Enchiriadis*—which contains among other things the first examples of written polyphony—starts with the distinction *à la* Aristoxenus between "articulated" and "singing" voice. The author takes cue from the analogy between language and music: letters make up syllables, syllables words and words speeches. Analogously, the "first foundations" of music are *ptongi* (sic), that is, musical sounds, which make up intervals, scales and ultimately give rise to the *cantus*.[140]

The elevation of the song to the rank of *musica humana* has the effect of somewhat bridging the gap between the theoretician and the performer. Aurelian, for example, compares the musician to the grammarian and the cantor to the reader.[141] But even the perspective of Guido of Arezzo (tenth-eleventh centuries) is actually not far from this. Expressing contempt for those who ignore the fundamentals of the art they practice, Guido condemns especially the singers ignorant of his innovative notational and mnemonic approach, who thus fail to understand music in a way that manifests itself in the exponential acceleration of the learning process.[142] These considerations must not suggest a diminished importance of the theme of cosmic harmony. John Scotus Eriugena (ninth century)[143] and other commentators to Martianus Capella, including Remigius of Auxerre, focused on the inconsistencies between the different versions of the harmony of the spheres, whose practical referent would be identified less and less with the ancient consonances and increasingly with the eight ecclesiastical modes.

---

138 Cf. Morelli (2007, p. 74); for similar ideas in Regino of Prüm see Pirrotta (1984, p. 7).
139 On music and grammar cf. Gallo (1991, p. 3 ff.), Bielitz (1977, *passim*); Morelli (2005, *passim*).
140 *Musica et Scolica enchiriadis* (1981, p. 3). The source is Boethius' *De institutione arithmetica*: cf. Bielitz (1977, p. 29 s.). The same analogy is expressed by Adrastus, quoted by Theon of Smyrna in Barker (1984, p. 213 f.).
141 Aurelian of Rêome (1784, p. 38 [vii]).
142 Guido of Arezzo (1985, p. 98).
143 Scotus Eriugena (1939).

As said, a new phase begins in the twelfth century. Scholars like Adelard of Bath and Dominicus Gundisalvi (Gundissalinus) are noteworthy for their translations from the Arabic, respectively of Euclid's *Elements* and the writings of Al-Farabi (ninth-tenth centuries), which introduced the distinction between *musica speculativa* and *activa*.[144] While Adelard takes up the topics of Boethius's sound physics,[145] Gundisalvi draws on the general definition provided by Isidore, but distinguishes between "practical" and "theoretical" music, dividing the latter into five parts.[146] Subsequent revisions of the encyclopaedic profile of music did not involve the abandonment of the traditional setting, but posed new problems concerning the best way to reconcile the new sources with the legacy of Boethius.[147] In Hugh of St. Victor's *Didascalicon* (twelfth century), music went back to the Boethian subdivision—the terms of which are set out with exemplary clarity—but enriched by reference to music as *ars:* people could already sing "before music" (which he understands as a science), but the latter is involved in perfecting notions.[148]

Things change when *Aristoteles physicus* comes into the urban culture of thirteenth-century universities. As known, *De caelo* rejects the Pythagorean idea of the harmony of the spheres, but equally important novelties came from *Physics* and *Posterior Analytics*, translated from the Arabic by Gerard of Cremona.[149] Following Aristotle, the mathematical analysis of music started to embrace the physical notions concerning the origin, propagation and perception of sound, along with considerations on movement and time. These issues are the subject of the reflections of Robert Grosseteste and Robert Kilwardby. According to Grosseteste, music deals with the sound number and is subordinate to mathematical harmony; on the other hand, in this original theory, sound is light built into thin air, and is present in the sound body as its quality.[150] For the Dominican Kilwardby, music is the science whose object is the *numerus harmonicus*. Music is a *res numeralis* and everything that can be measured with numbers has two natures, physical and mathematical. Kilwardby therefore recognizes in music a tension between physics and mathematics, even though he traces it entirely back to the latter: harmony relates to natural things (sounds), "*but not qua na-*

---

144 Cf. Dyer (2007, p. 16).
145 Adelard of Bath (1998, p. 130 ff. [xxi]).
146 Gundisalvi (1903, p. 97 f.).
147 Cf. Panti (2008, p. 206).
148 Hugh of St. Victor (1961, par. 1.11 and 2.12).
149 On the reception of Aristotle's *Politics* see Sachs (1989: *passim*).
150 Cf. Panti (1989, *passim*).

tural".¹⁵¹ Nevertheless, there were also different positions on the matter. Vincent of Beauvais (twelfth-thirteenth century) was influenced by the legacy of Albert the Great: for him, on the contrary, mathematics is subordinate to natural science, which it uses as a tool. The part of his treatise devoted to sound was significantly larger than that of his predecessors.

The work of Thomas Aquinas brought great innovation. In his commentary on *De caelo*, he defended the Aristotelian refutation of the music of the heavenly bodies against Simplicius's counterclaims. In his commentary (sixth century), translated from the Greek by William of Moerbeke, Simplicius contested the argument that the sound of the spheres would be powerful enough to damage the auditory organ: celestial harmony, for him, is beneficial by nature. Moreover, it is not inaudible because of habit: the reason why it eludes mortals (but not Pythagoras) is that the auditory organ is not refined enough.¹⁵² Aquinas responds to the first argument by claiming that a beneficial effect doesn't exclude destruction by excess: the sun is the source of life and yet the human eye cannot bear to look at it for long. As for the second argument, Aquinas replies that hearing grasps everything that can be heard: saying that hearing fails to perceive some sounds means mistaking the word "hearing" or the term "sound". So, the stars make no sound: it isn't imperceptible, nor is it such that it could damage hearing.¹⁵³ The authority of Aristotle and Aquinas had many consequences, including the influence over the idea of music expressed in Dante's *Paradiso*, where *coaptatio* (*harmonia*) is entirely spiritual and expresses itself in silence, which is the opposite of the powerful sound of the celestial machine.¹⁵⁴ As for Aquinas, the apical role of metaphysics in the classification of knowledge requires a reconsideration of the relationship between mathematics and music. As a science, music is part of the "intermediate sciences", in that it applies mathematical principles to sensible objects. But as it contains an operational aspect expressed in *melodias formare*, music is also seen as *ars*.¹⁵⁵

The Thomistic approach influenced Jerome of Moravia's *Tractatus de musica* (thirteenth century), which starts by listing the unnecessary difficulties arising from the use of the Greek terms for music theory. Echoing Johannes Affligemensis (Johannes Cotto),¹⁵⁶ Jerome defines music as "the movement of the voices

---

151 Kilwardby (1976, p. 58 [146]).
152 Aquinas (1952, p. 211 [2.1, 14.6, par. 425]).
153 Aquinas (1952, p. 212 [2.1, 14.7, par. 426]).
154 Cf. Pirrotta (1984, p. 32).
155 Aquinas (1972 p. 366 [*Lect*. 2, *quaest*. 1 ad iii]). Cf. Hirtler (1989, p. 36).
156 Affligemensis (1950, p. 58). Cf. Palisca (2001, p. 137).

that harmonize (*consonantium*) according to an appropriate proportion".[157] Then Jerome takes up the Thomistic criticism of celestial music. Pythagoras knew the mathematical relationships that describe the motion of planets, but because he claimed that he could hear their harmony he was using the term "sound" equivocally. What's worse, this misunderstanding extended to the very concept of music, whose subject actually is only "the sound itself". Everything in music goes back to sound: either because it is sound, or because it refers to it as its beginning and end.[158]

The fourteenth century polemic between supporters and critics of the *ars nova*, such as Johannes de Muris and Jacobus Leodiensis (Jacques de Liège), is a good way to see how music forms developed, and to highlight the role of polyphony as *musica mensurabilis*. In fact, since the twelfth century, music composition had become a refined intellectual activity, inspired by mathematics as well as the arts of the trivium. *Grammar* was mentioned above. As for *poetics*, Johannes de Grocheio (thirteenth-fourteenth century) introduced a sketched theory of genres by classifying music depending on what it was used for. Simple (or civil) music was made by laymen based on non-Latin texts; *musica composita* or *mensurata* was polyphony; finally there was ecclesiastical music.[159] Finally, in this period there was also a strict relationship between music and *dialectic*, considered in the light of the florid development of logic in that age. Guido of Arezzo had already hypothesized, based on the invention of linear notation, the possibility of purely graphical thematic variations, such as symmetry or specular inversion.[160] As Ernst Bloch and others noted, even more complex counterpuntal forms were modelled in analogy with the variations of a given judgment according to the manifold combination rules of scholastic logic.[161] This is the first time music and logic got close: this relationship would be very fruitful in the future.

The medieval counterpoint, whose practice was (sometimes too) close to an intellectual activity, renewed the combination of music and philosophy in an unprecedented way. One should read in this light Johannes de Muris's attempt to use Aristotle's *Metaphysics* to mitigate the distinction between music as science

---

157 Moravia (1864, p. 13f.).
158 Moravia (1864, p. 19).
159 Grocheio (1943, p. 47).
160 Cf. Gallo (1991, p. 10ff.).
161 Bloch (1993, vol. 3, p. 1075): "[...] a connection appeared which so far has not been pursued at all and yet maintains the proud rationality of counterpoint even today: the connection with *scholastic logic*, or *more precisely with its forms of combination*. It is significant that Boethius, the same writer who in his 'Ars musica' handed down the Greek science of music, translated and commented on Aristotle's *Logic* for the same world and in many cases for the same people".

and music as art, for the benefit of the latter.[162] This view was countered in *Speculum musicae*, where Jacobus Leodiensis argues in favour of the music of the spheres and defends Boethius from the accusation of having given a naive explanation of it.[163] In the framework of this conscious conservatism, there was also a strong affirmation of the superiority of the musician understood as a theoretician. Such positions, however, would become obsolete with the spread of the typically Renaissance figure of the theoretical and practical musician—a prelude to the fifteenth century professional musician. And yet, as we shall see, this process would fail to overwhelm *musica mundana*.

---

162 Muris (1972, p. 47).
163 Leodiensis (1955, p. 47 f.).

Second Chapter
Harmony and Disenchantment

1 Humanists and Scientists

In order to talk about music and philosophy in the Renaissance it might be useful to take up Boethius's tripartition. The *musica instrumentalis* underwent great changes: new theories and practices started to spread, deeply affecting its general framework. Furthermore, the anthropological sensitivity typical of humanists produced reflections on the *musica humana* in the light of medicine, magic and an early form of individual psychology. Finally, the ideal perfection of *musica mundana* was still a reference point, but some of its traditional meanings evolved. Of course, all these phenomena must be understood in view of a wider change: in the sixteenth century—and even more so in the seventeenth —the foundations of music were revised according to modern science, which was affirming itself. However, it would be wrong to imagine a sharp contraposition between the lingering paladins of the metaphysics of sound numbers and the neutral experimentalism of the new science. The situation was much more complex and nuanced than that.[1]

Since the fifteenth century, music was also affected by the important philological novelties that could be found in all branches of the humanities. Along the route from Byzantium to Venice, the Greek music textbooks made their way to Europe, where they were rediscovered and translated.[2] As a result, the traditional sources were significantly integrated: for instance, Aristoxenus's writings were acquired alongside those attributed to Euclid and Plutarch. Humanism, though, brought about a rediscovery of Greek music *theory*, not music as such—contrary to all other artistic fields, in fact, there weren't any instances of Greek music. On the one hand, this gave even greater importance to theory. On the other, the situation made it impossible to encourage the strict imitation of classical models, as there were no practical examples available. So, the myth of Greek music took hold based on anecdotes and theory, which would often foster the idea of its rebirth. This is notoriously one of the factors that marked the birth of modern Opera, conventionally taken to go back to year 1600, when Jacopo Peri (and part-

---

[1] For more on the topic addressed here see the essays in Gozza (ed. 2010).
[2] Cf. Palisca (1985, *passim*), which also contains an anthology of rare texts concerning this cultural transition.

ly Giulio Caccini) composed a *Euridice*.³ Sticking to what interests us here, the nostalgia for the lost music of the ancients had other relevant effects. Girolamo Mei, a reserved and overall underestimated humanist versed in ancient Greek music, influenced the Florentine Camerata and especially Vincenzo Galilei.⁴ So, much earlier than what would happen in literature, a *querelle* between the ancient and the moderns begun in music—one that would last and occasionally light up in sudden polemic heat up until the nineteenth century.

In the light of the above, it is not surprising that the anecdotes on the prodigious effects of music in the ancient world aroused much interest already in the fifteenth century. This tradition was especially studied in circles and academies in France and Italy, as well as by thinkers like Marsilio Ficino. In the closing pages of his Latin commentary to Plato's *Symposium*, Ficino insists that "divine madness is a kind of illumination of the rational soul, through which God draws the soul slipping down to the lower world back to the higher".⁵ The soul is indeed "filled with discord and dissonance; therefore the first need for the poetic madness, which through musical tones arouses what is sleeping, through harmonic sweetness calms what is in turmoil, and finally [...] quells dissonant discord and tempers the various parts of the soul".⁶ The particular relevance of music was due to the affinity between the airy nature of sound and the *spiritus*; the ancient analogy between music and medicine was updated thanks to the correspondence between the elements and the various voices of the counterpoint.⁷

The sixteenth century was a time of great progress in terms of music theory, mathematical instruments, and the natural philosophy of sound: among others, authors like Franchinus Gaffurius and Girolamo Cardano lay the basis for the significant developments of the century to come. A special role was played by Francis Bacon, as he was able to place reflections on music within an articulated philosophical framework. Unusually, Bacon complains about the discrepancy between music practice, well developed in the Elisabethan era, and theory, which instead wastes time on "mystical subtilties" that prevent one from identifying the real causes of sound.⁸ Therefore, he wishes for the two spheres to be reconciled to the benefit of theory. Indeed, the myth of Pan—a fable "pregnant with the mysteries and secrets of nature"—shows that "there seem to be two

---

3 See the contributions in Palisca (ed. 1989).
4 Cf. Palisca (1960, p. 13 and 40 ff.) and Palisca (2006, p. 41).
5 Ficino (1985, p. 230).
6 Ficino (1985, p. 231). Cf. Boccadoro (2010, *passim*).
7 Cf. Boccadoro (2010, *passim*).
8 Bacon (1881, p. 225).

kinds of harmony,—the one of Divine providence, the other of human reason".[9] Heaven and earth are separated and music falls within nature—personified by Pan, Echo's husband. In Bacon's view, the effects of music can be traced back to the "spirits", based on the hypothesis that hearing is the sense that influences them the most. Music, whose *tropoi* are strictly related to rhetorical ones, doesn't transmit its own ethos: even if it fosters a "variety of passions", it "generally [...] feedeth that disposition of the spirits which it findeth", thereby magnifying—so to speak—the existing state of mind.[10]

The changes of this age have been efficaciously described as an irreversible shift of the theoretical axis from "number" to "sound".[11] In order to analyse this long and rather complex process, it helps to focus on two important innovations. The first is the falsification of the myth of Pythagoras's hammers: by making a string twice as tight one doesn't get a higher octave. The second is the identification of the phenomenon of periodic *ictus* or "beats" in the air, which—it now started to be clear—musical consonances depend on. These (independent) changes were, so to speak, the *pars destruens* and the *pars construens* of the philosophical discourse on music in early modernity.

As for the first point, the credit goes to Vincenzo Galilei, a musician and scholar related to Giovanni de' Bardi's circle, and father of Galileo Galilei. He engaged in polemical dialogue with Gioseffo Zarlino, the greatest music theorist of the century, in relation to several issues: starting from the problem of the right intonation in singing and the tuning of instruments, they debated the "naturality" of intervals and the meaning of numbers in music. I wish to focus especially on the latter issue. In his *Istitutioni harmoniche* (1558), Zarlino overcomes the traditional exclusion of the intervals of third and sixth from the category of consonances by introducing the *"numero senario"*. Zarlino claimed that number six is omnipresent in nature: there are six Zodiac constellations visible in each hemisphere, there are six planets, six celestial circles, six natural properties and "offices" (size, colour, etc.), six kinds of motion, six ages of man and so forth.[12] This way, Zarlino takes up the idea that the subject of music is the "sound number",

---

9 Bacon (1884, p. 335 and 342).
10 Bacon (1881, p. 231–233). Cf. Gouk (2010, *passim*).
11 Cf. Gozza (ed. 2010). Cohen (1984) distinguishes between a "mathematical", an "experimental" and a "mechanistic" approach. Here I will focus on the achieved results rather than the methodologies used.
12 Zarlino (1558, p. 23 ff. and p. 21). To Vincenzo Galilei's *Dialogo della musica antica et della moderna* (Galilei 1581), Zarlino responded with *Sopplimenti musicali* (Zarlino, 1588). Cf. Walker (1978, p. 14 f.).

according to the (Augustinian rather than Pythagorean) hypothesis that "all things created by God were ordered by him by Number".

Amongst other things, Vincenzo Galilei opposes Zarlino with an argument that deserves to be quoted in full, as it sums up one of the revolutions of the modern age.

> If you believe that the weights Pythagoras attached to the strings to better hear consonances were the same as those of the hammers from which he had heard them before, now experience shows that this was not possible in any way. If you take two strings of the same length, thickness, and goodness, and you expect to hear the diapason [*scil.* the octave], you would have to attach on them weights that are not in double (as the hammers were) but in quadruple ratio.[13]

With these words—this was 1589—Pythagoras's discoveries in the forge were questioned for the first time since their description, which was made about one-thousand-five-hundred years before by Nicomachus of Gerasa. As slow as this process had been, it was now irreversible: independently of Vincenzo Galilei, Christiaan Huygens reached similar conclusions in 1661.[14] In the quoted passage, a significant and controversial part is the reference to "experience", which was seemingly denied by some errors committed by Vincenzo Galilei further on in his argument.[15] It has also been hypothesised that Vincenzo's experiments with weights attached to strings, which necessarily produce pendulum oscillations, might have aroused the interest of young Galileo.[16] Either way, one should not forget that in addition to being an erudite scholar Vincenzo Galilei was a valent lutenist, familiar with the manipulation and tension of strings. This constitutes a form of pre-scientific "experimentation", supported more by musical practice than by the adequate mathematical tools, but it is not necessarily irrelevant.

Indeed, this aspect is another interesting side to Vincenzo Galilei's research. Further developing the quoted observations, he started experimenting with the sounds and the acoustic characteristics of non-filiform bodies. Although little used in music, even bodies that differ much from strings, such as "striking rods, vases, copper and silver coins, and other things" can produce musical ra-

---

13 V. Galilei (1589, p. 104).
14 Huygens (1937, p. 362). Cf. Dostrovsky (1974, p. 173 f.).
15 Vincenzo Galilei associates the sounds related to the length of the strings, the weight of the weights stretching them and the volume of organ pipes with a linear, quadratic and cubic ratio. He is wrong in the third case, but the usual ratio of length and diameter of the organ pipes makes the idea plausible.
16 Cf. Drake (1978, p. 72).

tios like the octave; however, "these will be vague and not the determinate weight, size and number demonstrable with strings and pipes".[17] Weight, measure and number: the divine ordering instruments are here confused and indeterminate, and yet some elementary musical relations emerge. An element of irrationality creeps in below the ordered surface of the sound, demanding explanation. It is an important conceptual breakthrough. The focus shifts here not only from number to sound, but also from sound to the resonant body and its physical properties, usually different from those of the string. The possibility to get an octave from the most varied numerical ratios brings Vincenzo Galilei to a rudimentary phenomenology of the resonant physical nature, whose most illustrious predecessors can be found—ironically—in the Pythagorean school: for example in Hippasus, blamed by Iamblichus for divulging irrational numbers like the diagonal of a square.[18] Often accompanied by precise theoretical and aesthetic implications, this approach to the problem of sound was destined to recur several times in later periods.[19]

Vincenzo Galilei's discoveries might suggest that the time of the music of the spheres was coming to an end, but this would be a hasty conclusion. A look at the two greatest astronomers of the time, Johannes Kepler and Isaac Newton, proves that the new science did not necessarily contradict that ancient and deep-rooted metaphysical belief. In his *Harmonice mundi* (1619) Kepler develops the thesis of the harmony of the world in a new way. He claims that devotees of "Samian philosophy"—the reference is not to Pythagoras but to Aristarchus, who also came from Samos—namely heliocentrists, must not "envy" their enemies for the *harmonia mundi*, because "their joy shall be many times more perfect" thanks to the new system.[20] The elliptical orbits make it so that the planets' motion is characterized by a speed difference at aphelion and perihelion: each planet, therefore, does not produce a single sound, but an interval. So, Kepler's *harmonia mundi* turns out to be the much more perfect harmony of a polyphonic cosmos.[21] Its concern is not a static chord, but something that unfolds in the time set by the admirable harmony of elliptical orbits, the bearers of universal harmony. Hence the ordering role of the Sun, so typical of the Renaissance (think of the *Corpus Hermeticum*, Ficino, Campanella, Pico): Proclus had already

---

17 V. Galilei (1989, p. 185).
18 Iamblichus (1991, p. 47).
19 See below, chap. 3, par. 1
20 Kepler (1940, p. 185).
21 Cf. Fabbri (2003, p. 6).

compared it to Orpheus, but now the Sun becomes the "princeps" and director of the choir of the planets.[22]

Newton's position is no less singular. In the (unpublished) *Scholia classica*, Newton claims that Pythagoras, by putting different weights on the strings, understood that "the weights [*scil.* the applied forces] of the Planets towards the Sun were reciprocally as the squares of their distances from the Sun".[23] Thus, Pythagoras anticipated the discovery of Newton's own gravitational law. In fact, the weights were in proportional relationship not to the string lengths (which, in the analogy, correspond to planetary distances), but to the *square* of the string lengths: this is what Pythagoras must have found. It should be noted that here Newton attributes to Pythagoras the square proportion that, for strings, had been in fact discovered by Vincenzo Galilei. However, given that according to Macrobius' testimony Pythagoras put weights on his strings, Newton believes that Pythagoras *did* find—"*certum est*" he insists –) the correct (square) formula. The point, for Newton, is that "the Philosophers loved so to mitigate their mystical discourses that in the presence of the vulgar they foolishly propounded vulgar matters for the sake of ridicule, and hid the truth beneath discourses of this kind".[24] The vulgar argument, in this case, was the harmony of solid orbits, which led to the false Ptolemaic system; the truth is Newton's gravitational law, which thereby acquires an ancient and noble origin—though it would be obviously misleading to picture Newton as a renovator of ancient wisdom. The analysis of these cases doesn't show so much the presence of an "occultist" residue hindering the discoveries of the most brilliant scientists, but rather the conscious and clever attempt to adapt the new discoveries to the idea that the cosmos is perfect—which had alway underlain the metaphors of the *harmonia mundi*.

We can now move on to the *pars construens* of the new philosophical reflection on music. The contribution of the new science here was decisive, as it introduced the thesis that sound consists of repeated *ictus* ("hits", "beats") of the air. Around 1630 this principle was known to Beeckman, Galileo, Mersenne, Descartes and Huygens, mostly independently of each other and of Giovanni Battista Benedetti who formulated it first.[25] The *ictus* principle contains a rudimentary intuition of the concept of frequency that seems to do away with sound numbers, shifting the attention towards experimental physics. However, the calculation of

---

22 Kepler (1940, p. 244 ff.).
23 Newton (1966, p. 116); for the latin text of Newton's *Scholia classica* cf. Casini (1981, p. 41). Cf. Gouk (1986, *passim*) and, for a different interpretation from Gouk's, cf. Guicciardini (2013, p. 66).
24 Newton (1966, p. 117).
25 Cohen (1984, p. 75 ff.).

frequencies gives rise to numerical series that are simply the reverse of string lengths: an ascending octave shows, instead of the ratio 2:1, the ratio 1:2. This didn't entail a revival of abstract numerological speculations. Of course, as Galileo understood very well, one should describe how the motion passes from the vibrating string to the surrounding air, but the solution was still far away.[26] Still, the *ictus* principle draws the attention mainly to the means of transmission of the beats—that is, the air—which calls into play the study of sound *perception*. It is not that the soul spontaneously responds to harmony: it is the ear that is stimulated by the surrounding air according to rules that can be found by physiology or psychology. These rules might offer the key to explain the phenomenon of consonances.

This perspective became clear with Galileo. In the first day of his *Dialogues Concerning Two New Sciences* (1638), Galileo ends the discussion on some properties of the pendulum motion by speaking of sound. Starting from the phenomenon of sympathetic resonance, observed on the strings of a spinet, Galileo resumed his father's observations: "I see no reason why those wise philosophers should adopt 2 rather than 4 as the ratio of the octave [...]".[27] However, based on new observations, it could also be said that the octave in a sense is the ratio 2:1. In support of this "patricide", Galileo mentions the common experience of rubbing the rim of a goblet with a finger, which generates a sound and regular ripples in the liquid. When "the tone of the glass jumps an octave higher" one can see that "each of the aforesaid waves divides into two".[28] An even more reliable way to calculate frequency is to plane a metal object generating hisses, whose pitch can be measured thanks to the sympathetic resonance observed of the spinet's strings. So the fifth interval corresponds to the 45:30 (3:2) ratio, measured on the marks that the chisel leaves on the metal. As a result of these innovations, the focus shifts on the air and on the effect of vibrations on the ear:

> Returning now to the original subject of discussion, I assert that the ratio of a musical interval is not immediately determined either by the length, size, or tension of the strings but

---

26 See below, chap. 3, par. 1
27 G. Galilei (1914, p. 100f.).
28 G. Galilei (1914, p. 99). Following Walker (1978, p. 29), Cohen (1984, p. 88) criticizes Galileo, because the tone doesn't jump an octave higher by rubbing a rim of a glass. However, for Galileo "the same phenomenon is observed to better advantage by fixing the base of the goblet upon the bottom of a rather large vessel of water filled nearly to the edge of the goblet [...]". G. Galilei (1914, p. 99).

rather by the ratio of their frequencies, that is, by the number of pulses of airwaves which strike the tympanum of the ear, causing it also to vibrate with the same frequency.[29]

Only by keeping this in mind can one understand the nature of consonance and dissonance. The "unpleasant sensation of the latter" is due to "the discordant vibrations of two different tones which strike the ear out of time"; whereas consonance arises from "pairs of tones which strike the ear with a certain regularity". Finally, the visual analogy completes Galileo's discourse.

The main point has to do with physiology: the fact that the "pulses" in the same interval of time are "commensurable in number" makes it so that the eardrum is not kept "in perpetual torment, bending in two different directions in order to yield to the ever-discordant impulses". This "negative" definition of consonance as the absence of disturbance would be very popular in subsequent history. But Galileo also proposes a positive definition, one that allows for an embryonic classification of consonances. While the unison forces the eardrum to endure waves with a monotonous vibration, the octave interposes an additional pulse, but "in such a manner as to produce no disturbance", which makes it "rather too much softened" and lacking "fire". The fifth instead, "by its displaced beats" due to the 3:2 ratio, produces "a tickling of the ear drum such that its softness is modified with sprightliness, giving at the same moment the impression of a gentle kiss and of a bite".[30]

With his typical vivid imagery, Galileo thus inserted arithmetic observations deriving from frequency ratios into the framework of an elementary psychophysiology of consonance, full of promising perspectives and original solutions. But considering sound as air implies a series of cultural aspects that have an even wider scope.[31] Not only physics, but also what could be defined the musical anthropology of the time were very much affected. This is undoubtedly one way to understand Athanasius Kircher's Baroque encyclopaedia *Musurgia universalis* (1650), a text able to blend together with remarkable coherence elements from different disciplines: natural philosophy of sound, even in its most original physiological and zoological aspects; the Jewish origin of music (in terms of the old dispute, Jubal is placed before Pythagoras)[32] which, however, does not diminish the importance of the Pythagorean tradition, reinterpreted in the light of medieval and Renaissance sources, especially Zarlino; and finally the theory of mu-

---

29 G. Galilei (1914, p. 103).
30 G. Galilei (1914, p. 106 f.).
31 Cf. Gozza (2005, p. 238).
32 Cf. McKinnon (1978, *passim*).

sical composition.³³ In *Phonurgia nova* (1673), Kircher also explores the possibilities coming from the manipulation, transmission and amplification of sound, including the design of sound machines—far-fetched to some extent, but prophetically visionary in the awareness of the enormous impact of sound reproduction over human beings. This anthropological side of Baroque explains the renewed interest in the phenomenon of echo, with its extraordinary poetic but also scientific and technological value. As Marin Mersenne observes in the opening of his *Harmonie universelle* (1636), men are immersed in air like fish are in water, but unlike the latter they cannot get out of it, not even for a second.³⁴ This isn't just a suggestive image. The propagation of sound is similar to the dynamic of fluids: in the absence of void—like underwater—the struck air moves by transmitting the pulses.

Despite belonging to a specific scientific context, for Mersenne music isn't just any of the quadrivium arts, and he devotes more space to it than to any other topic. This can be already seen in his *Quaestiones celeberrimae in Genesim* (1623), where he embraces Kepler's criticism of Robert Fludd, and in the *Traité de l'harmonie universelle* (1627). But it is only after 1629 that Mersenne updated his views in the light of Isaac Beeckman's theory of *ictus* (*battements*).³⁵ Hence the *Harmonie universelle*, a very comprehensive musical encyclopaedia that holds a special place in the cultural landscape of the seventeenth-century. On the one side Mersenne develops his research with remarkable spirit of observation, managing for example to calculate the propagation speed of sound in air, and tackling many other phenomena with scientific spirit. On the other, being a monk of the order of Minims, who finds it very difficult to accept heliocentrism, he is always concerned with morality, which is expressed in many propositions and "corollaries" included in the book. In the section entitled *De l'utilité de l'harmonie*, Mersenne even offers a number of apologetic arguments in relation to the use of music for homiletics.³⁶ Like all sciences, music shows the glory of the creator: though not because it refers to the superhuman harmony of heaven, but because it is a free human creation and as such pleasing to God. Hence the adoption of the Keplerian contrapuntal conception of the *harmonia mundi*.

Apologetics and mechanism are therefore hard to separate. For example, Mersenne tried to demonstrate that frequency is the inverse of the strings'

---

33 On Kircher's *Musurgia universalis* cf. Pangrazi (2009, *passim*).
34 Mersenne (1636, p. 9).
35 Mersenne (1623, cols. 1557 f.). On Fludd cf. Ammann (1967, *passim*).
36 Mersenne (1636, p. 4 ff.). Cf. Fabbri (2008, p. 38).

length.[37] However, he derived from it that men are more dependent on God than a sound is on the body emanating it.[38] In the light of this moral meaning, one can understand the importance of a hierarchical classification of consonances —an issue that Mersenne had felt passionately about since his *Quaestiones celeberrimae in Genesim*. Descartes, instead, dismissed the whole thing by writing that deciding "to what extent a consonance is more pleasant than another" is like wondering to what extent fruit is better than fish.[39] For Descartes, one can establish whether a consonance is *simpler* than another, not whether it is sweeter or more pleasant (see below, par. 2). And yet, the issue is fundamental to Mersenne.

Consonances are all the more perfect the closer they are to the octave. This is similar to the "final cause of Morals" which determines the goodness of actions, which are "the better, the closer they are to it or the better they represent it, or the more they contain nobler relations and habits". The new physical notions on the air "beats" were welcomed by Mersenne also because they allowed him to justify this order. Indeed, an even more perfect consonance is the unison, of which the octave is the "doubling", or image, compared to the prototype. Aristotle had excluded unison from the category of consonances, and Galileo had relegated it to the last place for the above-mentioned reasons; Mersenne instead rehabilitated the unison as it "represents virtue and the treasures of divinity". It reminds us of the true meaning of music, which far from amusing the ear must bring us back "to the eternal things that keep an order so perfect" that there is no place in it for dissonance, as sins are only man's doing.[40]

In conclusion, one can note how the *pars destruens* and the *pars construens* of sixteenth-century music theory identify two models based on different aspects of sound, which would later diverge more and more up to becoming opposites. In other words, the passage from number to sound harbours two possible conceptions of sound itself: on the one hand the physical body, on the other air as its means of transmission. Interestingly, Galilei father and son ideally embody the unfolding of this dispute in the very brief time of a generation.

---

37 Dear (1988, p. 152; 2010, *passim*). Mersenne is of course far behind Galileo in terms of experimental skill: cf. Bailhache (1993, p. 75).
38 Mersenne (1636, p. 17).
39 Descartes (1933, p. 406).
40 Mersenne (1636, p. 115). See also Mersenne (1636, p. 29 and 42).

2 From Descartes to Leibniz

The critics tend to consider the *Compendium musicae*, Descartes's first unpublished work, as a testament to the breadth of his early interest, which does not have much to do with his mature production. Descartes gave it as a present to Beeckman in 1618; later, mistakenly suspecting plagiarism, he wanted it back. It would certainly be pointless to look for anticipations of Descartes's mature philosophy in his *Compendium musicae*.[41] However, the text has some bearing on his later writings both in philosophy and in mechanic science.[42]

First of all, Descartes identifies sound as the "object" of music. The end of music is "to please and to arouse various Affections in us", which are such that pleasure for music can also be provoked by sad melodies[43]. The physical origin of sound is considered irrelevant to music, which instead is equally influenced by variations in duration and pitch of the sounds. Once defined the field of investigation, Descartes starts listing the "preliminaries" (*praenotanda*) to the study of music. He begins by noting that all the senses can generate delight associated to the relationship with the object (1). The Aristotelian origin of this principle is shown by the reference to the possible disappearance of this relationship due to a disproportion of the object: gunshots and thunder are not music (2).[44] Once established that proportion is what matters when it comes to music, Descartes looks more closely at what proportions are preferable and why. His musical aesthetics revolves around the ease with which the sensible object is perceived: "[t]he object must be such, that it does not fall on the sense in too complicated or confusion a fashion" (3),[45] that is, its parts have to be in such relation as to result pleasantly proportioned (4–5). As we shall see, this happens when the proportion between the parts is "arithmetic, not geometric" (6). To be pleasing to the spirit, however, the object must not be caught too easily or with too much difficulty (7). Finally, "variety" is most pleasant in all things (8).[46]

The point is now to identify the music relations that best respond to such principles. Descartes believes that parts in arithmetic proportion ($a-b = c-d$) are perceived more easily than those in geometric proportion ($a:b = c:d$). In the former, in fact, "there is less to perceive, as all differences are the same

---

[41] Cf. Cohen (1984 p. 192ff.). It is particularly misleading to look here for anticipations of the *cogito*, as does Besseler (1959).
[42] Augst (1965, p. 120).
[43] Descartes (1961, p. 11).
[44] Descartes (1961, p. 11).
[45] Descartes (1961, p. 12).
[46] Descartes (1961, p. 13).

throughout. Therefore, in its attempt to perceive everything distinctly the sense will be not so strained".[47] Descartes discusses the issue referring to geometrical examples, based on which he concludes that "the mind is in this case constantly perplexed".[48]

These arguments are very important to understand the role played by the *Compendium musicae* within Descartes's thought. In the *Rules for the Direction of the Mind* (rule XIV), Descartes would insist on the importance of the imagination, as every quantitative consideration can be reduced to "that species of magnitude which is most readily and distinctly depicted in our imagination", that is, *extension*.[49] Indeed, even if something can be said to be "more or less white than another, and a sound more or less sharp than another", however "we cannot determine exactly whether the greater exceeds the lesser by a ratio of 2 to 1 or 3 to 1 unless we have recourse to a certain analogy with the extension of a body that has shape",[50] which is indeed the method adopted in the *Compendium musicae*.

I have already mentioned that the musically relevant aspects of sound are duration and pitch. Now, the principles of proportionality indicated by Descartes are functional to illustrate them both. Musical tempo must necessarily be made up of equal parts (based on preliminaries 4, 5 and 6), or else of parts that are in a proportion of 2 to 1 or 3 to 1. This doesn't hold for the exclusively rhythmical music of drums: as there is nothing but rhythm here, one can equally identify in it fifth- or seventh-type figurations. One could associate a different emotion to each type and speed of rhythm, but Descartes merely hints at it. As for pitch, Descartes introduces the issue in an original way: it can be considered

> principally under three aspects; sounds produced by different bodies at the same time; those which are produced successively in one and the same voice, and finally those which are produced successively by different voices or by different sounding bodies. By the first method consonances are produced, by the second method the steps, by the third those dissonances which are closer to consonances.[51]

Therefore, consonance solely relates to simultaneous sounds. In fact, sounds must be homogenous in simultaneity, or they would tire our ears, whereas for sounds emitted successively there is greater tolerability.

---

47 Descartes (1961, p. 12).
48 Descartes (1961, p. 13).
49 Descartes (1985, p. 58).
50 Descartes (1985, p. 58).
51 Descartes (1961, p. 16).

The phenomenon of sympathetic resonance leads Descartes to believe that "pitch is related to pitch like string to string".[52] The background of these elementary considerations is significant: Descartes sets aside the contraposition between continuous and discrete quantities (and the Aristotelian prohibition to move from one to the other) and focuses on the convergence between the two, which he will analyse in his *Geometry*. The *Compendium musicae*, which ends with an analysis of the various consonances as well as a series of rules to compose music, leaves much unsaid. But the general direction is chosen: the aesthetics of perception, explained based on the analogy with geometry, is the key to understand music.

In the next years Descartes went back to dealing with music on several occasions. It is no surprise that the topic emerges from his correspondence with Mersenne, especially in the years 1629–1630, when both philosophers studied the nature of sound.[53] Descartes's theory of "pulses", though, seems to be in contrast with the above-mentioned "geometrization", which involves emphasising the role of continuous magnitudes. Do physics of sound and musical aesthetics proceed separately? In fact, in both areas Descartes overcomes the opposition between continuous and discrete.[54] But where is the threshold between them? The answer must be sought in the physiological bases of the human mind, which is illustrated in the second part of Descartes's treatise *Le Monde*, which was left unpublished in 1633 because of Descartes's fear after Galileo's sentence.

Passing through the ear, the air pulses are transmitted unchanged to the ear filaments, which transmit to the brain the "slight shocks" that generate the auditory sensation. If the "shock" is one, it produces a muffled sound, which can only be relatively intense. If instead there are many shocks, as can be seen in the "vibrations of strings and of bells", which is then transmitted to the nerves, the sound will be louder or softer depending on the uniformity of the shocks, and higher or lower depending on how quickly they follow one another. The proportion of the shocks, therefore, is what determines musical ratios: double speed gives an octave, etc. This is how the soul finds pleasure in music, which is improved by variety as already mentioned in the *Compendium*, because "it is not absolutely the smoothest things that are the most agreeable to the senses, but those that titillate them in the best-tempered way".[55] The simplicity of ratios

---

[52] Descartes (1961, p. 16).
[53] Cf. the letters translated in Descartes (1991, p. 13–20).
[54] Fabbri (2008, p. 91).
[55] Descartes (2003, p. 47–49). Here Descartes seems to intuit the phenomenon of periodicity by favouring "smoothness", while a less regular succession causes "noise" to be mixed with the sound.

doesn't stand for special properties of music, nor does it improve the delight it brings. On the contrary, musical rhythms and pitches exemplify the same need to grasp the object clearly—something that is ubiquitous in Cartesian philosophy. So that the phenomenon is not reduced to a disheartening given, then, aesthetic dynamism is needed: hence the principle of variety.

Despite the relatively few passages devoted to it, music seems to have been very important to Leibniz. Nothing is more agreeable for human senses than musical attunement (*Einstimmung*)—a small taste of the kind found in nature.[56] As a consequence, Leibniz's famous sentence *musica est exercitium arithmeticae occultum nescientis se numerare animi* ("Music is the pleasure the human mind experiences from counting without being aware that it is counting") must be contextualised.[57] The general principle is clear: Leibniz accepts the idea that pleasure coming from consonances derives from the arithmetic congruence of *ictus*. So far there is nothing new, but Leibniz provides an explanation for this phenomenon based on his metaphysics. Only God, the supreme monad, can have a distinct knowledge of everything. The human soul, instead, knows everything only confusedly: strolling by the sea, we are aware of the overall rumble, whereas the noise of the individual waves, despite being heard, is not grasped distinctly.[58] Small perceptions are unperceived, but still have an effect: they help create the overall impression. Something similar happens in the perception of consonances. To be precise, Leibniz does not conceive of a composition of many small sound perceptions in an overall impression. After all, despite knowing some of Sauveur's writings,[59] Leibniz didn't seem to know about *sons harmoniques* (see below, par. 3). According to him, the coincidence of regular *ictus*, which remains unnoticed, generates the feeling of pleasure (*voluptas*). In other words, Leibniz's discourse is not related to the technicalities of the perception of sound, but only to the purely aesthetic sphere.

So as not to misunderstand the meaning of the above-mentioned principle, one has to ask a very important question: does musical pleasure arise *because* or *even though* we are unaware of being calculating? The correct answer is undoubtedly the latter:

> Music charms us, although its beauty consists only in the harmonies (*convenances*) of numbers and in the counting (of which we are unconscious but that which nevertheless the soul

---

56 Leibniz (1965b, p. 122).
57 Leibniz (1734, p. 241).
58 Leibniz (1898, p. 420).
59 Cf. Luppi (1988, p. 67).

does make) of the beats or vibrations of sounding bodies, which beat or vibrations come together at definite intervals.⁶⁰

So, it can be seen that the fundamental aesthetic principle is not *unawareness*—the "musical subconscious" that is sometimes attributed to Leibniz—but the regularity that wonderfully manages to affect the soul, even despite its obliviousness to it.

Indeed, the regularity that ennobles music is not only a matter of unaware calculation. For Leibniz, pleasure is the "feeling of a perfection" that we sense in ourselves or in something else. In the latter case, perfection is somewhat inscribed and "planted" in us: this happens when we contemplate the intelligence, virtue or beauty of another human being, or a work of art. In our aesthetic experience we are usually unaware of how this happens, so we just refer to an unspecified "something" that triggers it. Music is an excellent example of this "something". Someone hitting a drum with regular beats, a musical measure (*Tact*), or the cadence of a dancer please us because of the order they express. An equally regular order, albeit invisible, is in play when bodies resonate: it is transmitted through air to our hearing, generating a resonance (*Wiederhall*) in us such that it "stimulates our vital spirits". Hence the reason why music so easily affects the soul.⁶¹

However, Leibniz is perfectly conscious that variety is needed, and that harmony cannot exist incessantly. The metaphysical principle of *diversitas identitate compensata*—the idea that perfection has to involve the greatest number of simultaneously possible beings—implies the necessity of dissonance. The problem of the justice of God, addressed in *Theodicy* (1710), also involves some musical aspects. According to Leibniz, evil appears to us as such because, unlike God, we do not clearly grasp the whole edifice of creation in every part—past, present and future. It is as if we covered a painting with a sheet, with the exception of a small part: what can be seen there could easily seem pointless. Similarly, musicians mix dissonances with smooth harmonies in order to arouse the listener—to disturb him, as it were—so that he will be momentarily anxious about what is to happen, and will feel all the more pleasure when order is restored.

This passage leads me to discuss the question of intellectualism. In Leibniz, aesthetics appears as a form of knowledge, which is—literally—"slower" compared to intellectual knowledge. This shows that Leibniz does not profess extreme intellectualism: he is completely foreign to any form of contempt towards

---

60 Leibniz (1898, p. 422).
61 Leibniz (1965b, p. 86f.).

the senses, which are important and independent of the intellect. Nevertheless, there is no question that the aesthetic experience—as a form of knowledge—is inferior to intellectual and intuitive knowledge: aesthetic is the minor, not twin, sister of logic.[62] It is important to underline this aspect, because Leibniz's thought strongly influenced the "official" birth of aesthetics—which was thus christened in 1750 by Alexander Gottlieb Baumgarten, a student of Christian Wolff.

As we have seen, the reason for the importance of music, in Leibniz, isn't the unawareness of the calculation but the ordered complexity within arithmetic regularity. Therefore, as in the scholastic tradition, music is subordinate to arithmetics, whereas musical composition is related to the *ars combinatoria*: "one can show a man who knows nothing about music how to compose without making mistakes", even though the authentically aesthetic moment always requires the creative intervention of the imagination.[63] Indeed, the relationship between music and *ars combinatoria* was very often dealt with between the seventeenth and the eighteenth century. The problem of how to completely variate a series of notes, already present in Kircher, found practical application in very popular games aimed to invent or combine melodies.[64] In Mersenne, instead, the *ars combinatoria* was related to the moral issue: no one can take the best moral action, and nature cannot produce the best face or body, except for Adam, Our Lord or the Virgin Mary. What follows is that the only possibility for man, even in music, is the best combination of possible cases.[65] The potential tension between music and morality—which Mersenne tries to solve with the theoretical means available—are addressed with a very different approach by Leibniz.

Leonard Euler's divulgative writings appeared in the eighteenth century along with this line of thought. In *Letters to a German Princess*, published in the years 1768–1772, Euler develops the idea that musical pleasure is linked not only to a calculation, but also to a kind of musical puzzle. Euler illustrates with an effective graphical aid the physical foundations of the theory of consonance according to the traditional scheme of pulse coincidence. However, knowledge of the harmonic and rhythmic proportions of a song is not yet sufficient to explain the pleasure of music: "something more is wanting, which no one hitherto has unfolded".[66]

---

62 Cf. Bailhache (1999, p. 425).
63 Leibniz (1965a, p. 170).
64 Cf. Kassler (2001, p. 37 ff.).
65 Mersenne (1636, p. 104).
66 Euler (1802, p. 32).

Some insist on the value of dissonance: to really please us, the knowledge of proportions must "cost us something". But this is not enough either: according to Euler, the composer must have "have pursued in his work, a certain plan, executed in real and perceptible proportions". So, pleasure comes from "comprehending, beside the proportions, the very plan and design which the composer had in view". In this respect, music is akin to pantomime, where one guesses feelings and dialogues based on gestures, which are also pleasant to see. Therefore, musical enjoyment is reserved to a *connoisseur* who, in addition to perceiving the proportions, guesses the "plan" of the artist and feels the satisfaction that inevitably arises in the presence of an "intelligent ear".

3 Sounds and the Light of Reason: Rousseau

If the seventeenth century focused on the notion of *ictus*, the eighteenth was all about the so-called *sons harmoniques* (upper partial harmonic tones). This phenomenon had been roughly known since antiquity.[67] However, it wasn't until the late seventeenth century that there was a systematic study of it, so that the issue was no longer relegated to the sphere of *mirabilia* but was approached with a scientific spirit. Initially, the study of upper partial tones seemed to complicate things quite a bit, as they appeared to contradict the recently discovered law of frequency. However, the phenomenon acquired great importance because it hinted at the possibility to scientifically explain not only *consonances* but rather *harmony*, understood in the modern sense of theory of chords or tonal triads.

The first documents testifying to this new interest in upper partial tones include the contributions of John Wallis and Francis Robartes to the *Philosophical Transactions* of the Royal Society.[68] Academies played an important role in this process: institutions like the London *Royal Society* or the Parisian *Académie Royale des Sciences* spread the observations and experiments of scholars from different nations, contributing to the progress of the science of sound. It is no coincidence that the neologism "acoustics" (a science that would have a long and winding road ahead of it) is linked to the studies of Joseph Sauveur.[69] Sauveur was the first to clearly realize that the harmonic partial tones *always* resonate along with the fundamental one, when the string is left free to oscillate without any constrictions. Therefore, upper partials are not some strange peculiarity but

---

[67] Aristotle (2011, p. 385 [*Probl.* 19.13]).
[68] Dostrovsky (1974, p. 204f.).
[69] Sauveur (1701). See Auger (1948, *passim*) and Christensen (1993, p. 137ff.).

a constant component of sound itself, which reveals an unexpected multiplicity. In his report on Sauveur's exposition, the perpetual secretary of the Academy Bernard le Bovier de Fontenelle speaks of an "entirely new music system" destined to change "the ordinary practice of musicians".[70] Nature acts as a guide through this transformation: indeed, the music systems of all time have always been based on harmonics, even though the latter "had remained unknown". Almost to apologize for this belated discovery, Fontenelle adds:

> Therefore, it is not that nature in the past has not had the strength to push musicians into the system of upper partial. On the contrary, they fell into it even without knowing them, under the sole guide of their ear and their experience.[71]

Although Fontenelle takes up Descartes's observations on the simplicity of the proportions to justify people's different musical tastes, his words show all the strength of eighteenth-century musical "naturalism", a tendency that was far from obvious and indeed eccentric compared to the dominant aesthetic paradigm of imitation, which music was usually forced into.[72]

The triumph of *sons harmoniques*, though, was not as linear as one might think *a posteriori*. In his first work, Traité de l'harmonie (1722), Jean-Philippe Rameau didn't mention it, referring instead to Zarlino and Descartes. Rameau markedly privileged harmony over melody, showing the conviction that in every melody one can always hear the "fundamental bass", which is the "compass of the ear".[73] It was only later that Rameau related music theory to the phenomenon of upper partial harmonics, which makes every sound analogous to the corresponding perfect major chord.[74] Melody is not only logically and aesthetically subordinate to harmony: it is born from it.[75] The difficulty to explain the minor mode didn't change Rameau's faith in the general principles of his theory: at first he thought of an inversion of the generative process, then he resorted to a possible sympathetic resonance. In any case, only harmony reaches the soul, whereas melody stops at the senses. Coherently, Rameau thought that the music of the ancients was as "wrong" as their theory. How could the Greeks

---

70 Fontenelle (1701, p. 121).
71 Fontenelle (1702, p. 92).
72 Cf. Neubauer (1986, *passim*).
73 Rameau (1722, p. 3 ff.).
74 Rameau (1726, p. iv).
75 Rameau (1737, p. 28). Rameau suggests the analogy with Newton's prism: see Christensen (1993, p. 142).

not notice that thirds and sixths are consonant—he wondered with genuine bewilderment?[76]

Playing the *philosophe*, in the 1760s Rameau tried to narrate the origin of music by rewriting Rousseau's well-known image of the state of nature. In that situation, people did not speak—posited Rameau—but only used vocal inflexions: finding by chance the perfect major triad, they then used it in theory and practice. Otherwise it would be unclear why savages sing with the same intervals as us ("*aussi juste que nous*"). Rameau also wanted to relate the origin of harmony to Biblical genealogies. Having invented musical instruments, Jubal (*Genesis* 4.21) must have been aware of harmonic laws, therefore the inventor of singing was Adam. Such knowledge was "infused" into him by God, but went lost when Noah—understandably otherwise preoccupied after the Great Flood—entrusted two different sons with the tetrachord and with proportions, which thus ended up respectively in China (via the Tower of Babel) and in Egypt, whence they came to Pythagoras.[77] "All of this is probable", concludes Rameau in all seriousness.

Leaving aside this downward spiral, let's go back to 1748, when (perhaps following Rameau's refusal) Diderot asked a young Genevan recently arrived in Paris, known for a musical notation reform project, to collaborate in the drafting of the musical entries of the *Encyclopédie*. These entries, along with other musical writings by Jean-Jacques Rousseau, would cause Rameau's indignant reaction, giving rise to a controversy that would eventually involve all encyclopaedists.[78] After defending Rameau's theory at first, d'Alembert distanced himself from it.[79] There cannot be demonstrative evidence in music, contrary to what Rameau claims. Instead, one should forget about the whole "labyrinth of metaphysical speculations" on the causes of musical pleasure. D'Alembert also complains about the "ridiculous" abuse of geometry in music, because "experience" is the basis of everything. Nevertheless, "physical-mathematical" sciences like music do not necessarily depend on *one* experience: Rameau is a "precursor", but there is room for other experiences, like that of the "third sound" discussed by Giuseppe Tartini in 1754.[80]

---

76 Rameau (1750, p. 2).
77 Rameau (1760, p. 216 and 225 f.).
78 On this controversy see Cernuschi (2000); Fubini (1991a; 1991b).
79 Alembert (1752). The second edition (Alembert 1766) was "revue, corrigée et considérablement augmentée". In fact, d'Alembert introduces a *Discours préliminaire* (p. ii–xxxvi) expressing criticism towards Rameau.
80 These quotations come from Alembert (1766, p. xxx and xix).

Diderot's musical aesthetics is the closest to Rameau's theses. Drawing on Malebranche, Diderot however wants to read them largely based on Cartesian aesthetics.[81] A nice painting, a poem, or a beautiful piece of music please us because of the ratios, and one should beware of those who are too sensitive to music: based on the movements that harmony stirs in them, they sense the possibility of even stronger movements, up to envisioning the idea of "a sort of music that would kill them with pleasure".[82] What is particularly interesting is that Diderot comes to such an aesthetic thesis from his research in acoustics. Based on the usual analogy with architecture, in his *Principes généraux d'acoustique* (1748) he states that musical pleasure is given by the ratios between the sounds. However, differences in music taste derive from the greater or lesser ability to grasp the greatest possible number of ratios: this is why "the Barbarians' songs are too simple for us, and ours too composite for them".[83]

Rousseau would object to any conciliatory effort in this sense. The vibrating string does not at all only resonate with the upper partials corresponding to the simple ratios of the perfect major chord. On the contrary, as one can read in the *Dictionnaire de musique* (1768), it generates "an infinity of other sounds formed by all parts composing the resounding body".[84] Rameau's theory is therefore both under- and over-determined: it fails to explain the minor mode, and it arbitrarily privileges some upper partials over others, without providing any convincing reason. However, for Rousseau music always has a fundamentally philosophical value—a belief that goes well beyond his polemic with Rameau. On the one hand, the reason for this centrality is to be sought in the musical events that marked his life: from his youthful fantasies to the success at court of his composition *Le devin du village*, up to his return to Paris when Jean-Jacques only lived off his job as a music copyist.[85] On the other hand—which is what interests us here—one should note that Rousseau finds a deep and original link between

---

81 Cf. Charrak (2003, p. 174 ff. and 213).
82 Diderot (1751, p. 408): "[...] des hommes en qui toutes les fibres oscillent avec tant de promptitude et de vivacité, que, sur l'expérience des mouvements violents que l'harmonie leur cause, ils sentent la possibilité de mouvements plus violents encore, et atteignent à l'idée d'une sorte de musique qui les ferait mourir de plaisir".
83 Diderot (1748, p. 85).
84 Entry 'Harmonie', in Rousseau (2008, p. 374). This critical edition includes the different versions of those entries that Rousseau included both in *Encyclopédie* and in the *Dictionnaire*.
85 Cf. Starobinski (1971, p. 59) on Rousseau's youthful impersonations of an imaginary musician, and (1971, p. 176) on the success of *Le devin du village*.

music and anthropology. Not only is music a human phenomenon,[86] but it is also deeply rooted in human nature, of which it exhibits a distinctive trait.

Here I will look at the entries written by Rousseau for the *Encyclopédie*, which he later revised, supplemented and collected in his *Dictionnaire de musique*. The entry 'Musique' is a real hub in the intertwining of these texts. In the first version, published in *Encyclopédie*, Rousseau distinguishes between "speculative" and "practical" music. In the later version of the entry, appeared in the *Dictionnaire*, Rousseau added the further fundamental division of music into "natural" and "imitative". Natural music merely addresses "the physical aspect of sound", therefore acting on the senses by means of "more or less pleasant" sensations that do not reach the heart. Imitative music instead, by means of

> lively and accented inflections which, as it were, speak, expresses all passions, paints all pictures, renders all objects, subjects the whole nature to its ingenious imitations and thus brings to man's heart those feelings that are able to move him.[87]

Authentically lyrical and theatrical, this music "was that of ancient poems", supported by a very musical language (Greek vowels with an acute accent differ by a fifth from those with a grave one) that the moderns cannot even imagine.[88] This explains the effects of Greek music and the misunderstandings of the moderns:

> It is only in this [*scil.* imitative] music, and not in the harmonic or natural, that one should seek the cause of the prodigious effects it produced in other ages. So long as one seeks moral effects in the sole physics of sound, one shall never find them and will reason without understanding.[89]

This is how Rousseau undermines the alternative between melody and harmony. The point is not to carry on with the *querelle des bouffons* originated by the Parisian representation of Pergolesi's *Serva padrona*, whose lightheartedness was immediately set against the French lyrical tragedy.[90] Rousseau had indeed contributed to heating up the debate, precisely when the storm seemed to have passed, with the famous closing lines of his *Lettre sur la musique françoise:* "the French have no music and cannot have one, and [...] if they ever do have

---

[86] Rousseau (1966, p. 63): "Nature alone engenders little sound. And, unless one believes in the Harmony of the celestial spheres, it must be produced by living beings".
[87] Rousseau (2008, p. 462).
[88] Rousseau (1966, p. 24 ff.).
[89] Rousseau (2008, p. 462).
[90] Fubini (1991a, p. 92 ff.).

one, so much the worse for them".⁹¹ Rousseau didn't please anyone, as he attacked French tragedy without embracing the Italian cause: in his view, not even Italian is exempt from the loss of musicality that characterizes all modern languages.⁹²

Leaving polemics aside, it is worth insisting on the origin of music as it is described throughout Rousseau's texts. The first path leads to the anthropological topics of the second *Discourse* and of the *Essay on the Origin of Languages*. Here Rousseau sets "facts" aside to search for human nature, which he compares to the Platonic statue of Glaucus: so disfigured by marine encrustations that it looks like a beast more than a god.⁹³ To be precise, music did not appear in the state of nature: "the real savage never sang".⁹⁴ However, it played a crucial role in the immediately following phase: the "primitive" society. This is where Rousseau locates the birth of language, coinciding with the geographical spread of the human species. Where the climate was pleasant, human beings forgot about their own ferocity: the young voiced impressions deriving from their attraction to the other gender. Here "the first discourses were the first songs", because

> the melodious modulations of accent, gave birth to poetry and music along with language. Or rather, that was the only language in those happy climes and happy times when the only pressing needs that required the agreement of others were those to which the heart gave birth.⁹⁵

By contrast, in the hostile northern climates, the first utterance, with a very different emphasis, was not "love me" but "help me". Here is the origin of the bifurcation which is manifested in the alternative aesthetics of the century. The fracture between South and North goes back to a disjunction that took place with the very birth of language—and therefore of man.

We thus come to the second level of Rousseau's discourse, which highlights the historical hiatus between ancient and modern music. It only partly coincides with the anthropological gap between South and North, but undoubtedly complements it. According to Rousseau, the speculative and the practical parts of music went hand in hand in ancient times: everything revolved around a

---

91 Rousseau (1753, p. 328).
92 Rousseau (1966, p. 27).
93 Rousseau (2002, p. 1). The myth, modified here by Rousseau, is taken from Plato (2013b, p. 481f. [*Resp.* 611c–d]).
94 Rousseau (2008, p. 182).
95 Rousseau (1966, p. 50).

music that was deeply ethical and spoke to the soul, not the ear. This is what the presumptuous supporters of modern music often forget about.[96] Therefore, at a second and deeper level, the *querelle* on French music hides the polemic on Greek music. For Rousseau, musicians should not imitate ancient models (which they don't have, anyway) but make music as imitative as the ancient one. Music can be imitative as much as other arts, because it can put "the eye into the ear", so to speak, and imitate the invisible.[97] By realizing the deepest and most authentic form of mimesis, musicians do not paint the object but the state of mind that the object arouses in the listener.[98] What is left of the imitative paradigm refers to nature no longer understood as mechanical order in a Cartesian sense, but as a model from which man cannot be excluded.

So, music was originally imitative and expressive. However, since antiquity, it has undergone a process of progressive degeneration. As the enharmonic genre decayed, even in ancient Greece "the study of philosophy and the progress of reason deprive[d] language of its vital, passionate quality which made it so singable". What's worse:

> Greece was then full of sophist and philosophers, though she no longer had any famous musicians or poets. In cultivating and the art of convincing, that of arousing the emotions was lost. Plato himself, envious of Homer and Euripides, decried the one and was unable to imitate the other.[99]

Anticipating the line of reasoning that would later be adopted by Nietzsche,[100] Rousseau openly contrasted music and philosophy, strongly undermining the tradition that saw them as sisters. The explicit reference to Plato has special significance: the very philosopher who most of all identified music and philosophy reveals the falsehood of such association. Of course, Rousseau did not blame only philosophy: the loss of political freedom in Greece, the spread of Latin and finally the invasions of the Barbarians—whose speech, according to Emperor Julian, sounded like a frog croaking—were the final blow to music, which was then left, unrecognizable, to the mercy of modern harmony. These arguments might have exonerated philosophy, as it were, but Rousseau deliberately made a different choice—one that cannot be neglected or simply reduced to the polemics of his time.

---

96 Rousseau (2008, p. 469).
97 Rousseau (2008, p. 391); cf. also Rousseau (1966, p. 57).
98 Rousseau (2008, p. 391 f.).
99 Rousseau (1966, p. 68 f.).
100 See below, chap. 3, par. 5.

Indeed, Rousseau paradoxically associated the destiny of music to a crucial philosophical problem. Music is an exemplary illustration of the degeneration of language and, thereby, of the human being, but it also points to possible ways to remedy this. The lost music, which we can only imagine, arouses infinite nostalgia, which weighs like a shadow on musical enjoyment today. This music evokes human nature as it used to be, describing it with tones that cannot leave us indifferent. Nature mustn't be sought in acoustics experiments, but in the human heart.

4 Music and Play in Kant

The role of music in Immanuel Kant's *Critique of the Power of Judgement* (1790) is rather controversial.[101] Kant often speaks of music as an art that is not beautiful but only pleasant; he complains about the annoyance it can cause to neighbours, and theorizes that it is more about enjoyment than culture. For him, music is a matter of sensations that stirs something in our guts, like when we laugh at a joke. Therefore, it is not surprising that many music lovers have interpreted these theses as unacceptable: Kant seems to embody the prototypical philosopher obsessed with reason and deaf to music, mainly due to ignorance. Kant cannot be fully exonerated, due to his ambiguous and sometimes obscure argumentations on music, but this prejudice should nonetheless be set aside when analysing his work. Kant's specific knowledge of specific works of music, painting, sculpture, architecture or poetry, quite simply, has nothing to do with his critique of the faculty of judgment. After all, albeit with some difficulty, Kant doesn't expel music from his Olympus of arts.

Rather, Kant appears hesitant as to whether music is "beautiful" or "pleasant". To understand the issue it is important to note that, for Kant, aesthetic judgments can be pure or empirical. The latter express a "barbaric" taste that mixes the disinterested contemplation of beauty with "charms and emotions", compromising the universality of the judgment—one of its fundamental prerequisites.[102] Now, it seems that sounds fall precisely in the category of such

---

101 Guyer (1996, p. 206–207).
102 Kant (2002, p. 108–109). As for his references, it is unclear what Kant knew from direct sources and what from the *Allgemeine Theorie der schönen Künste* by Johann Georg Sulzer (Sulzer 1771). Cf. Nachtsheim (1997, p. 12ff.). As for acoustics, Kant only had the elementary knowledge available since the early seventeenth century, but this was no obstacle to his treatise.

"charms"; however, thanks to Euler, Kant knew that sounds also contain the mathematical regularity of the vibrations of the air.[103] Therefore, at a first level, establishing whether music is beautiful or pleasant for Kant means deciding whether sounds act directly on the ear or whether "reflection" can grasp some mathematical regularity in them. The first hypothesis is suggested by the speed of the vibrations: we only perceive "the effect of these vibrations upon the elastic parts of our body".[104] The second one, instead, is supported by the cases of people with perfect hearing that, however, do not associate to sounds any aesthetic quality—which proves that normally such an association does take place.[105] The general dilemma of music occurs several times in the third *Critique*, and Kant never seems to make a final decision—which has led to several interpretations. In general, it should be noted that pleasant art and beautiful art are not necessarily mutually exclusive: it would be hard for anybody to deny that some forms of music are pleasant at most. Kant eludes the decision claiming that, at present, there were no decisive elements to clarify the issue. More importantly, his theses on music are valid either way.

Luckily, the issue of the value of music doesn't only depend on the (unresolved) question of sound perception. Perhaps more important elements are derived from Kant's proposed classification of the arts. The philosopher addressed the problem in analogy with verbal communication, as follows. In speech, we blend "the word, the gesture and the tone" that correspond to "articulation, gesticulation, and modulation"; in turn, these aspects transmit respectively "thought, intuition, and sensation" to the listener.[106] Kant's semiotic considerations are extremely interesting, so much so that they help explain how "communication" works in aesthetics and, as we shall see, in music especially. By analogy with these three modalities, Kant distinguishes on the aesthetic level between "the art of speech, pictorial art (*bildende Kunst*), and the art of the play of sensations", the latter including music. It is often repeated that those are external sensations: Kant explicitly excludes that music may involve intimate feelings, which might be mistakenly suggested by the term "sensation" (*Empfin-*

---

[103] There is a philological issue related to a passage that was corrupted in the various editions: cf. Kant (2002, p. 108 fn.). A different reading can be found in Giordanetti (2001, p. 133 ff. and 200 ff.), who also discusses the main interpretations.
[104] Kant (2002, p. 202).
[105] Kant (2002, p. 202). See also Kant (2006, p. 52). Cf. Giordanetti (2001, p. 203 f.), where an interesting letter of Kant to Hellwag of 1791 is discussed.
[106] Kant (2002, p. 198).

dungen).¹⁰⁷ The play of sensations in music, for him, simply concerns the proportions of the degrees of "tuning" (*Stimmung*) or the "tension" (*Spannung*) of the senses, stimulated by the alternating auditory sensations.¹⁰⁸

After establishing the different kinds of fine arts by analogy with language, Kant classifies them. The first place goes to poetry, whereas the other ones depend on the point of view one adopts. Considering the "charm and movement of the mind", argues Kant, the second place goes to music, which can be naturally associated to poetry.¹⁰⁹ If, however, "one estimates the value of the beautiful arts in terms of the culture that they provide for the mind"—that is, the widening and refining of the faculties—then music occupies the lowest place. Nevertheless, Kant adds in brackets that it might have the highest place "among those that are estimated according to their agreeableness".¹¹⁰ Therefore, Kant's assessment is not absolute but changes considerably based on one's perspective: from that of charm, music is second, from that of culture it is last, from that of pleasantness it might be the first.

Let's look at music under the profile of "charm". Kant here offers his most articulate explanation of it. Contrary to poetry, music leaves nothing to reflect on because it speaks without concepts, by sensation alone. For this reason its effect is deep but transitory. Music's charm lies in the fact that it can "move the soul"—something it does even better than poetry, at least in terms of intensity. But what is this capacity of music based on? The analogy with the semiotics of language is crucial in Kant's long and complex line of reasoning. I shall here divide it in single passages, for sake of simplicity.

(1) In oral speech every single expression takes on a given "tone", based on the context, which "more or less designates an affect" of the speaker.¹¹¹ (2) The listener therefore doesn't only grasp the meaning of what is said, but also the tone: thus an affection is aroused in him that gives rise to "the idea that is expressed in the language by means of such a tone".¹¹² It is fundamental here to understand "idea" in the Kantian aesthetic sense of representation of the imagination "that occasions much thinking though without it being possible for any determinate thought, i.e., concept, to be adequate to it"; accordingly, "no lan-

---

107 Kant (2002, p. 198). On sensation as "objective representation of the senses" cf. Kant (2002, p. 92). On the *Empfindung* in Herder and Hegel see below, chap. 3, par. 3. Cf. also Fugate (1966).
108 For a history of the idea of *Stimmung*, a word related to *Stimme* ("voice") and *stimmen* ("to be correct"), cf. Spitzer (1963, *passim*).
109 Kant (2002, p. 205).
110 Kant (2002, p. 206).
111 Kant (2002, p. 205).
112 Kant (2002, p. 205f.).

guage fully attains or can make intelligible" aesthetic ideas.[113] (3) The whole of these expressive tones, i.e. the "modulation" (in this Kantian sense of "intonation", or "general tone" i.e. of a speech), is a sort of "language of sensations universally comprehensible" that music uses "in all its force" in the absence of semantic elements—which instead are not universal, but vary in different languages.[114] So, music is defined a "language of the affects"—but its is important not to misunderstand this expression. As seen, (1–2), affects are both (i) the content conveyed by the "tone" and (ii) the means to express "aesthetic ideas". Now, for Kant affects do not have aesthetic meaning *qua* contents (i). Unlike the Baroque *Affektenlehre*, they are irrelevant to the *aesthetic* experience as such—at most, they are a nuisance in that regard. They only matter to the judgment of taste insofar as they lead to aesthetic ideas (ii).[115] (4) Given that in music aesthetic ideas do not adhere to determined concepts or thoughts, as happens in poetry, the adopted form is not the linguistic one, but "the form of the composition of these sensations (harmony and melody)" in an aesthetic idea "corresponding to a certain theme, which constitutes the dominant affect in the piece". (5) This harmonic and melodic form follows a mathematical rule: communication, in the language of affections, depends on the "proportionate disposition" of the sensations.[116] Even if there is no concept in this mathematical relation, it is the sole cause of the "satisfaction that the mere reflection on such a multitude of sensations accompanying or following one another connects with this play of them as a condition of its beauty valid for everyone". (6) Finally, one should restate that mathematics as such plays no role in charm and movement of the mind: it is only the *conditio sine qua non* of grasping multiple sensations in a whole, without which they could not support the aesthetic idea.[117]

This is a very complex passage and it is worth explaining. "Tones"—which are also present in language—are used alone in music, and therefore transmit "affects", which convey aesthetic ideas, with great power (hence the movement of the mind) (1–3). In music, though, such ideas are not associated to a concept —as happens in poetry—and this explains the lesser duration of the aesthetic effect of music (4). Without a concept to relate to, the totality of thoughts contained in an idea is supported by the "dominating affect" that orients it towards the "form" of sensations themselves (not towards the concept), which is determined by the mathematical proportion (5). So, the beauty of mathematical proportions

---

113 Kant (2002, p. 192).
114 Kant (2002, p. 206).
115 Cf. Dahlhaus (1953, p. 346); Zoltai (1970, p. 220 f.).
116 Kant (2002, p. 206).
117 Kant (2002, p. 206); see also (2002, p. 228).

strengthens the idea so that it doesn't dissolve—as it would—in cacophony. This mathematical beauty, however, is in a way an improper surrogate of the concept, as—unlike the latter—it is not entitled to be the object of aesthetic contemplation (contrary to what was posited by Leibniz). Therefore, it must be said very clearly that Kant's is no *Affektenlehre*, but a semiotics of the affects. In the light of the critique he carries out, Kant deprives affects of any aesthetic function: they only matter as they mediate aesthetic ideas. However, as we will see, affections will turn out to play a very important role in a different sense.

This way, music can legitimately be understood as a beautiful art. It doesn't have the highest place because the "play of thought" that is "aroused by it in passing" by it is the effect of "an as it were mechanical association".[118] Poetry strengthens the mind, making it feel independent of nature insofar as it can judge it "in accordance with aspects which it does not present in experience". One cannot say the same about music. Without a concept, the mind has to turn to the mathematical rule, which supports the idea mechanically and not freely—as mentioned. So, there cannot be that feeling of superiority of the spirit, granted by the poetic imagination, because in music it is left to a mathematical rule that affects both composer and listener.[119]

As for the other perspectives on the classification of the arts, music has the last place if one considers culture. Pictorial arts, with their lasting effect, are much superior to it. Indeed, they proceed "from determinate ideas to sensations", whereas music, as seen, proceeds "from sensations to indeterminate ideas".[120] For this reason, if they are "involuntarily recalled by the imagination", the impressions of music are rather wearisome. In the second edition, Kant adds to this some considerations on the impoliteness of music, as it exceeds the limits of space annoying those who are exposed to it. It is well-known, in fact, that Kant was exasperated by the singing coming from the nearby jail: his hard concentration on philosophical matters was disturbed by the inmates of Königsberg, who were seeking a legitimate distraction. In general, this aspect of Kant's conception is rather disappointing: the scarce cultural value, for him, depends on its lack of concepts, which hinders any lasting effect of cultural refinement.

Finally, music is considered from the standpoint of agreeableness and here it seems to be superior to all other arts. After analysing the difficult balance between idea, affection and mathematical proportion, Kant analyses the parallel

---

118 Kant (2002, p. 205).
119 At the same time, though, this "inferiority" to nature doesn't make music akin to the sublime: the latter is always related to thought and to the supremacy of reason over sensibility, whereas in music what happens is the exact opposite.
120 Kant (2002, p. 206–207).

play of affects. As we have seen, the latter are just a vehicle for aesthetic ideas, but once evoked one cannot simply brush them off. The *Affektenlehre* comes back into play here, but Kant takes it down a very unexpected road. To understand this, one has to adopt an anthropological—rather than aesthetic—point of view. This is where Kant introduces some of his most interesting ideas on music, giving a new value to the dimension of bodiliness. The mental movement induced by the affections, as seen, is very strong, but it doesn't arouse a lasting enough reflection to produce a cultural refinement. The strong energy released therefore falls onto the body, so to speak.[121] Since Galileo and Descartes, thinkers had resorted to physiology to explain the perception of sounds in consonances; this aspect was very important also in the British tradition, especially in Edmund Burke.[122] However, Kant's approach is overall different.

Kant admits that there is a difference between what pleases judgment and what pleases sensation: a great pain might give subtle pleasure, as happens, say, to a widow who feels ennobled by her grief.[123] The same happens with the play of sensations. Even if there is no real pleasure for the object, there is a specific delight of the senses, which can grow up to involve the emotional dimension. This brings to the fore a central notion to Kant's entire aesthetics: play. Consider "the play of chance" in cards games and similar, which arouse affects of hope, fear, joy, anger and so forth, "even though nothing has been either gained or learned".[124] However, such games are not beautiful: "by contrast", Kant goes on, "music and material for laughter" "are two kinds of play with aesthetic ideas or even representations of the understanding, by which in the end nothing is thought, and which can gratify merely through their change, and nevertheless do so in a lively fashion".[125] Regardless of its beautiful or merely pleasant nature, music always has this supplementary dimension of lively playfulness.

The effect of music, in this sense, is akin to that of laughter: in both cases one "plays" with intellectual representations (jokes) or aesthetic ideas (music).

---

121 According to Kivy (1993) Kant repeats the classical theory of the affections, which then through aesthetic ideas (the only new aspect introduced by Kant) act on the body. Aesthetic ideas for Kivy, are therefore the vehicle of the affections. However, what happens in Kant is precisely the opposite. The physiological effect does not come from the idea—otherwise it would be much stronger in poetry—but is the result of the fact that the idea is ill-supported in music: only "mechanically" by the mathematical form.
122 Burke (1757, par. 4.11).
123 Kant (2002, p. 208).
124 Kant (2002, p. 208). Gambling is excluded though.
125 Kant (2002, p. 208).

Through them "in the end nothing is thought", and therefore their gratification can only come from the change they present. This proves that

> animation in both cases is merely corporeal, although it is aroused by ideas of the mind, and that the feeling of health resulting from a movement of the viscera corresponding to that play constitutes the whole gratification in a lively party, which is extolled as so refined and spirited. It is not the judging of the harmonies in tones or sallies of wit, which with their beauty serve only as the necessary vehicle, but the promotion of the business of life in the body, the affect which moves the viscera and the diaphragm, in a word the feeling of health (which otherwise cannot be felt without such a stimulus), which constitutes the gratification in which one discovers that one can get at the body even through the soul and use the latter as the doctor for the former.[126]

In the *Analytic of the Sublime* Kant already explained that the "agreeable exhaustion" following the "agitation by the play of affects" is not related to the sublime, but is "an enjoyment of our well-being arising from the restored equilibrium of the various vital forces". The same happens with massage, which "the voluptuaries of the Orient find so comforting", getting their bodies "as it were kneaded". The difference is that here the "moving principle" is mostly external, whereas with affects it is internal.[127]

These observations have often put critics in an awkward position: some have seen them as yet another sign of Kant's musical incompetence, others have tried to minimise them as "merely" anthropological—as if this made them *ipso facto* irrelevant. On the contrary, it would be extremely shortsighted to think that Kant associates music to something—jest, the body—it should be ashamed of. It is worth recalling that Augustine already related inferior numbers "not to the carnal lust but solely to his bodily health".[128] However, to stick to the eighteenth century, we have seen that Euler compares the pleasure of music to the solution of an "enigma" (see above, par. 2); Burke associates rapid modulations—which are "contrary to the genius of the beautiful in music"—to the rise of "mirth, or other sudden and tumultuous passions".[129] Lichtenberg also observes that wit and music have something in common, namely that one becomes more

---

[126] Kant (2002, p. 208–209). For Hermann-Sinai (2009, p. 448) this implies, for instance, that "my gut contracts and relaxes according to the Sicilian rhythm"(i.e. 6/8): the body should adapt to compositional forms, which, however, it cannot do. But in Kant the body's internal balance is recovered after being subverted by intense affections of any kind (not according to *Kompositionstopoi*), as shown by the examples of sermons and tragedies. Laughter doesn't imitate the form of jokes—it follows from it. And the same holds for music.
[127] Kant (2002, p. 155).
[128] Augustine (2002a, p. 93–95).
[129] Burke (1757, par. 25).

demanding with experience.[130] In addition, one should note that the German term *Witz*—which Kant associates to music—has a wide and complex meaning, more than jest or wit. Wolff used it to translate *ingenium*, which is related to the term "genius" that was so important to Kant's aesthetics.[131] For the Romantics, *Witz* hinted at the "lightning" that links finitude and infinity so that, even without resorting to Freud, art is but a "higher form of prank"—as Adorno would note, quoting Thomas Mann.[132] Most of all, the physiological meaning of music would be taken up by the later Nietzsche (see below), with very different tones from Kant's. These remarks might be insufficient to claim that this is the most promising part of Kant's reflection on music, but should be enough to avoid the misunderstanding that associating music to *Witz* means degrading it.

Of course, Kant separates *ingenium* and *iudicium* because the former is a mere play without concepts. So *Witz* forces reason into the abyss of a "nothingness" in which it flounders, paralyzed in apnea, as it were, until the laughter breaks out in the body and the intellect can breathe again, restoring the usual paths of meaning. Music brings into play a similar *mechanism*—a term that should be understood literally. The difference is that in jokes "the play begins with the thoughts" and then extends to the body, whereas in music the movement goes "from bodily sensations to aesthetical Ideas [...], and then from these back again to the body with redoubled force".[133] Given that they have a different origin but a common end, one could say that both music and *Witz* turn a legitimate expectation of reflection into "nothingness". However, with music the proceeding is less instantaneous: the back and forth between body and mind results in a longer lasting effect. In music there is no sudden revelation, but a delayed suspense effect that eventually affects the body. This doesn't describe the aesthetic *ratio* of music, but is for Kant a necessary component of its effects. This way, music relates us to our own life, not existentially but biologically, making us feel alive in a way that normally doesn't happen.

---

130 Lichtenberg (1958, n. 223).
131 Cf. Gabriel (2005, cols. 983 ff.).
132 Adorno (2002c, p. 185).
133 Kant (2002, p. 209).

Third Chapter
The Century of Music

1 Romantic Acoustics

Critics have acknowledged long ago the impossibility to clearly define the borders of "Romanticism". The plurality of categories[1] that are applied to a relatively small period of time shows how hard it is for historians to classify that time. In the case of music, things are even more complicated because of the interaction of three factors: the development of a compositional practice, of a musical aesthetics and of an acoustic physics all classifiable in various ways as "Romantic". The temptation to find common traits and trace family lines is therefore understandably strong. Unfortunately, however, these more or less simultaneous phenomena were largely independent from one another. The drive to ubiquitously apply the reassuring paradigm of "feeling" should therefore be set aside in the name of a detailed reading of the texts.[2]

Musicological studies have shown that the romantic musical aesthetics doesn't derive from the experience of Romantic music, but is modelled (e.g. by Hoffman) upon the style of Viennese "classics", or based on literary suggestions completely devoid of direct music references (Wackenroder, Tieck). This aesthetics highlights the sentimental effect of instrumental music, whereas musical Romanticism—from Schubert to Berlioz and Liszt—often explores the territories of *Lied* or "programme music".[3] And the situation is no less complex in terms of the physical foundations of music. Acoustics plays an important role in Romantic science, being present in many of the most important authors of the time. For the sake of thematic continuity, I shall discuss musical aesthetics in the next chapter and start with the philosophical consequences of Romantic acoustics.

Johann Gottfried Herder's ideas offer a privileged vantage point to understand the evolution that took place in Germany at the time. Herder expressed his opinion on musical aesthetics for the first time in 1769, in the fourth volume of *Kritische Wälder*, and resumed the topic thirty years later, in *Kalligone*, with

---

[1] Speaking of German Romanticism, e.g. *Spätaufklärung, Empfindsamkeit, Sturm und Drang, Vorromantik, Frühromantik, Goethezeit, Romantik*, etc.
[2] The view that "the romantic aesthetic was an aesthetic of feeling [...] is one of those resilient prejudices of the history of ideas that are so deep rooted that the historian hardly stand a chance of exterminating them": Dahlhaus (1991, p. 70).
[3] Cf. Wiora (1965, p. 18); Dahlhaus (1988, p. 86 ff.).

very different tones. Drawing on Rousseau, at first Herder privileged melody over harmony, because the simple tone can arouse a deeper and more touching feeling than the "heavy Gothic harmonies and the scholastic ratios" of northern musicians.[4] Like a silver arrow, the tone goes up to the most hidden recesses of the soul, where no ray of light can penetrate, and evokes a "sensation"—not in the Kantian sense, but as a correlate of an intimate movement of the soul—which is the root of beauty in music. In *Kalligone* (1800), which he wrote in response to Kant's *Critique of the Power of Judgement*, he took a very different, almost opposite position. Leaving "tone" and "sensation" aside, Herder proceeds to an aesthetic appreciation of "sound" (*Klang*), which brings out the "inside of things"—both animate and inanimate—that would otherwise remain hidden. While sight tells us about the surface of things, sound as "universal expression of the elastic nature in motion", communicates the inside, the "passions" (*Leidenschaften*) of nature.[5]

The strings oscillate by sympathy with the corresponding sound; animals use cries to call the others to rescue: human musical activities are no exception to this rule. It is not surprising that this late Herderian rehabilitation of harmony hides no nostalgia for Rameau. Far from exalting the omnipresence of the major triad in sound, Herder resumes an argument used by Rousseau in the *Dictionnaire*,[6] stressing that "with one tone all tones are given", just as white light contains all colors. The tones no longer act isolated on their specific "sensation", but all contribute together to close the "tone circle" (*Tonkreis*) that is the horizon of all musical possibilities. This interpretation, observes Herder, is reflected in Chladni, a physicist who has "even" made "visible" the internal structure of the tonal material.

To understand the significance of this reference it is necessary to consider certain scientific developments of the time. Eighteenth-century acoustics was characterised by the opposition between two great schools of thought as to the origin and propagation of sound: the supporters of the "sound tremors" and those of "oscillations". According to the first, the cause of sound lies in the tremblements of every small part of the body, while the total oscillations, for example of a string, act—so to speak—as a flywheel, increasing the strength and duration of the sound.[7] According to the second, instead, sound originates

---

[4] Herder (1878, p. 108).
[5] Herder (1800, p. 62 and 64).
[6] See above, chap. 2, par. 3
[7] Sauveur, Carré, La Hire, Diderot, d'Alembert and Rousseau are part of this group. Hegel will also adhere to it in his own way (see below, par. 3).

from macroscopic oscillations of the string, which produce tremors as a consequence.[8] The first school of thought is supported by the idea that tremor can be transmitted more or less unchanged from the vibrating body to the air. By contrast, Newton was the greatest inspirer of the "oscillationists": recognizing periodic waves of compression in the air, he theorized a discontinuity in the transmission of the string's motion to the air.[9] Also in the light of the geographical distribution of the two parties, it is easy to see that—in this respect—the dispute was a chapter in the opposition between Cartesians and Newtonians. Descartes's physics and physiology were the methodological archetype of the theory of tremors, as they allowed for the continuous transmission of motion; instead, the discontinuity proposed by Newton, not surprisingly rejected by those who endorse the "tremorists" (including Euler, d'Alembert, Lagrange) with unusually harsh tones, was the "acoustic counterpart" of the action at a distance of the gravitational force.

It is no coincidence then that the scientific dispute on the vibrating string ended up involving issues related to the very definition of sound. Considering the sound of bodies such as rods or bells, which emit "extremely disharmonious" simultaneous partial tones, Daniel Bernoulli concluded that the series of upper partial harmonics "should not serve as a principle for music systems".[10] We recognize here the line inaugurated by Vincenzo Galilei with the experimental study of non-filiform three-dimensional bodies. The question was once again topical because the eighteenth century rationalism cultivated the dream of tracing the acoustic behavior of bodies of any shape back to that of the vibrating string. A famous example is the unfortunate gaffe made by no less than Euler, who in 1739 associated the acoustic behaviour of a cylinder to that of a bundle of strings of equal length. But even in 1753, in *The Interpretation of Nature*, Diderot stated that the geometrician "only needs to extend the calculation of the vibrating string to the prism, the sphere, or the cylinder, to find the general law of the distribution of motion in an impacted body".[11] In late eighteenth-century acoustics, however, the exact opposite occurred: it was impossible to trace the motion of solid (non-filiform) bodies to the equations of the vibrating string, so thinkers began to reverse the argument. Perhaps the motion of the string was rather a special case of a more complex law, which regulates the acoustic behavior of sound bodies of any shape and size. It should be recognized that this attitude,

---

8 This group includes Daniel Bernoulli (who draws on Brook Taylor), Giordano Riccati and Chladni. For the mathematical aspects see Truesdell (1960, *passim*).
9 Newton (1687, p. 418–423 [2, 48.38]). Cf. Dostrovsky (1974, p. 209 ff.).
10 Bernoulli (1753, p. 152 s.).
11 Diderot (2000, p. 52). Cf. Truesdell (1960, p. 320 ff.).

in the long run, would promote the dissolution of acoustics into the mechanics of solids, with the consequent loosening of its relation with the theory of music.[12] But for the moment, this hypothesis had a good reception in Germany at the turn of the century, in the light of the new Romantic conception of nature described in Herder's *Kalligone*. This was the general situation that allowed for the development and popularity of Ernst Florens Friedrich Chladni's work.

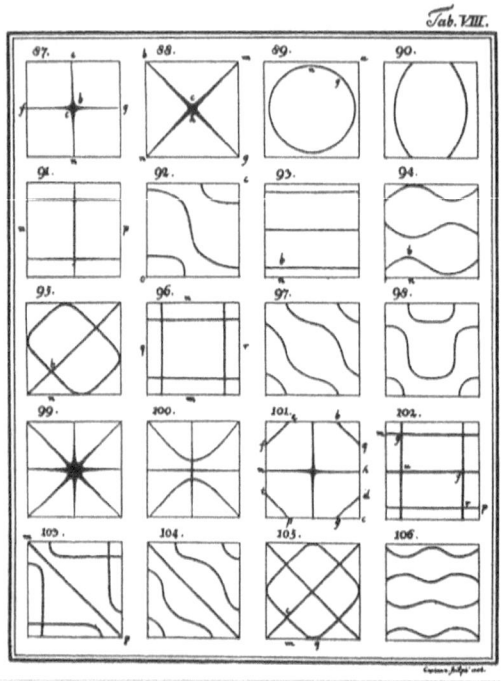

Figure 1: Sound patterns from Chladni (1787).

Chladni was a typical exponent of the purely experimental science of the Romantic era. In physical acoustics[13] he introduced two novelties: a method for the visualization of sound oscillations and the consequent redefinition of the concept of sound. Sprinkling dust over some glass plates fixed at the center and "playing them" with a violin bow, Chladni got the dust to deposit itself on the slightest vibration points, thus drawing the lines that make up the famous

---

12 Cf. Szabó (1977, p. 407 ff.).
13 Besides, Chladni also successfully investigated meteors and fireballs.

and impressive-looking *Klangfiguren* ("sound figures", or sound patterns; see fig. 1).[14]

Although the method is in a sense similar to that by which harmonics are obtained, the sounds in this case follow entirely different arithmetic progressions, which also contain intervals like the minor third—a source of many difficulties for Rameau.[15] As regards the definition of sound, Chladni is explicit: his experiments show that the upper partial harmonics are not an "essential character of sound", and that one cannot deduce from their existence "the fundamental principles of harmony".[16] The series of upper partial harmonics of a string does not represent a property *of sound*, as if the latter "contained" partial harmonic tones. It must rather be stated that several independent oscillations *coexist* in the same physical body, oscillations which are composed in a complex oscillation. The pattern of partial tones (harmonic or non-harmonic) is none other than the characteristic of the physical system in question: its acoustic footprint, we could say.

Systematically exposed in *Akustik* (1802), the first handbook in history exlusively devoted to this science, these ideas had a really strong impact.[17] But Chladni popularized his views also by performing all over Europe with the musical instruments (the Euphon and Clavicylinder) he invented based on the instrument invented by Benjamin Franklin, who called it *Harmonica*, later known as *Glasharmonika*. No wonder the ethereal sounds of these *verrophones*, originated by the rubbing of rods or glass cylinders, made a great impression and were associated with the studies on the "animal magnetism" and mesmerism. Inspired by Lichtenberg's experiments on magnetic fields, Chladni's figures also seemed similar to natural affinities such as those governing electromagnetic phenomena, and aroused keen interest in the latter's discoverer Hans Christian Ørsted. Chladni was an authority in the field of acoustics also for Hegel and Schopenhauer. Even though Helmholtz partly drew on Chladni's experiments, the positivist suspicion towards Romantic science has contributed to relegating the acoustic discoveries of the Wittenberg physicist to the sphere of erudite fun facts. For instance, Chladni's *Klangfiguren* appeared in Thomas Mann's *Doctor Faustus:* they were part of the para-scientific domestic experiments of Adrian's

---

14 Cf. Ullmann (1996, p. 17 ff.).
15 See above chap. 2, par. 3
16 Chladni (1787, p. 70 f.).
17 Chladni's *Die Akustik* (Chladni 1802) was translated into French (Chladni 1809) and posthumously reprinted in 1830 (Chladni 1830).

father, an example of an animist and "demoniac" root typical of the German curiosity for nature.[18]

The aim of the above considerations is to show that Chladni, today much unappreciated, was very influential at the time. Ritter, Ørsted, Jean Paul, Herder, Goethe, Novalis, Görres, the later Kant and Hegel were some of the thinkers who were familiar with Chladni's figures. Without taking his studies into account it is therefore hard to understand—or worse, it is likely to misunderstand—a significant part of the scientific and philosophical reflection on music of the time. A relevant example of this influence is offered by Johann Wolfgang Goethe. In 1808 he exchanged letters on musical matters with the composer Carl Friedrich Zelter, who justified the major mode with the "division of the string", considering the minor third as the artificial result of altering the major third. Goethe responded by comparing art to a city built on a rugged terrain that the founders have cleared and settled, reusing excavated material, adapting the caves to work as cellars: the piano and the organ, in which one can no longer distinguish nature from artifice, are similar to this city.[19] In other words, Goethe rejects the absolute value of the string's division: like the Newtonian prism, whose role is reduced in *Farbenlehre*, the Pythagorean monochord is not enough to explain the origin of the tonal system. One should rather show the origin of the minor mode in an experimental way. Chladni was obviously the inspirer of these thoughts: Goethe knew him, and had received his works and experimental instruments as a gift. His interest in Chladni's figures also shows in the sketch of his *Theory of Sounds*, unfortunately unfinished and unpublished.[20]

Novalis' philosophical and scientific writings, whose value is today finally recognized, achieved a reconciliation between the objective and subjective sides of sound. For Novalis, these two levels correspond to "chemical acoustics" and "transcendental acoustics".[21] The first aspect refers to interesting developments of Chladni's figures, appreciated by Novalis in many respects, not least because of the symbolic elements (one of the first acoustic figures is a cross: see above, figure 1) that also fascinated a physicist like Johann Wilhelm Ritter.[22] The "transcendental" aspect of acoustics identified by Novalis is equally interesting. A keen Fichte scholar, the young Novalis (who always stayed young, as he

---

18 Mann (1996, p. 27): "with what eyes one would have looked on the man from Wittenberg who [...] had invented the experiment of visible music?" Among those who occasionally refer to Chladni's figures, see also Nietzsche (1979) and Benjamin (1998).
19 Goethe (1808, p. 60).
20 Goethe (1810, p. 285–295).
21 Novalis (2007, p. 56 and 153). Cf. Martinelli (2005, *passim*).
22 Ritter (2010, p. 475).

died at age 29) tried to overcome the Fichtean opposition between I and non-I by defining reality an "oscillation" between those two poles. The aesthetic implication of this thesis is remarkable: in perception we receive the "figures" from nature, whereas in art we become active subjects. Making a "reversed use of the senses", therefore, the musician listens "actively"—from the inside, just like the painter projects his inner vision onto the canvas.[23]

Therefore, it must be noted that for Novalis the aesthetic gesture mainly has a symbolic value, *contra* any expressive or sentimental paradigm. Novalis justifies the primacy of music over the other forms of art with the claim that music is not even remotely imitative. Coherently with these theses, and in line with his time, Novalis favours instrumental ("absolute") music: "the music of dance and songs is not the real music. It is rather its degeneration. Sonatas—Symphonies—Fugues—Variations: this is the true music".[24] However, this claim should be read together with other passages, which seem to point to a different direction: "The human voice is, as it were, the principle and ideal of instrumental music".[25] How to interpret these seemingly contradictory statements? The word 'voice', for Novalis, "expresses a self-constituting thing",[26] that is, the spontaneity of the self. The sound of a voice comes from the subjectivity itself, affirming its aesthetic and ethical freedom. This explains the alleged "ideal" function of voice for instrumental music: the voice, the original source of any aesthetic and musical intention, is where music is "deduced" in the "acoustic-transcendental" sense. In analogy with the Kantian "I think", Novalis prospects a kind of "I sing" that must accompany all my musical performances, including those used in instrumental music.

This renewed attention to the voice requires the integration of Chladni's concept of sound, giving air once again a major role, although in quite a new sense. The interaction of the airy and bodily dimensions of the sound corresponds to the presence and balance of vowels and consonants in language. On an aesthetic level, the rehabilitation of the air element is expressed in the frequent references to the Aeolian harp: a musical instrument whose strings resound to the blowing of the wind without human intervention. Being based on a structurally similar mechanism to that of human speech, the Aeolian harp for Novalis becomes the symbol of the identity of man and nature, expressed in the story of the unveiling of the Goddess's statue in *Disciples of Sais*. That instrument is therefore

---

[23] Novalis (1997, p. 72). Cf. Moretti (1991, p. 40).
[24] Novalis (1968, p. 685 [no. 669]).
[25] Novalis (2007, p. 57 [no. 382]).
[26] Novalis (2003, p. 182 [no. 634]). Cf. Leusing (1993, *passim*).

the very essence of Romanticism: "A fairy tale is really a dream picture—devoid of all coherence—An *ensemble* of wondrous things and happenings—a *musical fantasy* for instance—the harmonious effects of an Aeolian harp—*Nature herself*".[27] Also, "Nature is an Aeolian harp—She is a musical instrument—whose tones in turn are the keys of higher strings in us".[28] Ignited by the most recent philosophical and scientific discoveries, and fully indifferent to sentimentalism, Novalis' philosophy of music represents one of the peaks of the Romantic period.

Schelling's insistence on the meaning of rhythm in his 1802–1803 lectures gathered in *The Philosophy of Art* is explained by the need to philosophically justify ("deduce") the difference between ancient and modern art, placing classicism and Romanticism in their respective domains. Schelling distinguishes "figurative arts" (music, painting and plastic arts) from the "verbal arts" (lyric, epic and drama).[29] His classification is clearly biased in favour of the *redende Künste*: figurative arts do not express their content semantically but work on their very material. The position of music is somewhat ambiguous: it has the lowest place and yet, for this very reason, it is the closest to the Absolute in its origin.

This ambiguity echoes in the difference between ancient and modern music, to explain which Schelling distinguishes three elements: rhythm, modulation and melody. By recursively applying (in his typical procedure) the triad of figurative arts to this distinction, Schelling finds that rhythm is the "musical" element of music, modulation is the "pictorial" and melody the "plastic". This explains, at least formally, his famous claim that *"rhythm is the music within music"*[30]—which would otherwise appear rather enigmatic. However, it should be noted that the point of the whole operation is to "scientifically" explain the "opposition of ancient and modern music": and this is where rhythm plays an essential role. Being essentially rhythmic, Greek music was authentic. Modern music, instead, is first of all harmonic and is therefore degenerate. If it is clear that these ideas partly derive from Rousseau (the *Dictionnaire* was Schelling's main source), so is the fact that Schelling uses them in a new context. Like all things classic, the music of the ancients is only about what is necessary, while that of the moderns also speaks of what is merely accidental. Greek music highlighted its nature of "real" (asemantic) art by underlining the rhythmic element, whereas the *hybris* of modern music lies in aiming for a superior unity that is out of its reach. "The ancients—notes Schelling—roundly attributed to rhythm the greatest aesthetic power": beauty in music comes from rhythm. However,

---

27 Novalis (2007, p. 171 [no. 986]).
28 Novalis (2007, p. 169 [no. 966]).
29 Schelling (1989, p. 202ff.).
30 Schelling (1989, p. 111).

"we must separate out everything else in music that is stimulating or exciting. Tones, for example, are also significant in themselves. They can be cheerful, gentle, sad, or painful". The reference to Kant's theses on the ambiguous "charm" of sounds is here obvious. But Schelling takes them to extreme, up to de-sounding music so as to make it pure rhythm: "when we view rhythm we must completely abstract" from any other element of music.

> Its beauty is not material and it does not require the merely natural affectations residing within tones in and for themselves in order to be absolutely pleasing and to enchant a receptive soul.[31]

Sounds are quintessentially impure, and the modern harmonic music is the true opposite of the ancient rhythmic one.[32] The primacy of rhythm thus involves, in Schelling, the adoption of "classicism" in the strict sense: it is not a preference for Haydn or Mozart, but the longing for the unknown music of the Greeks.

2 From the Romantics to Schopenhauer

As mentioned, many thinkers of the time were completely independent of the Romantic acoustics. This, indeed, is the time when music aesthetic became an autonomous discipline, freeing itself both from the philosophy of nature and from general aesthetics. Some indications on how this process began can be found in the work of Wilhelm Heinrich Wackenroder, who published *Confessions from the Heart of an Art-Loving Friar* in 1797, while his *Phantasies on Art for Friends of Art* were published posthumously by his friend Ludwig Tieck in 1799.[33] In these works, what's striking is the frequent dualism between the intensity of the musical experience and its mathematical basis: "from what sort of magic potion does the aroma of this brilliant apparition rise up?—I look,—and find nothing but a wretched web of numerical proportions, represented concretely on perforated wood, on constructions of gut strings and brass wire".[34]

Science of sounds and aesthetic experience of music surely diverge here. In part, this can be traced back to the biography of Wackenroder, who studied music with poor results with the aforementioned Zelter and Johann Friedrich

---

[31] Schelling (1989, p. 110).
[32] Schelling (1989, p. 113): "The predominating element in contemporary music is harmony, which is precisely the opposite of the rhythmic melody of antiquity".
[33] For a critical assessment cf. Schubert (1970, p. 12ff.).
[34] Wackenroder (1970b, p. 341).

Reichardt. Perhaps Wackenroder's literary alter ego Joseph Berglinger was expressing his contempt for the pedagogic tools of the time. Being very passionate about music, Berlinger wants to study it but is disappointed with the "compelling mathematical law" regulating melodies, the "awkward scaffolding and cage of grammar of the art".[35] It is therefore easy to understand Wackenroder's disinterest for any attempt to pursue such studies: one should merely acknowledge that between "the individual, mathematical, tonal relationships and the individual fibers of the human hearth an inexplicable sympathy has revealed itself",[36] that's all. Indeed, an "eternally hostile chasm is entrenched between the feeling heart and the investigations of research, and the former is an independent, tightly sealed, divine entity, which cannot be unlocked and opened up by the reason".[37] The feeling cannot be explained except by feeling itself: those who spoil beauty with their "relentless searching for Purpose and Cause" are "not concerned with the beauty and divinity of the things themselves but with concepts, as the boundaries and husks of the things [...]".[38]

Contrary to what a hasty interpretation may suggest, it must be said that the Romantic movement often embraces views that are diametrically opposed to this veto on theorising. Defined by Friedrich Schlegel "the art of this century",[39] music is indeed very often seen as an exercise similar to philosophy. Schlegel further notes that he who "has a sense for the marvelous affinities among all arts and sciences" will not consider music naturalistically, i.e. as a "language of affects"; rather, he will reflect upon "a certain affinity between the pure instrumental music and philosophy", as demonstrated by the analogy between a varied music theme and the "object of a meditation within a series of philosophical ideas".[40]

Wackenroder's intimate "confessions" obviously lead very far from such affirmations. However, his description of the music experience is much less naive than one might think. Feeling is not only a subjective impression, but also the means to a knowledge that goes far beyond the ineffability of music. First, Wackenroder insists on the presence and richness of "images"[41] evoked by listening to music. This stimulation of the imagination on the part of "pure sounds" generates a "childlike joy", which has the effect of soothing the pain of living: "O then

---

35 Wackenroder (1970a, p. 294).
36 Wackenroder (1970b, p. 359).
37 Wackenroder (1970b, p. 363).
38 Wackenroder (1970b, p. 363).
39 Schlegel (1981, p. 258 [no. 43]).
40 Schlegel (1967, p. 254 [no. 444]).
41 Wackenroder (1970b, p. 338).

I close my eyes to all the strife of the world—and withdraw quietly into the land of music, as into the *land of belief*, where all our doubts and our suffering are lost in a resounding sea".[42]

And there's more: music also elevates the spirit towards a superhuman form of love, close to divine bliss. This last point deserves attention, because the relationship between music and religious faith in Wackenroder is very close. Distraught by the death of his father, Berglinger composed for Easter a sublime Passion of Christ: "with its penetrating melodies that embrace all the pains of suffering" this will always be a "masterpiece".[43] Indeed, sacred music, the most noble kind of music, raises its praise to God. Exhausted by this extreme effort and "wonderful paroxysm", Berglinger then fell prey to a severe "nervous debility", like a "harmful dew", and finally died "in the springtime of his years".[44] As Rudolf Haym noted, the "Gospel of art" (*das Evangelium der Kunst*) had never been preached with such tones in Germany before Wackenroder.[45] It is a suitable image: music becomes religion and the yearning for the divine explains the fact that Wackenroder never refers to any composer or piece. It is easy to note that the references cited above, comparable to the religious and indeed pro-Catholic feeling of many Northern Protestant Romantics, go in a completely opposite direction to the exaltation of instrumental music. Tieck is rather distant from these trends: more radically than Wackenroder, he distinguishes between pure instrumental and vocal music, favoring the latter as part of an aesthetics of the sublime.

The exaltation of feeling in some of Wackenroder's most famous pages is significantly marked by images of *resurrection*. Music is "like a phoenix" that is pleasantly circling; or the unfortunate "child lying dead" whose soul is transported into the celestial ether, where it savours the "golden drops of eternity".[46] Wackenroder stages even a kind of apocalypse of musical feeling:

> Whenever all the inner vibrations of our heartstrings,—the trembling ones of joy, the tempestuous ones of delight, the rapidly beating pulse of all-consuming adorations,—when all these burst apart with one outcry the language of words, as the *grave* of the inner frenzy of heart: then they go under a strange sky, amidst the vibrations of blessed harpstrings, in transfigured beauty as if in another life beyond this one, and celebrate as angelic figures their resurrection.[47]

---

42 Wackenroder (1970b, p. 339).
43 Wackenroder (1970a, p. 301).
44 Wackenroder (1970a, p. 301).
45 Haym (1870, p. 119).
46 Wackenroder (1970b, p. 338).
47 Wackenroder (1970b, p. 364).

If now we analyse what music feeling looks like after this transfiguration, we'll be quite surprised. Language describes the "secret river in the depths of the human soul", while music "causes it to flow past of ourselves".[48] But the description of happiness, peace, joy, etc. evoked by music does not invest directly the effect aroused in the mind of the listener. Rather, it is the above-mentioned fantasy that fills the sounds with magical figures: "through the overwhelming magic of its *sensual force*", it arouses all of its "wonderful, teeming hosts, which populate the musical strains with magical images and transforms the formless excitation into distinct shapes of human emotions, which draw past our senses like elusive pictures in a magical deception".[49] In other words, we experience a phantasmagoria of feelings when the imagination is free to work: these feelings are part of the rich collection of images that music evokes.

To be clear, some feelings are also genuinely "felt", in music. A composer might make music out of her deep pain and make it artistic; then, once the pain has gone, she can listen to it and exult "like a child" over her "so magnificently glorified heart".[50] But the truly distinctive and exclusive feeling of the music experience, on the contrary, lies in a transfiguration and sublimation of individual feeling. Music reaches its peak in those "divine, magnificent symphonic pieces"—here the reference is to instrumental music—"in which *not one individual emotion is portrayed*, but an entire world, an entire drama of human emotions, is poured forth".[51] In the welter of images the mind is abstracted until it sees in a dream all the manifold human emotions that "incorporeally celebrate a strange, indeed, an almost mad pantomimic dance for their own pleasure, like the unknown, enigmatical sorcerer-goddesses of Fate".[52] The most sublime instrumental music therefore arouses a kind of transfiguration of human feelings into something that combines them, and at the same time transcends them. After briefly glimpsing the abyss of the demonic, the soul is filled with this feeling and resolutely takes the road that leads to the divine.

A keystone in the formation of the Romantic view of music is Ernst Theodor Amadeus Hoffmann's review (1810) of Beethoven's *Fifth symphony*, which later appeared modified in other, more widespread, works as *Beethoven's Instrumental Music*.[53] Hoffmann starts by noting that, given the magnificence of the piece, the usual review would not suffice. Then he clearly establishes that instrumental

---

48 Wackenroder (1970b, p. 365).
49 Wackenroder (1970b, p. 366f.).
50 Wackenroder (1970b, p. 345).
51 Wackenroder (1970b, p. 368). My italics.
52 Wackenroder (1970b, p. 370).
53 Hoffmann (1810 and 1917).

music is the most Romantic art—indeed the only purely Romantic one—and has theoretical priority. It gives access to a new world, which has nothing in common with the sensible one; however, this happens only if music does not attempt to imitate feelings or even external events. The passions that are expressed both in Opera and in real life are transformed by the magical power of music: wrapped in the purple glow of the Romantic, they are elevated to infinity. Although he refers to the triad of Haydn, Mozart, and Beethoven, Hoffmann believes that only the latter is a purely Romantic—and therefore truly musical—composer. Beethoven's instrumental music opens the realm of the immense and the incommensurable: wrapping us with concentric coils, it destroys everything in the soul except the infinite *Sehnsucht* in which all pleasure arises and passes. Beethoven's art incorporates but doesn't destroy the determined feelings—love, hope, joy—that burst in our hearts in the full harmony of "all the passions".[54] Albeit with different accents, we find here a theme that was already present in Wackenroder: that of a higher fusion and sublimation of the passions in music.

Only eight years after Hoffman's review, Arthur Schopenhauer's first edition of *World as Will and Representation* was published (1818–1819). Gone unnoticed at first, it was successful with the third edition of 1859, in a now completely different philosophical and musical context. These external circumstances are probably the reason behind the power and ambiguity of Schopenhauer's philosophy of music. According to young Schopenhauer, the feelings aroused by music in the Romantic soul have a solid metaphysical basis. This, however, implies understanding them very differently. Far from uniting in a yearning for the overhuman, feelings maintain their separate names but become markedly metaphysical and abstract.

> [M]usic does not express this or that particular and definite pleasure, this or that affliction, pain, sorrow, horror, gaiety, merriment, or peace of mind, but joy, pain, sorrow, horror, gaiety, merriment, peace of mind *themselves*, to a certain extent in the abstract, their essential nature.[55]

The philosophical context of this thesis is well-known. The core of Schopenhauer's philosophy is the concept of will, which is for him the Kantian thing-in-itself. The world as phenomenon is "representation" but, at the same time, it is also fully "will". This is the basis on which Schopenhauer takes up the association between music and philosophy: "supposing we succeeded in giving a per-

---

54 Hoffmann (1917, p. 128).
55 Schopenhauer (1969a, p. 261). I adopt this translation because no other includes the *Supplements* so far.

fectly accurate and complete explanation of music which goes into detail", we would have obtained "a sufficient repetition and explanation of the world [...] and hence the true philosophy". Even more explicitly, paraphrasing Leibniz, Schopenhauer says that music is not an exercise in arithmetic, but in metaphysics, performed by the spirit whilst unaware of its philosophizing. In music we become philosophers without realizing it, because behind the surface of phenomena we grasp the ultimate reality—the will. Therefore "we could just as well call the world embodied music as embodied will". This aspect should be carefully considered: music does not imitate or express nature, that is, the world of representation. World and music are *parallel* manifestations of the will: music is quite literally *another world*. Given their common origin, between music and physical world there is only a relation of "analogy".

As has been noted many times, Schopenhauer's illustration of this analogy is not very convincing. Harmony and the fundamental bass are related to each other as living beings and the planet that hosts them; the score for four voices corresponds to the natural kingdoms (mineral, vegetable, animal, human), and so on.[56] Strictly speaking, however, the correspondence between music and the will cannot be demonstrated. Schopenhauer instead invites us to surrender to the impressions of music, where this truth urges us to a pure exercise of a philosophical nature.

However, this exercise hides a problem, because the will seems to embody the very negation of musical harmony. It refers to the blind and yet vain struggle of living beings, whose constant desire achieves nothing. There are only rare times of "suspension" of the will, often given precisely by musical enjoyment. At the same time, though, Schopenhauer presents his metaphysics of music as an "interpretation" of Pythagoras's philosophy of numbers.[57] Schopenhauer takes for granted the old "theory, generally known and by no means overthrown by recent objections, that all harmony of the tones rests on the coincidence of the vibrations".[58] Consonance is based on the coincidence of the vibrations while dissonance is due to irrational mathematical ratios, when the vibrations contrast and refuse to be at one. Indeed "what resists our *apprehension*, namely the irrational relation or dissonance, becomes the natural image of what resists our *will*; and, conversely, the consonance or the rational relation, by easily adapting itself to our *apprehension*, becomes the image of the satisfaction of the *will*".[59] How

---

56 Schopenhauer (1969a, p. 258 ff.).
57 Schopenhauer (2014, p. 36).
58 Schopenhauer (1969b, p. 450) [*Supplements*].
59 Schopenhauer (1969b, p. 451) [*Supplements*].

can rationality and consonance be the image of what satisfies the Schopenhauerian will, understood as above? The reader finds here a seemingly unsolvable contradiction.[60]

The pages where Schopenhauer tries to solve this problem are extremely original, and yet often neglected. Schopenhauer draws on one last analogy, which he defines "remarkable", between music and the objective world. To understand the matter, one must start from the conflict between individual and species as to the relationship with the will. Since the will objectifies itself in each individual, the world becomes a "permanent battlefield of all [...] phenomena of one and the same will", which reveals its "inner contradiction with itself". Indeed, by conforming to the will, every individual is opposed to the others, which also conform to the will. This self-contradiction, which is the reason behind the tragic nature of human existence, finds perfect correspondence in music. In fact, Schopenhauer notes, "a perfectly pure harmonious system of tones is impossible not only physically, but even arithmetically. The numbers themselves, by which the tones can be expressed, have insoluble irrationalities".[61] Schopenhauer is thinking of Pythagorean intervals, which do not allow for a complete music system ranging over several octaves. Hence the necessity of temperament that manifests in music a contradiction similar to that of the social world. If individuals are consistent with the desire that dwells in them, they are no longer consistent with others; in parallel, if sounds are correct with respect to the keynote, they are no longer such in respect of one another. Schopenhauer concludes:

> Therefore a perfectly correct music cannot even be conceived, much less worked out; and for this reason all possible music deviates from perfect purity. It can merely conceal the discords essential to it by dividing these among all the notes, i.e., by temperament.[62]

With a fine image, sounds are likened to theatre actors, who play different characters every time: the *Tonic*, the *Dominant*, the *Leading tone* (1st, 5th, 7th), etc. The tragic masks of sounds-actors, who play on the stage of the tempered system, show the individual's pain of being forced to adjust to a system of conventions, which mitigates conflicts but denies his true nature. The music we hear might be harmonious, but its deep structure is tragic as such. The Pythagorean music system—perhaps for the first time—is *not* taken to embody unreachable

---

60 Cf. Ferrara (1996, p. 188).
61 Schopenhauer (1969a, p. 265f.).
62 Schopenhauer (1969a, p. 266). Conversely, Herbart believed that tempered intervals are *psychologically* perfect, while the supposed superiority of the Pythagorean ones depends "inaccuracies of the ear". Herbart (1811, p. 102).

perfection, and this is the very reason why Schopenhauer exalts it: it is unable to produce a complete music system.

The analysis of this moment in history would be incomplete without a reference to the illuminating observations about music that Søren Kierkegaard entrusted to the first volume of *Enten-Eller* (1849). The focus here was mainly on Mozart's *Don Giovanni*, which for Kierkegaard plays the epochal role of expressing the very essence of music. Among the Greeks—says Kierkegaard—sensuality was not understood as a "principle", that is, as "spiritually determined", because they lacked the historical background needed for this to happen. With a "boldly venturesome" claim we must instead recognize that Christianity is what introduced sensuality in the world.[63] Precisely by banning eros, in fact, Christianity (negatively) conferred it the spirituality it didn't have with the Greeks. Hence the "erotic sensual genius": an exclusively modern idea that is expressed at best in music. This is why Kierkegaard can claim that Mozart's *Don Giovanni* is the absolute musical work, in which form and content perfectly coincide: it is not a work like any other, but the only one that stages sensuality and therefore, as it were, music itself.

Being quite honest about his musical incompetence (which is quite rare among philosophers) Kierkegaard proceeds to an analysis based on analogies and differences between music and language. The latter can be perfected: from prose—very far from music—one can get to poetry, which is almost at one with it. This ascent from prose to poetry seems to indicate the possibility of getting ever closer to music and therefore to perfection. However, notes Kierkegaard, this is an illusion, "unless it is assumed that saying 'Uh' is more valuable than a complete thought". It is true that language fails to grasp "the immediate" as such, as belonging to the dimension of the instinct. But this is a flaw of the immediate, not of language. The immediate is foreign to the spirit and takes on a sensual aspect, and that's why it can be expressed in music: "in the erotic sensual genius, music has its absolute object".[64]

Kierkegaard scorns at how often his contemporaries indulge in the association between music and images. For him, the only exception to this view is the *Ouverture* of *Don Giovanni*, where the omen of the protagonist's destiny is announced by Mozart with a sort of brief musical lightning—a glow on the horizon heavy with dark clouds. The epochal role played by *Don Giovanni* excludes any talk of "absolute music", but Kierkegaard is rather unfavourable to synaesthesia, because sight and hearing get in each other's way. As a consequence, he concen-

---

[63] Kierkegaard (1992, p. 30).
[64] Kierkegaard (1992, p. 33).

trates on listening music only, even at the cost of acting rather bizarrely. He confesses that "I have resorted to an out of the way corner of the theatre where I could hide myself totally in music". In the end, after a long search:

> I stand outside in the corridor; I lean against the partition separating me from the auditorium and then the impression is most powerful; it is a world by itself, apart from me; I can see nothing but am near enough to hear and yet so infinitely far away.[65]

It is a telling passage, because the infinite distance achieved with the maximum effect of music recalls the situation of suspension typical of Kierkegaard's philosophical concept of *Angst*. And focusing on Kierkegaard's way of listening rather than the character of Don Giovanni—widely analysed in *Either Or*—makes it possible to present the *demonic* side of music from a particular standpoint. There is no need to recall the final punishment for the unrepentant seducer, but this does not imply that music, in its aesthetic function, is an expression of the demonic plunging itself into the abyss of hell. In describing the demonic character of music, Kierkegaard remarks "with secret horror":

> How terribly this art, above all others, often lacerates its votaries, a phenomenon which oddly enough seems to have escaped the attention of the psychologists and the multitude, except when they are startled now and then by a despairing individual's shriek of terror.[66]

To combat these excesses, Kierkegaard doesn't suggest listening to music in a "technical" way, like an expert. He responds to the demonic by means of the emblematic "partition" separating him from the audience. Hidden in the corridor, protecting his "despairing" individuality from the seduction of music, Kierkegaard is hesitant in front of the charm of music. He is reminiscent of Donna Elvira, caught between loving and cursing her seducer: "She is in distress at sea; her destruction is imminent, but it does not concern her; she is not aware of it; she is perplexed about what she should save".[67]

3 Hegel and Trembling

Georg Wilhelm Friedrich Hegel's interest in music is mainly related to his system of arts, for reasons shown in his lectures on aesthetics. For him, the artist turns

---

65 Kierkegaard (1992, p. 80).
66 Kierkegaard (1992, p. 41). For more on the "metaphysical and impersonal" characteristic of the demonic in Kierkegaard cf. Mathieu (1983, p. 22).
67 Kierkegaard (1992, p. 156).

the idea into a sensible manifestation in view of some end. Depending on the relationship between idea and sensible manifestation, Hegel distinguishes three forms of art: symbolic, classic and romantic. In the system of arts, the first two are architecture and sculpture, the last is the triad of painting, music and poetry. Architecture prepares the space by building a temple, sculpture gives determinacy to the divine by representing it as a statue; but then with romantic art the human community makes its appearance, and we already seem to hear it sing.

To understand the role of music as an intermediate element within the triad of romantic arts, though, one has to keep in mind the dual development characterizing Hegel's articulation of fine arts. This development can be seen both in the progressive spiritualization of sensible matter—from heavy stone to the lightness of poetry—and in the progress of the spiritual element expressed in that matter. The perfect correspondence between form and content of classical art is therefore not enough: on the contrary, the spirit struggles to manifest its freedom in the stillness of marble. To express itself, the spirit has to depart from matter and reach its proper dimension: interiority. As the first romantic art, painting is the first step in this direction. While not suppressing it entirely, it reduces spatial exteriority to pure visibility thanks to the use of colour, which allows the artist to express particular feelings and representations that are unaccessible by sculpture.

This is where music comes in. Music overcomes the spatiality left in painting and further perfects the path towards interiority, completely eliminating bodiliness and spatiality from art. The "ideality of matter [...] appears no longer as spatial but as temporal ideality". Indeed, music uses sound as its matter, which "releases the Ideal, as it were, from its entanglement in matter".[68] This is a fundamental step forward: poetry will not make use of a different material, but will simply use it differently, so that sound will be degraded to mere sign and content will find its best determination. Sticking to music, its place within the romantic arts thus depends primarily on the structure of the sound. In this regard, Hegel provides more details on the transition from spatiality to temporality:

> The cancellation of space therefore consists here only in the fact that a specific sensuous material sacrifices its peaceful separatedness, turns to movement, yet so vibrates in itself that every part of the cohering body not only changes its place but also struggles to replace

---

68 Hegel (1975a, p. 88).

itself in its former position. The result of this oscillating vibration is sound or a note, the material of music.[69]

These words can be better understood in the light of the *Philosophy of Nature*, the second part of the *Encyclopaedia of the Philosophical Sciences*,[70] where the passage from material spatiality to material temporality happens through *vibration*. Vibrating due to the external shock, the coherent parts of the body loose their cohesion, and then get back to their original state. Thus, sound manifests the higher ideality that is present in nature and is destined to appear more and more clearly in the organic world.

It is easy to see in this conception of sound the legacy of the eighteenth century doctrine of "sound tremors", which I have discussed earlier (see above, par. 1). However, Hegel uses it within a completely different philosophical framework. In fact, sound is produced in a way that is analogous to the master-slave dialectic, one of the most famous parts of the *Phenomenology of Spirit*. The resonant body acts like the slave, who endures the violence of his master but isn't crushed by it; he submits to his master, but in so doing he prepares to overthrow him. It is significant that both in *Philosophy of Nature* and in *Phenomenology of Spirit* Hegel uses the same verb, "to tremble" (*erzittern*): the servant's conscience "has trembled in every fibre of its being, and everything solid and stable has been shaken to its foundations".[71] The fear of death leads the servant's consciousness to internal dissolution in trembling. But the devastation of absolute fear is preserved as a negative sign of otherness, which the slave's consciousness will externalise in the "formative" action of working.

In the light of the above, one can see how peculiar Hegel's view of sound and music is. In this sense it can help to recall that for Herder sound was the most typical expression of suffering—and music, as a consequence, was the expression of passion (*Leidenschaft*). For Hegel, instead, suffering is part of the process, but the body's *active reaction* is fundamental. His Berlin lectures on the *Philosophy of Nature*, collected by his students, include a masterful definition of sound: "The plaint of the ideal in the midst of violence, but also its triumph over the latter since it preserves itself therein".[72] The *Klage des Ideellen* is the voice of the idea, alienated and imprisoned in matter, at the time when (like the slave) it trembles.

---

[69] Hegel (1975b, p. 890).
[70] Hegel (2004, p. 136 ff.).
[71] Hegel (1977, p. 117). Cf. Nowak (1971, p. 46 and 52–58).
[72] Hegel (2004, p. 139).

So far I have only analysed the first aspect of the matter. Going back to the *Aesthetics*, one should ask what corresponds to sound (i.e. the material of music) in terms of spiritual content. Indeed, it is clear that marble and colour can welcome the forms of real objects, whereas sound, despite its greater ideality, cannot.

> What alone is fitted for expression in music is the object-free inner life, abstract subjectivity as such. This is our entirely empty self, the self without any further content. Consequently the chief task of music consists in making resound, not the objective world itself, but, on the contrary, the manner in which the inmost self is moved to the depths of its personality and conscious soul.[73]

The content expressed by the musical sound is not the external world, but subjectivity itself. The subjectivity that manifests itself in music, however, is devoid of any content: it is an "empty self". In terms of the effects of music, this entails the total identification of the listener with the temporal flow of the sounds. One can lose oneself also in a statue or a picture, but while never forgetting the distance that separates the subject from the object of contemplation. In music, though, one is completely immersed in sound—at least at a first level. In fact, Hegel acknowledges that the expert might listen differently, in a more detached manner, judging what he hears by the virtue of his knowledge of the musical laws. This happens mostly with pure instrumental music. However, for Hegel this type of listening goes against the nature of music, which is thus left empty and devoid of spirit.[74]

The interiority achieved in music, therefore, is still basic due to its excessive adherence to the object, which ends up flattening subjectivity onto the flow of sounds. Under the aesthetic profile, the "emptiness" of the musical self demands compensation—it wants to be filled. For Hegel the composer has two ways to find the content he needs: he can add lyrics to the sounds, or express his "mood in the form of a musical theme". In this case, the succession of sounds in time must be accompanied by "a content, i.e. a spiritual feeling felt by the heart, and the soul of this content expressed in notes".[75]

In this context, the term used by Hegel (*Empfindung*) must be translated as "feeling", but this doesn't imply any associations with Romanticism.[76] We have already come across the term *Empfindung:* in Kant it defines music as art of ex-

---

[73] Hegel (1975b, p. 891).
[74] Hegel (1975b, p. 892 and 953f.).
[75] Hegel (1975b, p. 895 and 908).
[76] Cf. Heimsoeth (1967, p. 167); Kulenkampff (1987, *passim*).

ternal sensations, whereas in early Herder it refers to pure inner sensation.[77] Hegel instead chooses on a dialectic conception of the term, whose roots must be sought in the chapters on Anthropology and on Psychology of the *Philosophy of the subjective spirit*. In Anthropology the "sensation" (*Empfindung*) is a "dull agitation" of the spirit that awakens from the natural dimension: the soul finds an already existing content (such as color or sound) and takes it as its "most characteristic property".[78] In Psychology the *Empfindung* refers again to an auroral stage, in which the relationship with a content takes the form of a mere individual peculiarity, which isolates the subject.[79] In both cases Hegel's use of the concept designates a state of self-referential immediacy of subjectivity: the spiritual is reflected in an interiority produced by a sort of naive self-deceit. The feeling that the composer puts into his music, therefore, doesn't fill it enough from the aesthetic point of view. In fact, as Hegel notes in *Aesthetics*, the "region" of music is the "relatively formal interiority". This points to the partial aesthetic failure of music, which lacks a content and cannot find an appropriate one either by having lyrics (as it works only partly) or by the input of feeling, which doesn't bring subjectivity out of itself.

To be sure, in the analysis of specific musical means Hegel seems to envisage a possible revaluation of music thanks to the melodic dimension. Melody, in fact, gives music a "soul", as it blends rhythm and harmony, of which it is the dialectic synthesis. Harmony has to do with mathematical ratios (which Kant has already considered a *condicio sine qua non*) and relations between chords. Hegel compares the harmonic structure of music to that of the skeleton: the rigidity of the bones does not prevent bodily movement, but facilitates it.[80] Also, harmony is the terrain on which melody exists, the "free sounding of the soul in the field of music". Hegel is inspired: melody is the

> poetic element in music, the language of the soul, which pours out into the notes the inner joy and sorrow of the heart, and in this outpouring mitigates and rises above the natural force of feeling by turning the inner life's present transports into an apprehension of itself, into a free tarrying with itself, and by liberating the heart in this way from the pressure of joys and sorrows [...].[81]

Right here, where Hegel is closest to a positive view of the aesthetic effect of music, however, some elements appear that point in the opposite direction.

---

77 See above, par. 1 and chap. 2, par. 4.
78 Hegel (1978, p. 153). Emphasis omitted.
79 Hegel (1978, p. 119 ff. [par. 447]). Cf. Heimsoeth (1987, p. 160 ff.).
80 Hegel (1975b, p. p. 929 f.).
81 Hegel (1975b, p. p. 929 f.).

On the one hand, Hegel admits that a truly intimate portrait of this aspect exceeds the musical knowledge that he was able to acquire; after all, not much can be evidenced from professional musicians who are often insignificant people. But above all, the limit is objective: as much as music embraces a spiritual content and expresses its inner movement, such content is seldom "definite and detailed".

In spite of these difficulties, the Hegelian conception of music as art of temporality and interiority would have very serious consequences in the subsequent philosophy of music. It wouldn't be long before the bleak emptiness of Hegel's musical self filled with new contents and meanings: expanding up to encompass historical time, this "temporality" would eventually give music a whole new sense.

4 Musical Science and Aesthetics

The deepest instances of Hegelian thought in the field of music, however, were destined to unfold their potential at a later stage. Around the middle of the nineteenth century, the most innovative drives were united by the opposition to idealism in the name of a more scientific approach. We must therefore turn our attention to two independent phenomena, even if partly related: scientific developments and those of musical aesthetic, culminating respectively in the work of Hermann von Helmholtz and in that of Eduard Hanslick.

Let's start from the development of scientific psychology, many of whose protagonists—Herbart, Fechner, Lotze, Wundt, Lipps, Stumpf—proposed theories of consonance and other aspects of music.[82] Johann Friedrich Herbart is among the first to insist on the need to re-establish psychology in a scientific sense. The psychology of music, which Herbart cultivates competently, acquires a paradigmatic value because it shows the inadequacy of the prevailing philosophical systems perfectly exemplifying the mathematical rigor that characterizes the spiritual mechanisms. Abandoned all reference to sensations, Herbart emphasizes the interplay of "representations" that appear in the internal theater of the mind and which are subject to quantification starting from the mutual interaction and "inhibition". The "tone representations" (*Tonvorstellungen*) are defined in what Herbart calls "musical fantasy" (*musikalische Phantasie*): the pure inner perception of sounds, in which the musical ratios are offered in absolute evi-

---

[82] On these authors Cf. Martinelli (1999, p. 83 ff.).

dence, safe from the inevitable approximations typical of physical sounds.[83] Herbart imagines tone representations located along an interior "tonal line": a kind of psychological monochord where the musical ratios are represented in their geometric precision, allowing for a correct calculation of consonance and dissonance relations. Despite the difficulty of Herbart's mathematical formulas, too complex to catch on, his thought had considerable success especially in the Habsburg Empire, where the general hostility to Kantian and Hegelian philosophy would be strengthened as a result of the philosophy of Franz Brentano.[84]

To understand the further developments of scientific psychology one has to look at what happened in acoustic science. Chladni's thought had been taken up by scientists like Wilhelm Weber, who would influence Johannes Müller (among others). However, the scientific framework of acoustics was quickly changing. Apparatuses such as the "rotating siren" opened up new possibilities, while the controversy between Georg Ohm and August Seebeck put the spotlight back on the phenomenon of upper partial harmonics. Noting that these are mostly imperceptible, Seebeck contested the central role that Ohm had granted them.[85] In this context, after his success in physiological optics, Hermann von Helmholtz decided to address the issue to prove with ad hoc experimental devices (the "resonators") the physical reality of the decomposition of a sound wave in it elementary components, in Ohm's sense. Most of all, Helmholtz uses the different intensity of partial harmonics to explain the differences in the timbre of different instruments: each partial tone exists in the compound musical sound "just as truly, and in the same sense, as the different colours of the rainbow exist in the white light proceeding from the sun or any other luminous body".[86] As happened in the romantic period, acoustics and colour theory were strictly related, but with an opposite perspective: the analogy with Newton's prism here doesn't discredit but rather canonizes Helmholtz's resonators, giving them higher scientific respectability.

Physical acoustics, though, was only the first step. Helmholtz aims at a doctrine of tone sensations as the physiological basis for a music theory. Bypassing Herbart's mental representations, Helmholtz thus embraces the so-called "physiological" neo-Kantianism of the time. Indeed, Helmholtz believes that, through physiology, he will be able to solve the "wonderful and significant mystery" of why simple number relations result in consonances. Helmholtz identifies in

---

[83] Herbart (1810, p. 100). Cf. Moro (2002, *passim*).
[84] See below, chap. 4, par. 3.
[85] Cf. Turner (1977, *passim*).
[86] Helmholtz (1912, p. 48). Cf. Vogel (1994, *passim*); Hiebert (2014, p. 47 f.).

the inner ear a series of "fibers" adapted to vibrate in resonance, each for their own specific frequency: the auditory system is likened to a piano whose strings are left free to resonate and connected to the nerve fibers that transmit impulses to the brain. The ear-piano analyses every sound in its elementary components, finally providing an explanation to the two-thousand-years-old "enigma" proposed to science by Pythagoras.[87]

An important role was also played by psychology, which involves some of the most controversial points of Helmholtz's doctrine. One of them is the ear's ability to perceive—albeit with difficulty—partial harmonics, whereas the eye can never decompose white light as Newton's prism does. To explain this anomaly, Helmholtz first introduced a distinction between sensation and perception;[88] then he took up Leibniz's distinction between perception and apperception.[89] The greatest perplexities, though, were aroused mainly by Helmholtz's auditory theory. In fact, according to Helmholtz, each one of the thousands of nerve fibers involved would be endowed with a "specific energy", that is, an intrinsic capacity, different for each fiber, to evoke "sensations" corresponding to a given pitch. Many critics saw this as an excessive positivist "analysis", which would end up arousing opposite reactions in the long run. Thanks to Herbart and Brentano, psychology—especially in Austria—would rather underline the structural, non-elementary, aspects of music perception. In line with Ewald Hering's and later Ernst Mach's criticism of Helmholtz's theory, authors related to Brentano like Christian Ehrenfels and Carl Stumpf would pave the way to the overthrowing of Helmholtz's reductionism and the birth of Gestalt psychology.[90] In general, though, the historical role of Helmholtz's theory wasn't affected by these developments. Helmholtz truly ended a series of millenary speculations on the mathematical, physical and physiological foundations of music perception: from now on, philosophy would no longer address these topics. This is the epochal role played by Helmholtz in the present context. By solving these issues (even if, of course, science would carry on with its investigations), Helmholtz indirectly pushed philosophical reflection towards new problems.[91] In short, Helmholtz's solution to Pythagoras's enigma marked the end of "pythagoreanism" (in its various meanings) as the necessary ingredient of any respectable philosophical explanation of music.

---

87 Helmholtz (1912, p. 15 and 229).
88 Until the third edition: Helmholtz (1870, p. 101).
89 In the fourth edition: Helmholtz (1877, p. 106).
90 Cf. Ash (1995, p. 60 ff.).
91 At the time, Spencer's and Darwin's ideas on the origin of music echoed in the work of Edmund Gurney: cf. Budd (1994, p. 56 ff.).

In this sense, it is significant that another work—completely different from, but comparable to, Helmholtz's *Lehre*—also appeared in the same period: namely, Eduard Hanslick's *On the Musically Beautiful* (1854). Hanslick wasn't a philosopher nor a scientist, but a music critic who taught, and later got tenure, at the University of Vienna *honoris causa*. From the sociological point of view, this was a novelty. Related to subjective evaluation by nature, music criticism in the early nineteenth century stayed purposely clear from the objective language of science —"musicology" (*Musikwissenschaft*)—but Hanslick mastered it.[92] Furthermore, Hanslick aimed specifically at the *musically* beautiful, not at beauty in the special case of music. Thus, musical aesthetics parted from the more conventional aesthetic of music—the *Aesthetik der Tonkunst* that, according to the subtitle of his book, Hanslick wanted to reform, so that the usual armchair "system-building" would finally give way to "research".[93]

Hanslick has two theses: a negative one (music doesn't arouse or express feelings) and a positive one (the musically beautiful is specific of sounds, without further conceptual references). The first point must be adequately contextualized: Hanslick doesn't rule out the presence of feelings from music, but protests against their interference with science, because focusing on feelings prevents scientists from drawing "musical laws". His language is clearly positivistic, but it shouldn't be misunderstood: far from calling for other sciences (physiology, psychology, etc.), Hanslick wants to adopt their methods. But if music doesn't act on feelings, what effects does it have? One should be careful here not to hastily jump to a strong version of Hanslick's "formalism": there are no feelings, therefore there are only forms of sounds. In reality, Hanslick doesn't fail to speak of the effect of music over the human soul: it doesn't affect feelings or the intellect, but something in between—the "imagination" (*Phantasie*). Faced with the beautiful, imagination doesn't engage in mere contemplation, but in "active understanding". These lines are often interpreted as an example of Kant's legacy. However, Hanslick proposes a rather psychologistic version of music's reception, which has little to do with Kant: representation and judgment, in Hanslick's view, occur so swiftly that they hide the presence of "several intermediate processes".

For Hanslick, the *medietas* of the imagination individuates the realm of music: focusing on the intellect or on feelings means misunderstanding music in a logical or pathological sense. Therefore, Hanslick's rejection of sentimentalism doesn't entail an intellectualistic position. For Hanslick it is wrong to iden-

---

92 Cf. Fubini (1991b, p. 195).
93 Hanslick (1986, p. 2). For an introduction, cf. Grey (2011, *passim*).

tify the peculiarity of music in its effect over our feelings, which is historically conditioned. It is thus absurd to claim that feelings are the "content" of music. In this regard, Hanslick refers to something that—after Brentano—was called "intentionality": like all mental acts, feelings are always addressed to an object, e.g. love to the loved one, and so forth. And yet, for Hanslick, it isn't so in music. Indeed, otherwise we would refrain from listening much of the music repertoire: "if every dull requiem, every noisy death march, every plaintive adagio had the power to make us sad, who would want to go on living?"[94] Music cannot even properly imitate visible objects, nor does it express feelings in the abstract sense as in Schopenhauer. Rather, Hanslick notes, music can express the dynamic of feelings with its own means: "music can imitate the motion of a psychic process according to its various phases—presto, adagio, forte, piano, crescendo, and diminuendo. But motion is only a property, an aspect of feeling—not feeling itself".[95] In the sixth edition of *The Musically Beautiful* (1881), Hanslick indicated Herbart, an opponent of the aesthetics of feeling, as a forerunner for this negative part of his theory.[96]

Hanslick's positive thesis is usually defined "formalism". The musically beautiful, claims Hanslick, "consists simply and solely in *tones* and their artistic combination". Hence the famous definition: "the content of music is tonally moving forms". Beautiful forms are not only present in music: the arabesque, the kaleidoscope, leaves and flowers please us as such, with no need for content. But these are just examples that Hanslick makes to get closer to the musically beautiful, which is so hard to put into words. Hanslick doesn't say that music has the same aesthetic value as an arabesque. Music expresses something, but this something is made up of musical ideas:

> A musical idea brought into complete manifestation in appearance is already self subsistent beauty. It is an end in itself, and it is in no way primarily a medium or material for the representation of feelings or conceptions.[97]

Thus, there are musical ideas, which do not require anything else to be justified within aesthetics. The widespread "contempt for the sensible", which for the ancients was fueled by morality and for Hegel by the idea, is what makes most peo-

---

94 Hanslick (1986, p. 4, 6 and 66).
95 Hanslick (1986, p. 9).
96 Cf. Tedeschini Lalli (1993, p. 46 ff. and 153). Hanslick was close to Robert Zimmermann, a leading figure of the Herbartian school in Prague.
97 Hanslick (1986, p. 28 f.).

ple blind to this fact. Now, it is true that Beethoven doesn't compose for "the labyrinth or the eardrum". However, Hanslick insists that

> the auditory imagination [...] which is something entirely different from the sense of hearing regarded as a mere funnel open to the surface of appearances, enjoys in conscious sensuousness the sounding shapes, the self-constructing tones and dwells in free and immediate contemplation of them.[98]

As a consequence, Hanslick rejects the idea that the musically beautiful consists in symmetry or mathematical proportions.[99] He is more open to the role of feelings, provided that imagination is "by no means an isolated domain": drawing its "vital impulse" from sensations, it expands to intellect and to feeling, which however are "peripheral" to the authentic conception of the beautiful. The jurisdiction of these peripheral domains, therefore, resides outside musical aesthetics: physiology and psychology may well have their say about the effects of the musically beautiful, but never about the musically beautiful itself.

So, Hanslick outlines a theory of musical composition and experience. The composer is driven by "an inner singing, not merely an inner feeling", which he gives shape to progressively, "like a crystal". In other words, the composer "composes and thinks [...] in tones". Experience can also be understood in two different ways. While the amateur is overwhelmed with feeling, raptured by the "naturally beautiful", which is part of, but doesn't coincide with, the musically beautiful, the cultivated artist keeps the sentimental aspect to the minimum. For Hanslick, the most important source of pleasure is "the mental satisfaction which the listener finds in continuously following and anticipating the composer's designs, here to be confirmed in his expectations, there to be agreeably led astray".[100] As said, this process is subconscious because it happens too swiftly; Hanslick calls it "reflection for imagination", and it clearly happens mostly in instrumental music, "because only instrumental music is music purely and absolutely". In opera, instead, music joins poetry in a "morganatic marriage" (where children have no right to their parents' inheritance).

Once again we come across the issue of instrumental music, which is so important that it deserves some clarifications. First of all, one should note the ambiguity of an expression that Hanslick didn't use but is today very widespread: "absolute music". It has been noted that the expression is due to Richard Wagner, and that it goes very well with his conception of drama: music is absolute in

---

98 Hanslick (1986, p. 30).
99 Hanslick (1986, p. 41 and *passim*).
100 Hanslick (1986, p. 64).

that it is "free" from its original bond to poetry. But even if one sticks to more neutral formulations, this conception introduces asymmetry in the very notion of music.[101] In the end, the idea that music is eminently instrumental (and then one can add to it lyrics and/or interpretative "programmes") is largely illusory. Supporters of "absolute music" consider "pure" instrumental music superior to vocal music, as it implies lyrics. Strictly speaking, though, the exception shouldn't be the voice as such, but the arbitrary interpretation given by the "programme", which is supposedly conveyed by the lyrics. And yet this exception is no less arbitrary: it is enough for listeners not to understand the words (say because they don't speak the language) for it not to hold.

This brings me to the issue of the spiritual value of music according to Hanslick, in the light of the final pages of *The Musically Beautiful*. Music can only have spiritual value within the doctrine of moving tonal forms: Hanslick speaks of a "creation of the mind out of material compatible with the mind". These are the final words of all the editions of the book, after the third. In the first edition, though, Hanslick added that this spiritual content relates the musically beautiful to "all great and beautiful ideas": music does not act only through beauty, but also as "sound image of the great movements of the cosmos". By means of "deep and secret natural relations", the meaning of music transcends the sounds and "in the work of human talent also hints at the infinite", so that "man finds the whole universe in music". As shown by these variants, after 1865 the spiritual content of music loses this cosmic-metaphysical flavour. Without these references to the resonance of the "great and beautiful ideas" in the musically beautiful, Hanslick's position seems formalistic by subtraction, as it were.

This issue also appears in the work of a very influential philosopher at the time: Hermann Lotze. In his *Geschichte der Aesthetik in Deutschland* (1868) Lotze develops the hypotheses he already made in a timely review of Hanslick's book. Music, for Lotze, is not about feelings, but can and must arouse them. Music can suggest with a figure the "form of the movement" with which the snow falls, but it cannot precisely evoke the snow falling, rather than something else related to it.[102] No interpretation is compelling: we can very well not connect the given piece to the falling snow, but it is true that we can hardly connect it to a hurricane raging on the ocean: there is always a "limited range" of sensible choices. What applies to the snow also applies to feelings: they are not determined, but made probable by a given piece of music. According to Lotze, though, one shouldn't seek feelings "at all costs", but only those that produce "the exhibition

---

101 Cf. Dahlhaus (1991, p. 20).
102 Lotze (1868, p. 480).

of an objective relationship". Music does not offer a personal well-being, yet it must guarantee a "living reality" to the "value" of those relationships. Intentionality, namely the presence of an object which a feeling is for, in fact, muddies its purity.

Lotze observes that in grief, for instance, there can be an element of selfish bitterness because it happened to us and not someone else. In music, instead, feelings appear in a pure form. Therefore it is true that in music there are only sound forms, but they appear beautiful because they remind us of the "countless good things" that have appeared in an analogous form. Music purifies feelings by making us accustomed to experiencing them in their highest form, thus acquiring an ethical function. It is therefore not surprising that Lotze would be critical of the music of his time. Lamenting the particular inclination for music that was so widespread in Germany, Lotze fully embraced Hanslick's polemic against sentimentalism. Lotze stigmatizes especially the constant "going down into in this yet unformed world", which causes a "pernicious atony" of all those forces that the newly unified nation should instead target for other purposes.[103] This critique of German musicophilia is of course aimed at Wagner, anticipating a position that Friedrich Nietzsche would reach after a tortuous and fascinating path.

5 The Case of Nietzsche

His experience as an amateur composer, his controversial relationship with Wagner and the constant references to music scattered across his works testify to the importance of this art in the life and thought of Friedrich Nietzsche. Nevertheless, it wouldn't be correct to consider it one of the core themes of his philosophy—as is the case with Rousseau or, later, Adorno. There are good reasons for this: the part specifically devoted *to music* in his writings on Wagner—both the early enthusiastic ones and the later critical ones—is indeed relatively small. Many references to music scattered elsewhere appear quite disappointing—so much so that one is tempted to believe (mistakenly) that Nietzsche knew nothing about the matter. The truth is that, in Nietzsche, music often points to issues that transcend it: ancient Greece and Germany in their intertwined destiny, history and politics, "decadence" and the possibility of redemption, then disenchantment and finally "life", seen (as in Kant) in its markedly physiological components and (as in Plato) in its dawn and twilight.[104]

---

103 Lotze (1868, p. 483 and *passim*).
104 Cf. Most (2008, p. 420 ff.); Sorgner (2011, *passim*).

Preceded by several unpublished works and followed by much controversy, *The Birth of Tragedy* (1872) introduced the distinction between the "Apolline" and the "Dionysiac", which correspond to plastic art and music. Artistic perfection in tragedy is achieved by the interaction of these two elements, but what prevails overall is the Dionysiac, which, for Nietzsche, is Beethoven's *Hymn to Joy* imagined as a painting, placing "no constraints on one's imagination as the millions sink into the dust, shivering in awe, then one could begin to approach the Dionysiac".[105] Apolline music, instead, is gentle notes on the lyre: it keeps away the typical nature of Dionysiac music ("and hence of music in general") namely "the power of its sound to shake us to our very foundations, the unified stream of melody and the quite incomparable world of harmony".[106] This reference is enough to show how Nietzsche's definition hardly applies to Greek music as we know it. A professor of Classical Philology at the University of Basel, Nietzsche was probably aware of this. Forcing the contrast between Apollo's lyre and Marsyas' aulos, Nietzsche shows that he is mainly thinking of *his* age, which the second half of the work deals with: the book is not so much about the birth of tragedy, but rather about its desired *rebirth* from the spirit of music.[107]

Wagner and Schopenhauer are the obvious protagonists of this rebirth. Following Schopenhauer, Wagner has affirmed the need to evaluate music with entirely different parameters from those used for other arts. The point is to break free from the tyranny of the beautiful form, which is Apolline and thus improper in music. Nietzsche's identification of the principle of the tragic, the recomposition of the Apolline and Dionysiac, is preceded by a very long quotation of Schopenhauer's most famous passages about music.[108] Tragedy enriches music with myth, leading it to perfection; music returns the favour by giving myth renewed energy. Nietzsche recognizes the hypothetical nature of this reconstruction, given that we do not know what kind of music accompanied the tragic texts: as an "example" of the interaction of Apolline and Dionysiac he then mentions the third act of Wagner's *Tristan und Isolde*. This reference marks a true turning point in the *Birth of Tragedy*. Nietzsche first refers to simply listening to the orchestra, which leads "to the heart of the universal will", to "the raging desire for existence": in the following confusion, the Apolline element of Wagner's lyrics comes to the rescue.[109]

---

[105] Nietzsche (1999, p. 18).
[106] Nietzsche (1999, p. 21).
[107] Most (2008, p. 425).
[108] Nietzsche (1999, p. 77–79).
[109] Nietzsche (1999, p. 100).

The idea of an aesthetic rebirth originating from the recovery of ancient theatre is far from new, but Nietzsche's reference to the "German spirit" gives the theme new declinations. Going back through the history of Greek civilization, the German spirit goes from the Alexandrine age to the Classical. But how does Nietzsche justify this German-Hellenic allegiance? First of all, thanks to German music, born "out of the Dionysiac root" of the German spirit, "from Bach to Beethoven, from Beethoven to Wagner".[110] Ignited by this spiritual power, then, German philosophy with Kant and Schopenhauer was able to "destroy scientific Socratism's contented pleasure in existence" and establish "*Dionysiac wisdom*".[111] So, in Nietzsche, there is a very strong bond between *German music* and *German philosophy*, something that has to lead to a "new form of existence, the content of which can only be guessed at from Hellenic analogies". Nietzsche concludes:

> Yes, my friends, believe as I do in Dionysiac life and in the rebirth of tragedy. The time of Socratic man is past. Put on wreaths of ivy, take up the thyrsus and do not be surprised if tigers and panthers lie down, purring and curling round your legs. Now you must only dare to be tragic human beings, for you will be released and redeemed. You will accompany the festive procession of Dionysos from India to Greece! Put on your armour for a hard fight, but believe in the miracles of your god![112]

Richard Wagner in Bayreuth is a journey from contemporaneity to the Greek world. The theatre founded by Wagner in 1872 witnessed the rebirth of the project "to found the State upon music".[113] While the work praises Wagner comparing him to famous men like Alexander the Great, Nietzsche privately harbours serious reservations on Wagner who, in his view, mainly attempts at political power.[114] In parallel, Nietzsche already cultivates some doubts about Wagner's actual musical talent.

Nietzsche now considers in more detail the historical development of music. For a long time music primarily aimed at giving "expression in sound to a mood, a state of determination or cheerfulness or reverence or penitence".[115] The static nature of this music, however, made it uninteresting—something that the composer tried to avoid, for example, by combining contrasting different moods.

---

110 Nietzsche (1999, p. 94).
111 Nietzsche (1999, p. 95).
112 Nietzsche (1999, p. 98).
113 Nietzsche (1997, p. 217).
114 Nietzsche (1992, p. 384). This fragment [32.71] is not included in the English translation (Nietzsche 2009).
115 Nietzsche (1997, p. 240).

Yet "[a]ll these are still rude and primitive stages of music. The first law originated in fear of passion, the second in fear of boredom".[116] Thus, this interplay of oppositions has to eventually come to an end: the ethos thus gives way to pathos with Beethoven.[117] Still using conventional language, Beethoven, however, remains affected by a residual darkness. Only Wagner breaks free from all the encumbrances of the ethos in favor of a greater "clarity". A powerful "symphonic intellect" capable of taming and merging conflicts, Wagner makes the music plastic, as if at last it was no longer ashamed of being seen from all sides.

As a musician, then, Wagner takes every degree and every shade of feeling with the utmost firmness and determination;

> he takes the tenderest, most remote and wildest emotions in hand without fear of losing his grip on them and holds them as something hard and firm, even though to anyone else they may be as elusive as a butterfly. His music is never indefinite, indicating only a general mood; everything that speaks through it, man or nature, has a strictly individualized passion; storm and fire take on the compelling force of a personal will.[118]

However, as has been said, even then Wagner and his audience—the "Germans"—gave Nietzsche reason to doubt the yearned-for spiritual rebirth. Since 1872, there had been issues with the "star friendship" between the philosopher and the composer, much like two ships that, after a stop in the same harbour, resume their divergent routes.[119] I don't need here to go into the complex personal relations between the philosopher and the composer (and his wife). What matters is that soon Nietzsche had all the elements for a position that necessarily implied a different philosophy of music.

To understand the issue it is useful to start from *The Case of Wagner*, an essay published in 1888, five years after the death of the composer. Wagner (and Schopenhauer like him) is now depicted as an illness, a pernicious neuroses, to the point that "[t]o turn my back on Wagner was for me a piece of fate".[120] The illness in question is *décadence* (which Nietzsche inevitably refers to in French): the hate for life, which Wagner arouses and amplifies. "Wagner increas-

---

[116] Nietzsche (1997, p. 241).
[117] Nietzsche (1997, p. 240). The distinction between ethos and pathos had been relaunched in 1795 by Christian G. Körner in Schiller's journal "Horen": cf. Dahlhaus (1988, p. 88).
[118] Nietzsche (1997, p. 242).
[119] Nietzsche (2001, p. 225 f.). However, Wagner is not mentioned in this aphorism entitled *Star friendship* [no. 279], that might refer to Franz Overbeck instead (cf. the editor's commentary in the footnote, p. 226).
[120] Nietzsche (1911a, p. 17).

es exhaustion—*therefore* he attracts the weak and exhausted to him",[121] with a hypnotic music able to overexcite a tired soul. On the one hand, Nietzsche criticises Wagner's Christian symbolism, compassionate morality and the obsession for "redemption"—all typical elements of his later works. On the other hand, he addresses Bayreuth, a theatre for the masses that only produces mundane entertainment. As an antidote to Wagnerism, Nietzsche proposes nostalgia for a sunny, mediterranean music: "The return to Nature, health, good spirits, youth, *virtue!*"[122] This music is not found in Italian Opera but in Bizet's *Carmen*. Bizet is described as a genius able to discover a part of the South in music with "this southern, tawny, sunburnt sensitiveness".[123] On the other hand, Wagner's style is also described in detail: by "overthrowing" and "elevating" people, Wagner gives the masses "the sublime, the profound, the overwhelming".[124]

In his analysis of Wagnerism, Nietzsche makes an increasing use of physiology. Some musical instruments have to persuade "the guts", while others captivate the "spinal cord"; symmetrically, Bizet is praised among other things because his music "does not sweat".[125] The philosopher isn't being ironic or argumentative. The physiology of music is of fundamental importance, even more exalted in the paragraphs of the *Gay Science* taken up in *Nietzsche Contra Wagner*, the last thing Nietzsche wrote before surrendering into madness. The work, an anthology of earlier writings, is intended to illustrate Nietzsche's permanent attitude to Wagner: "we are antipodes".[126] Aesthetics here becomes "applied physiology": Wagner's music has such an effect that "I can no longer breathe with ease", and the foot "immediately begins to feel indignant at it and rebels".[127] Wagner exacerbates the nerves mainly due to his cheap use of "passion". Inverting the previous exaltation of pathos as a result of the development of the history of music, Nietzsche now mercilessly defines passion (*Leidenschaft*) as "the acrobatic feats of ugliness on the tight-rope of enharmonic".[128] Passion is related to Wagner's musical idealism, which translates into the pernicious precept to never give the listener any relief. The grandeur of those who aspire to make us see everything through the magnifying glass, then, turns into its opposite: Wagner is the "greatest musical *miniaturist*", expert in "his elaboration

---

121 Nietzsche (1911a, p. 28).
122 Nietzsche (1911a, p. 12).
123 Nietzsche (1911a, p. 20 f.).
124 Nietzsche (1911a, p. 29).
125 Nietzsche (1911a, p. 19).
126 Nietzsche (1911b, p. 57).
127 Nietzsche (1911b, p. 59).
128 Nietzsche (1911a, p. 31).

of detail".[129] Wagner himself thought that what he wrote was "*not music alone*"— but "*no musician would speak in this way*", comments Nietzsche.[130]

So, this is how Nietzsche's judgment of Wagner was established. However, considering the role Nietzsche gave earlier to the "German masters", some further doubts arise. What interests me, in fact, is not so much the case of Wagner, but rather Nietzsche's ideas about music—or, as it were, *the case of Nietzsche*. One must therefore ask if, in parallel to the judgment of Wagner, Nietzsche has really changed his opinion or feeling about music in general. The answer is yes, but it requires some clarifications, because the numerous positive references to Bizet might be misleading. The same could be said of Nietzsche's praise of melody over harmony,[131] which seems to point to the eighteenth century.

The situation, in fact, is more complex. On the one hand, the rejection of Wagner's music would seem to put things in place, saving modern music from Wagnerism. However, this does not happen: Nietzsche does not maintain his judgment on German music, only excluding Wagner. On the contrary, what he expresses is the acknowledgment of a generalized decline: "not even a God can save music".[132] Music is a late art, the latest of all chronologically speaking, born "at a time when the culture to which it belongs is in its autumn season and beginning to fade". In short, music cannot be cured "from the main fact [...] of being modern". Without the "physiological assumption" of "good music" that inspired dance, Wagner's audience can only swim, or rather clumsily reel in a foreign element.

Showing a Platonic influence that also emerges from his use of the term "theatrocracy" to criticize Bayreuth's philistinism, Nietzsche understands music as a useful remedy for when life is blooming or declining. In the first case there is an overabundance of life and therefore a desire for Dionysiac art, in the second there is instead an impoverishment of life and one wants "repose, quietness, calm seas, or else the intoxication, the spasm, the bewilderment which art and philosophy provide", treacherously obtained by Wagner and Schopenhauer by "revenge upon life itself". The way to go, for Nietzsche, is clearly the first.

> [H]ave *relief:* as if all animal functions were accelerated by means of light, bold, unfettered, self-reliant rhythms, as if brazen and leaden life could lose its weight by means of delicate

---

[129] Nietzsche (1911a, p. 34).
[130] Nietzsche (1911a, p. 41).
[131] Nietzsche's own musical compositions (think of *Hymnus an die Freundschaft*) were the very negations of these principles.
[132] Nietzsche (1911a, p. 53).

and smooth melodies. My melancholy would fain rest its head in the haunts and abysses of *perfection*; for this reason I need music.[133]

The reference to animal functions and their "acceleration" falls within the line of reasoning inaugurated by Kant and developed in nineteenth century scientific physiology (from Lange to Helmholtz) of which Nietzsche is a passable connoisseur. Again, in Nietzsche the effect of music soothes and consoles the body, as "there is no such thing as a soul".[134] But this is a weak solution, a palliative even for Nietzsche himself. The philosopher grasps, as it were, the very making of the historical fact that the development of music, in its upward flight, is approaching a turning point after which there will no longer be a "modern music" as it was understood till then. It is not that Wagner is this turning point: he has rather accelerated the ruin of music. There are simply no longer the preconditions for musical education, even the best one, to take root and be fruitful.

It is legitimate to ask whether Nietzsche contemplates a solution to these difficulties. In a first sense, the way out can only be anthropological:

> In itself it is not impossible that there are still *remains* of stronger natures, typical unadapted men, somewhere in Europe: from this quarter the advent of a somewhat belated form of beauty and perfection, even in music, might still be hoped for.[135]

In the best case scenario, Nietzsche continues, we have nothing but a few exceptions, that is, the "honesty" that is still possible in miniature. Nietzsche has learned not to trust in German music, and yet he still has the dream about music "being redeemed from the north" so as to achieve "more profound and powerful, perhaps more evil and mysterious music".[136] This would be a "supra-German" music "whose rarest magic consisted in no longer knowing anything of good and evil—although, perhaps, some sailor's homesickness, some golden shadow and delicate weakness might run across it every now and then".[137] This music welcomes the belated fugitives who no longer understand those concepts. This omen cannot help raising questions about the music to come.

---

133 Nietzsche (1911b, p. 59).
134 Nietzsche (1911b, p. 59).
135 Nietzsche (1911a, p. 46f.).
136 Nietzsche (2002, p. 147).
137 Nietzsche (2002, p. 148).

Fourth Chapter
Dissonances

1 Bloch and the Art of Utopia

The early 1900s were a period of great development for both music and philosophy. The crisis of the tonal system, as well as the artistic and scientific interest in extra-European musical traditions and phenomena like synaesthesia, strengthened the idea that Western tonal music was only one amongst many possible ways to construct a musical language. New technologies—like the phonograph, the gramophone, and the radio—exercised an influence on the mode of fruition of music, and questioned the very nature of a musical event. As for philosophical reflection, inquiry into the meaning of music turned towards history, rather than nature, and this happened at a time when history became more turbulent and unsettling than ever before. An important document in this regard is Ernst Bloch's *The Spirit of Utopia*, published in 1918—thanks to an enthusiastic report by Otto Klemperer, who reviewed the manuscript for the publisher—and revised in 1923 after Bloch's conversion to Marxism. The dense section dedicated to music is not to be interpreted as a philosophical companion to socialist expressionism, however. Bloch does not apply a type of philosophy to a type of music. Rather, this "inwardly utopian"[1] art form plays a central philosophical role within Bloch's work. Indeed, subjectivity can detach itself in the sounds of music, becoming capable of dreaming and elevating itself to the most important things—to the Apocalypse of the meaning of its own terrestrial predicament. *The Spirit of Utopia* examines this problem by developing both a philosophical *history* and a philosophical *theory* of music, following a bipartite structure, something especially evident in the first edition.[2]

Bloch's "philosophical history" of music focuses on modern music, because all that precedes it is presented as insignificant. According to Bloch, not only the Persians, the Chaldeans and the Egyptians, but even the Greeks had no "*music worth mentioning*".[3] This is not an aesthetic judgment but rather a thesis in the philosophy of history. These peoples, however, compensated for their lack

---

[1] Bloch (1985a, p. 137). References will be to the English translation of two chapters on music respectively from *The Spirit of Utopia* (Bloch 1995a) and from *The Principle of Hope* (Bloch 1995b). For further details cf. Palmer (1985, p. vii); for a complete translation of the two works see Bloch (2000) and Bloch (1995).
[2] See the first edition: Bloch (1918, p. 80).
[3] Bloch (1985a, p. 136).

of music with "clairvoyance" (*Hellsehen*): they had a "secure heaven filled exclusively with visible and objective things", allowing them to be in close contact with transcendence.[4] This attitude projects the barycentre of meaning towards the outside, and it is therefore incompatible with an authentically musical soul. The music of the Greeks, so often idealized by philosophers, is divested of its mythical halo, being interpreted as the expression of a wholly different spiritual attitude. At the same time, Bloch detests the "false, *purely astronomical theory of music*"[5] and the correlated mathematical conception of sound. And he similarly despises the infertile "formal mysticism" that is preserved by the medieval conception, still linked to astral music and numerological speculation—yet surprisingly still ready to exert its influence over modern thinkers like Schelling or Schopenhauer. These doctrines mistakenly apply the scheme of the "divining vision" to music, while the latter has simply nothing to do with it.

It must be noted that Bloch later felt the need to integrate these theses. In *The Principle of Hope* (1953–1959), the origin of music is placed in the myth of the nymph Syrinx: pursued by Pan, Syrinx was turned into the reeds of a river, which the god cut in different lengths and tied together creating the pastoral flute still called by the name of either of the two protagonists.[6] Syrinx's presence is also her absence: music, Bloch notes, "originated in yearning and it began very much as a *call into what has been forgone*".[7] At first, one may read this absence as the distant lover for whom the shepherd is singing, but the panic origin of music entails that "we cannot help hearing a summons in the singing".[8] Here Bloch points out an alternative to Nietzsche's dichotomy between Apollonian and Dionysian, one that emerges from the balance between "atmosphere" (the nymph's presence/absence) and "proportion" (the different length of the reeds). Dionysus and Apollo therefore play their part, but are both subordinated to the human need that originated music, which determines the supremacy of a modest rural whistle over the noise of the sacred instruments of religious and civil power.

Bloch thus reaches a more pondered judgment on the cosmic-mathematical conception of music, which comes from dividing the two aspects that were joined in the myth of Syrinx: "whereas music as a mood remains buried within the soul and seems the most chthonian of all the arts, so-called *musica mathematica* be-

---

4 Bloch (1985a, p. 136).
5 Bloch (1985a, p. 121).
6 Ovid (1951a, p. 51f. [1, 690–710]).
7 Bloch (1985b, p. 196).
8 Bloch (1985b, p. 196).

comes wholly Uranian and steps off in heaven".⁹ Originally human, music is dislocated and decentralized, hidden underground and elevated to heaven. The extrahuman order however does not completely deny the human content of music: the harmony of the spheres, Bloch admits, also lets nature resonate as "humanly significant". Pythagoreanism "held sway for all too long", but eventually "taught the musical work to think a very great deal of itself".¹⁰

The music of the spheres, in its medieval developments, can be read as the hatch of an ambitious utopia disguised under as quite the opposite:

> Ideal time (*Wunschzeit*), and consequently real utopia, infiltrates this changing harmony of the spheres, the avowed harmonic-integrity of Creation, only inasmuch as one conceives its ideal space (*Wunschraum*) as being filled not simply with the music of angels but with that of a *future Jerusalem*.¹¹

This allows us to link back to the moment, in the modern era, when the "clairvoyance" was dissolved. Modern man voids this image of its mystical character and, in music, turns, in Hegelian fashion, towards interiority.

Bloch's inquiry into the history of modern music, then, begins with the problem of how we listen to ourselves in music. Bloch distinguishes three levels: (1) the "endless singing-to-oneself" (*das endlose vor sich Hinsingen*),¹² which gives origin to dance and chamber music; (2) the "uniform song" (Mozart, Bach); and (3) the schema of "open-ended song", including Opera, choral works and symphonies (Wagner, Beethoven, Bruckner).¹³ The discussion of these topics, which I cannot examine in depth here, ends with a reflection about the "bitter feeling [...] that tormented Mozart, Schubert and Beethoven before their deaths —namely the feeling that they really should begin now, that they had not yet written a single note". However, it is from this bitter feeling for the unfinished that the utopian meaning of music stems. This is examined by Bloch in the section titled "The philosophical theory of music".¹⁴ Here he offers a philosophical interpretation of the characteristic elements of musical language: sound ("means"), harmony ("formula"), rhythm ("form"), counterpoint ("ideogram"),

---

9 Bloch (1985b, p. 201).
10 Bloch (1985b, p. 214).
11 Bloch (1985b, p. 217).
12 Bloch (1985a, p. 14).
13 Bloch (1985a, p. 15). This subdivision is influenced by the two "cultures" (Bach's fugue and Beethoven's sonata) described by August Halm (1913), who is also highly praised by Adorno (2002, p. 201).
14 Bloch (1985a, p. 90). The first edition has "transcendental" instead of "philosophical" theory of music.

then again sound as a "phenomenal", and finally the "thing-in-itself" in music. For each of these section, the text is introduced by some opening aphorisms, that display a certain continuity and which I will cite by assigning them a Roman numeral (i–vi).

First of all, Bloch claims that "nothing in this realm can sound by itself" (i). This anti-naturalistic thesis states that sound, in general, has a meaning due only to human intervention, rather than to its own objective structure, mathematical or otherwise.[15] It is a matter of discerning ourselves in sound, a "question of feeling extensively" (ii): this is the purpose of harmony. Every harmonic system is also a means of amplification, aimed at the "unerring continuation of 'tonal', i.e. man-lent instinct, the man-lent vitality of notes".[16] As for rhythm, the "musical beat, otherwise, does not seem to be wholly divorced from the reflecting process" (iii).[17] What Bloch means here is that musical mimesis, in which a human aspect is represented (i.e. a historical or sentimental content) has its origin in rhythm. There is indeed a profound correspondence "which structurally connects the symphonically framed and the remaining productively historical events".[18] Musical tempo and historical time tend to converge: this is what makes possible the explicit comparison between music and philosophy, linked not by their origin, but by their shared future goal. Thanks to counterpoint, a parallel broadening of the horizon is realized in the spatial dimension: for "if we do not also advance, no note will" (iv).[19] If left by itself, sound only walks a few steps, soon stumbling onto the tonic, unless its mobility is increased by an idea that is "productive of movement" and authentically melismatic. We arrive at a conception of sound as a phenomenal movement: indeed, if we do not "advance with the note, nothing can continue singing" (v).[20] Only insofar as it is "used and radically broken down by human beings" can sound morph the dissolution of the visual relationship with the divine into "a favourable, personally intimate sense, in the more luminous sense of the concept of a spirit-realm, a concept so uncanny in itself".[21] But this result is not to be taken for granted: "only a few people, however, actually reach the stage of pure self-hearing" (vi).[22] Bloch targets the expert listener, intent on performing a formal anal-

---

15 Bloch (1985a, p. 93).
16 Bloch (1985a, p. 98).
17 Bloch (1985a, p. 99).
18 Bloch (1985a, p. 103).
19 Bloch (1985a, p. 104).
20 Bloch (1985a, p. 115).
21 Bloch (1985a, p. 118).
22 Bloch (1985a, p. 124).

ysis, and determined to be "objectively" musical. On the contrary, music must question subjectivity. A new "I" has to take shape inside every musical form, the subject of a "metaphysics of divination and utopia" to which we approach "only in our dreaming", even if "it is as near to us as it could be".[23]

Bloch's reflection, then, finds its completion in the oneiric character of music, albeit in a peculiar sense. The dream of music "leads into the heart" insofar as it is an omen of that which still has to happen: in Jean Paul's words, cited by Bloch, it is "a nostalgia not for an old country we have left behind but for a virgin one, not for a past but for a future".[24] Hence a new articulation of the relationship between music and philosophy: "what is still a fervent stammering at the moment will one day share in the eloquent language of music, in increasingly expressive certainty", showing that the "ultimate purpose of music and philosophy is purely the articulating of this basic mystery, this first and last question in all things".[25] The musical "thing in itself" does not resemble Schopenhauer's demonic will but is simply defined as "'appearing' in sacred yearning alone", and therefore authentically musical. Then the times have changed:

> Music, miraculous and transparent, will have achieved with surpassing art, beyond the grave and the point where this world ends, the first disposition of the human face divine and the quite different naming of a divine name, the name both lost and undiscovered.[26]

2 Adorno: Philosophy of Music

The work of Theodor Wiesengrund Adorno represents a watershed in the history of the philosophy of music. In his writing, the constant tension between dialectic and ethics is supported by an extraordinary musical competence, unprecedented in the history of philosophy. Thomas Mann famously depicted him as a man refusing "to choose between the professions of philosophy and music. He felt that he was actually pursuing the same thing in both divergent realms".[27] Adorno's

---

23 Bloch (1985a, p. 131). Emphasis omitted.
24 Bloch (1985a, p. 132).
25 Bloch (1985a, p. 133).
26 Bloch (1985a, p. 133).
27 Mann (1961, p. 43). In his American exile, Adorno was Mann's neighbour and advisor for the crucially important musical parts of the novel. Cf. Schmidt (2004, *passim*). On Adorno's remarkable skills as a pianist Mann reports: "Then Adorno sat down at the piano and, while I stood by and watched, played for me the entire [i.e. Beethoven's] *Sonata* Opus 111 in a highly instructive fashion". Mann (1961, p. 48). Furthermore: "his knowledge of tradition, his mastery of the whole

considerable fortune of a few decades ago is now being followed by unjustified neglect. In part, this is due to the obsolescence of some categories typical of the critical sociology of the Frankfurt School. Specifically, Adorno's popularity was affected—first positively and then negatively—by the *Philosophy of Modern Music* (1949), whose two-part structure (Schoenberg and Stravinsky as "progress" and "restoration") expresses the need to enter a dialectic dimension within "modern music" (*neue Musik*).[28] This element, added to the polemical debates within the musical avant-garde movements he engaged with upon his return in Germany from the exile in United States, has put some distance between his thought and the concerns of musicology, busy setting itself free from philosophy while and moving towards a less ideological study of musical phenomena.

Despite the importance that Adorno assigned it, an interpretation focused on his reading of *neue Musik* appears, today, rather limited. A different angle of Adorno's position emerges, in part, in light of the posthumous publication of the fragments remaining from his project of a book on Beethoven, upon which he worked for decades, without ever finishing it. The title itself shows an interesting shift in Adorno's interests. If the essays on Schoenberg and Stravinsky converged towards his *Philosophy of Modern Music*, Adorno planned to give his Beethoven book the more ambitious subtitle *The Philosophy of Music*.[29] I will therefore start with this text in order to analyse Adorno's thought, without forgetting that the book was never published for objective reasons. The promise to offer a reconciliation of man and nature, which Adorno sees in Beethoven's music, turns out to be an impossible goal, in its historical reality no less than in its dialectical formulation. In its incompleteness, Adorno's *Beethoven* exemplifies its object in a paradoxically adequate manner.[30]

Before looking at these issues, it might be useful to start from a theme that is only seemingly marginal: the concept of "national" music addressed in the *Introduction to the Sociology of Music*. Adorno does not shy away from a reflection on the German element in music, something I already mentioned when talking about Nietzsche, highlighting its problematic nature. In the early sixteenth century, during the music Renaissance in Italy, German choral music was still medieval—posits Adorno. Since then, the German element in music has "always kept an archaic, prenational touch". This is why German music was later able to tran-

---

historical body of music, is enormous. An American singer who works with him said to me: *It is incredible. He knows every note in the world*". Mann (1961, p. 48).
28 Cf. Witkin (1998, p. 141–143).
29 Adorno (2002a, p. 10). "The Beethoven study must also yield a philosophy of music"
30 Cf. Tiedemann (2002, p. xii).

scend itself and speak "the language of humanity".[31] This is how Adorno justifies the primacy of German music, from Heinrich Schütz to the mid twentieth century: the compenetration between the prenational and the national phases explains the concept of "totality", which around 1800 brought music to "converge with the speculative systems and their idea of humanity". The overturning of perspectives, compared to Nietzsche's early ideas, is palpable. The German element is not the Dionysian/irrational, but rather the pre-modern, and medieval: it does not clash with the Latin element, but rather merges with it. Hence the historical figure of Mozart, in whose music the Italian, vocal element decouples instrumental music "from the rattling mechanics of rationalism" and "turns itself into a carrier of humanity", while the "German construction principle" (coming from Bach) helps melody to reach unity in diversity. Mozart, then, inaugurates the Viennese tradition, whose traits are discernible up to Webern. However, with Mozart the detachment of music from a character of mere pleasantness is still incomplete.

The complete coincidence of speculative systems with early nineteenth-century German music is reached only with Beethoven, considered "the musical prototype of the revolutionary bourgeoisie", while at the same time championing a music that "has escaped from its social tutelage and is aesthetically fully autonomous". The musical element of the reprise, to mention only one decisive example, shows Beethoven's intention to justify what has happened as the "result of a process", analogously to what happens in "social practice" and, on the philosophical level, to the concluding section on "absolute knowledge" in Hegel's *Phenomenology of Spirit*.[32] By repeatedly comparing Beethoven and Hegel, Adorno intends to start a reflection on music and philosophy which deserves our undivided attention for the unprecedented way in which the composer is given priority over the philosopher. Beethoven's music and Hegel's philosophy have precise formal correspondences, but the first towers over the second insofar as he already expresses a critical potential that overcomes that of thought. This is due to the intrinsic superiority of music itself, in which the apotheosis of the subjective must always objectivise itself in the material, soaring above the concept, and thus implying its own critique. Beethoven's music—and particularly his later style—already contains, at least potentially, a negative dialectic.

Leaving aside Adorno's justifications for the comparison between Beethoven and Hegel, it must be noted that this exercise points to a general strategy: the mutual approach and the near identification of music and philosophy as an end-

---

31 Adorno (1976, p. 158 ff.).
32 Adorno (2002a, p. 44).

point for the evolution of music. But on what grounds does this mutual approach take place? Here a mere sociological perspective will not suffice, nor is it helpful to refer to the alleged similar effect of socio-economical conditions on the work of both the composer and the philosopher—all the more because "in Beethoven's music society is conceptlessly known, not photographed".³³ What is instead necessary—as Adorno knew very well—is an analysis of the deeper relations between music and philosophy, and of the conditions of possibility for their encounter. In order to simplify a rather dense topic we could say that the two poles around which the essence of the relationship between music and philosophy rotates are those of *truth* and *humanity*. In the panorama of philosophical disciplines, these primarily refer to logic and anthropology.

As for the first aspect, Adorno takes a decisive step forward as opposed to the stances willing to acknowledge a "play" of sensations or representations in music—such as Kant or nineteenth-century psychology. There is surely something like this in music, but it is

> a play with logical forms as such: those of statement, identity, similarity, contradiction, the whole and the part; and the concreteness of music is essentially the force with which these forms imprint themselves on the material, the musical sounds.³⁴

However, in music, the combination of these elements does not take the typical forms of discursive logic (predication, subordination, etc.): musical synthesis is "constituted solely by the constellation of its elements". Hence Adorno defines music as a "*logic of the judgement-less synthesis*". Elsewhere, he suggests an even stronger affinity between music and language. In tonal music there is something akin to concepts (chords, as symbolism of "primitive concepts") and even to judgments: the thetic value, the self-affirmation of music *qua* music expresses a sort of "this is so" (*das ist so*), wholly equivalent to an existential judgment. The difference is that music gives up any semantic role, thus becoming "demythologized prayer".³⁵

Far from being explained as *adaequatio* or "correspondence", the "truth" of music has its roots in its capacity to suspend empirical reality. Its very beginning, the tautological fact of its "being music", immediately creates a second, autonomous reality. The *a priori* moment, the self-determination that is implicit in

---

33 Adorno (2002a, p. 43). On the critical equivocation of Adorno as sociologist of music see Jay (1984, p. 142f.).
34 Adorno (2002a, p. 11).
35 Adorno (2002b, p. 114); Adorno (1978, p. 251–256). See also the editorial note in Adorno (1978, p. 680).

any existence, lies entirely in the beginning. Clearly taking up the dialectical movement of being and nothingness of Hegel's *Logic*, Adorno interprets all of Beethoven's music is an attempt to reclaim the emptiness of its beginning. Considered as a "totality", after its echo has stopped reverberating, music is eminently subject to appearance, but as long as it persists in its "immanent movement" it is the most free of all artforms:

> Its remoteness from reality does, it is true, cast on the latter a reflected, conciliatory glow, but keeps music itself purer of subservience to reality [...]. Once it has consented to be music at all, it can, to an extent (that is, as far as it is not aimed at consumption), do as it thinks fit.[36]

Music's suspension of reality does not encourage an escape towards the realms of fairy tales or metaphysics. On the contrary, it is a condition of possibility for music's emancipation from the duty of mirroring social relations. Music is not passively dragged along by the flow of time: it wholly dominates it, even if only between its beginning and its end.

The oneiric character of musical representation comes into play here, allowing Adorno to offer a personal reading of the opposition between formalism and the aesthetic of expression. Even though the logic of music seems to lead towards a refined kind of formalism—wherein "play" pertains to abstract logical forms—Adorno unexpectedly recuperates an aspect of the opposite doctrine. Sounds can indeed represent something determinate, but only within the limits typically imposed by dreams. In the flow of sound, images do appear, but "only in scattered, eccentric flashes, vanishing at once" since they acquire a meaning only "in their transience". This is evident in romantic music. In the first movement of Schubert's *Symphony in C major* we have, for a few instants, the feeling of being "at a rustic wedding", but "once imbued with that image", music proceeds in a completely different manner:

> We are at the rustic wedding, then are carried away in the musical flood, heaven knows where (it may be similar with death—perhaps the affinity between music and death has its locus here).[37]

As can be clearly seen, the comparison between music and logic does not entail any form of intellectualism. Rather, it is necessary to interrogate the musical page, searching for its truth content—an analysis that gives up any consideration

---

36 Adorno (2002a, p. 7).
37 Adorno (2002a, p. 8).

related to beauty, not to mention "pleasantness". The truth of music goes beyond the contingencies occurring before and after the musical fact, like the composer's psychology and the public's reception. Yet, at a sociological level, Adorno pays careful attention to these phenomena. The study of the fetishization of the musical object in "regressive" listening supports his reflections on pop music, jazz, radio, and movie soundtracks. And even if what he says about these phenomena in *Introduction to the Sociology of Music*[38] is not always flattering, Adorno still has the merit of interrupting the traditional silence of philosophy on these topics. The mastery over nature and the growing logicization of highbrow music bring us back to the fact that "truth" in music bypasses any reference to nature. Adorno does believe that music has an originally comforting function, but limited to a pre-aesthetic level.[39] Naturalism is no longer possible: neither in a mathematical sense, nor in an harmonicist perspective. The tonal system is not nature, but *second* nature, that is, an "illusion rooted in history". Musical material, however it may be intended, has an essentially historical character.[40]

Once outside of the material of music, though, the concept of nature is destined to return in a dialectical form, expressed in the concept of humanity. This leads to the abandonment of the level of logic in favour of that of anthropology, a term to be interpreted in regards to the specific meaning given to it by Hegel's philosophy of subjective spirit.[41] The vocabulary employed by Adorno, who speaks of a "soul" which "opens its eyes" to the world, awakening from the slumber of its alienated dimension, leaves no doubt. But Adorno's anthropology, compared to Hegel's, is turned upside-down: it is not the latent spirituality of nature unveiled in the soul, but rather the neutrality of spirit. It is nature, not spirit, that "opens its eyes" and finds itself in the "soul", which is not a substance but a historical gesture, ever repeated in music:

> Nature, having become the ego, opens its eyes as ego (not in the ego, as its regressive part) and becomes aware of itself qua ego as nature. This moment—that is, not the breakthrough

---

38 Cf. the thoroughgoing critical analysis by Witkin (1998, p. 161–180).
39 Adorno (2002a, p. 7). On nature, history, and myth see Paddison (1993, p. 29 ff.).
40 Adorno (2007, p. 11). Cf. also Adorno (2002c, p. 90): "With the elimination of the principle of representation in painting and sculpture, and of the exploitation of fragments in music, it became almost unavoidable that the elements set free—colors, sounds, absolute configurations of words—came to appear as if they already inherently expressed something. This is, however, illusory, for the elements become eloquent only through the context in which they occur".
41 See above, chap. 3, par 3.

of nature but its awareness of difference—is closest to reconciliation as also to lamentation.[42]

The reference to a soul in an anthropological sense explains how music is linked, as it already was for Hegel, to the characteristic act of giving life. The greater naturalness and immediacy of voice makes it, paradoxically, less suited than an instrument to the dialectical process of recognition of the self in the other. What needs to be accomplished in incipient music is work, an overcoming, a "technique" necessary to the musical substance itself. The original phenomenon of any musical dialectic is that "the instrument *is* animation".

Adorno once again re-elaborates a classic problem—absolute music—in an unusual way. While the music we imagine in the silent workings of our mind is always vocal, in its concrete development it needs to repeat the original "gesture" with which nature, made "I", awakens in its beginning:

> In musical terms, humanity means: the permeation of the instrumental with spirit, reconciliation of the alienated means with the end, the subject, within the process, instead of mere humane immediacy.[43]

All of this, Adorno observes, is characteristic of Beethoven. On the other hand, the contemporary "cult of the vocal against the instrumental" indicates "the *end* of humanity in music". The descriptive subtitle *The Philosophy of Music* begins to feel justified: it is precisely from Beethoven's onwards that many of the philosophical traits of music are revealed.

These precepts, clearly, should not be interpreted in a regressive sense, not merely because the value of modern music is not lessened by this level of argumentation, but mostly because of the unavoidable ambivalence of humanity. The promise of a free subjectivity appears strictly bound to the mastery over nature realized in the musical phenomenon, something particularly evident in the *tour de force* of Beethoven's instrumental technique. But this "mastery" can all too easily reveal the unsettling aspect of authoritarianism, many traces of which are displayed by music. 'To master' is a verb often used to describe the specific talent of the composer, and indeed Luther praised Josquin des Prez for having bent the notes to his own will.[44] With the mastery of the means of musical composition, enslaving musical matter, the truth of music runs the risk of becoming its un-truth. Totality imposes its unlimited right upon the parts, emptying of pur-

---

42 Adorno (2002a, p. 173).
43 Adorno (2002a, p. 173).
44 Adorno (2007, p. 65). See also Bloch (2000, p. 36).

pose the animating gesture in which music consists. Even more radically, in the *Dialectic of Enlightenment*, Adorno and Horkheimer interpreted the Homeric episode of the Sirens as the *locus* of the original schism: on the one hand the "landowner" Odysseus, who is tied on his ship as he "listens to a concert, as immobilized as audiences later"; on the other his subordinate companions, to whom he prescribes the only other possible way: do not listen to "the temptation of the irrecoverable", something possible only if one is not "unable to hear".[45]

Is there then another chance of rehabilitation, another way between the wax in the rowers' ears and the preclusion of pleasure self-imposed by Odysseus? And, most importantly, does this third possibility lie in music—or at least in *neue Musik?* In light of Adorno's work, it is not possible to give a decisively affirmative answer to this question. But it would be ungenerous not to recognize, in the entirety of Adorno's philosophy of music, an effort to clear a path.

Where Adorno appears to be the closest to a positive proposal is, once again, in the analysis of a typically anthropological phenomenon: crying. This is not to say that Adorno falls into sentimentalism: crying breaks the interior shell of subjectivity, perforating its dense core from the inside. If, for Hegel, it announced the creation of the social "world" by the objective spirit—in an embryonic form later destined to find its perfection in the voice—for Adorno, on the contrary, this path leads the soul to dissolve itself, in a backward journey towards nature.

> The beginning of music, in the same manner as its end, extends beyond the realm of intentions—the realm of meaning and subjectivity. The origin is gesticulative in nature and closely related to the origin of tears. It is the gesture of release. The tension of the face muscles relaxes; the tension which closed the face off from the surrounding world by directing the face actively at this world disappears. Music and tears open the lips and set the arrested human being free. The sentimentality of inferior music indicates in its distorted figure that which higher music, at the very border of insanity, is yet able to design in the validity of its form: reconciliation. The human being who surrenders himself to tears and to a music which no longer resembles him in any way permits that current of which he is not part and which lies behind the dam restraining the world of phenomena to flow back into itself. In weeping and in singing he enters into alienated reality. "Tears dim my eyes: earth's child I am again"—this line from Goethe's *Faust* defines the position of music. Thus earth claims Eurydice again. The gesture of return—not the sensation of expectancy—characterises the expression of all music, even if it finds itself in a world worthy of death.[46]

---

45 Horkheimer/Adorno (2002, p. 26 f.).
46 Adorno (2007, p. 128–129). The citation *"Die Träne quillt, die Erde hat mich wieder!"* is from Goethe (2014, p. 22 [v. 780]). See also Adorno (2002a p. 6).

The last few comments that can be added, as a *coda*, cannot but focus on the relationship between music and philosophy in Adorno's oeuvre. His philosophy of music is a dialectic whose "negative" value can be highlighted not only with respect to Hegel, but also—and far more meaningfully for what pertains to the musical sphere—to Plato. Philosophy is no longer the supreme music: on the contrary, music has become supreme philosophy. Music is not lacking as opposed to philosophical discourse; it is better than the latter when it expresses, and thus accomplishes, the promise of a non-alienated humanity, reconciled with nature not through the labour of the concept, but rather through musical work. But this is possible only when—from Beethoven to Schoenberg—music carries the self-impressed seal of truth.

3 Phenomenologies of Listening

The task of presenting the main philosophical trends of the latter part of the twentieth century can be accomplished by moving backward, starting from certain contemporary results, in order to identify their origins. A first signpost is the long established dichotomy between analytic and continental philosophers, to which one can trace many of the contemporary differences in method and language. When applying this general interpretive schema to this specific case, however, some clarifications are needed. First of all, it is necessary to broaden the geographical and linguistic focus of analysis to France and to English-speaking countries. Partly due to the tragic pressure of historical events, the close link between German music and German philosophy—whose fates had long been intertwined—was broken. Hence the interplay of different styles and traditions, not just philosophical but also musical. This also contributed to a deflation of the analogies between music and history, more or less explicitly based on the myth of the overall linear development of music, at least in its more preeminent representatives. One should also consider the development of new musicological approaches, based on cultural anthropology, psychology, and neuroscience, for example. Despite certain detectable links, these studies were not conceived as functional or allied to the philosophical discourse (on the contrary, they sometimes tended to antagonize it), and thus they indirectly contributed to circumscribing the object of philosophical reflection on music to a relatively narrower, but no less fertile field, within which one can distinguish the two great analytic and continental families mentioned above.

Analytic philosophy will be discussed later. I will first consider the continental tradition, which for our purposes can be mainly characterized by the pre-eminence of the theme of *listening*. To listen does not simply mean to hear, but rather to adopt an intentional attitude. The modalities of this attitude have been defined mostly within the phenomenological movement, but its more remote origins should be sought in the Jewish tradition, and the privilege it assigned to the auditory dimension over that of the visual. The philosophical theme of listening does not only or mainly refer to music, but rather to the Word (human and divine, and especially the poetic word), implying the dimension of silence as a precondition for the appearance of the transcendence of the Other. Given the breadth of the theme (which, in part, exceeds my present concerns) I will limit myself to discussing a few phenomenological ideas revolving around the theme of listening, without attempting to make a comprehensive assessment. In particular, I will analyse some themes developed within phenomenological circles and Brentano's school, to then focus on Vladimir Jankélévitch, a thinker not fully reducible to the phenomenological school but open to various influences, most evidently that of Henri Bergson.

When considering these themes one cannot avoid a few observations about Carl Stumpf, who was a student of Brentano and Lotze, and Husserl's teacher in Halle. Both a philosopher and a gifted musician, Stumpf elaborates the doctrine of "tonal fusion" (*Tonverschmelzung*), which is essentially the tendency of two simultaneous tones to appear as one single sensation.[47] From a philosophical point of view, Stumpf develops a synthetic model of the constitution of objectivity which influenced Husserl and Meinong.[48] From a musical standpoint, Stumpf's doctrine supports an alternative conception to Helmholtz's naturalistic stance,[49] taking up argumentative models that were common in ancient philosophy, in particular in Aristotle. In his *Tonpsychologie* (1883 and 1890) Stumpf does not quite elaborate a new psychology of music. Rather, he contributes to a conscious integration of the doctrine of "tonal fusion" with work in the field of ethnomusicology done by Stumpf himself, by his student Erich Hornbostel, and others like Curt Sachs—as well as, occasionally, Max Wertheimer.[50] It is no coincidence that in Berlin, in 1900, Stumpf founded the Phonographic Archive: a collection of recordings (phonograph cylinders and gramophone records) of songs and music of various provenance.[51] The decisive psychological factor, according to Stumpf, is not any mathematical affinity perceived by the

---

47 Stumpf (1890, p. 128). In the first chapter I have shown that Archytas already claimed that only "one sound is perceived in consonance". The main antecedent of Stumpf's tonal fusion, however, is Aristotle's *mixis*. For both constructs see above, chap. 1, par. 1 and par. 3.
48 Cf. the essays in Fisette/Martinelli (2015).
49 Cf. Kursell (2008, *passim*).
50 Stumpf (2012).
51 Cf. Simon (2000, *passim*).

ear, but rather the tendency to fuse sounds together: that inertial moment, so to speak, which makes us mistake a melody to the octave for a single voice. The basic mechanism of musical meaning, then, is formed in a sphere that is independent from that of arithmetical relationships, upper partials, etc. As an anthropological constant, detectable in some of the most diverse musical systems, the *Tonverschmelzung* can offer an explicatory principle capable of transgressing the limits of European tonal music. This explains the growth of the Berlin school of "comparative musicology" whose human, scientific, and material patrimony was then scattered, for obvious reasons, by German National Socialism.[52]

In both Munich and Göttingen, Edmund Husserl's influence gave rise to philosophical circles where certain applications of phenomenology to musical themes were explored. The phenomenological method prescribes the "bracketing" of the physical or phenomenological datum relative to sound, in order to focus on the essence of the musical phenomenon itself, in pure intuition. In Moritz Geiger this path goes through the rejection of any Wagnerian ecstasy, of any sensuous addiction to music made by dreamy people who scorn form and construction and pursue music as a source of reverie.[53] This anti-subjectivist attention to the aesthetic object is a common trait in the phenomenology of music. Waldemar Conrad underlines the ideal nature of the musical object, which awakens, in the listener, an intuitively adequate apprehension through a progressive "fulfilment" (*Erfüllung*) of the initial impression.[54] A whistled melody will be first played on a piano, then rehearsed by an orchestra of amateurs (whose imperfect execution does not alter the object, but represents it in an incomplete way), finally finding its final form in an ideal, perfectly adequate, symphonic execution.

The ideality of the aesthetic object is a common postulate in Brentano's school: it can be found in the musical aesthetics flourishing in Alexius Meinong's school, in Graz. For example, against the idea of musical creation as a mere "composition", in the sense of "putting notes together", Alois Höfler claims that valuable melodies are "discovered", rather than created, by the musician.[55] Melodies with a particular aesthetic value enjoy a kind of super-temporality, making them Platonically pre-existent to their formulation, and ontologically analogous to the "states of affairs" (*Sachverhalte*). In this sense, their ontological status surpasses that of ordinary melodies, just like an existential judgment, e.g. "A *exists*", belongs to a higher logical order than the simple affirmation "that-

---

[52] Cf. Martinelli (2014, p. 398).
[53] Geiger (1928, p. 8f.).
[54] Conrad (1908, p. 74).
[55] Höfler (1912, p. 225). Cf. Martinelli (2010, p. 174).

A".⁵⁶ For Stephan Witasek, on the other hand, attention is turned to the modalities of listening, which allow one to differentiate the intellectual from the emotional aspects. Witasek acknowledges two kinds of feelings: the pleasure caused by music and the emotional character (*Stimmung*) of the piece. The listener of a sad piece has *real* aesthetic enjoyment, but is not *really* sad. The problem is to explain how the piece expresses sadness: this happens because the intentional object (the piece as heard) is itself emotionally neutral. I project my elementary feeling—which is a *"phantasy"* feeling (technically speaking, they refer to a hypothetical assumption rather that to a judgement)—into the melody, thus giving shape to a truly "expressive" melody. The latter in turn generates a feedback that finally enables me to feel a *"real"* feeling, whose intentional object is the melody *plus* my original assumption-related feeling.⁵⁷ So Witasek defends a modification of the *Einfühlung* theory,⁵⁸ very different from that made famous by Theodor Lipps—who, incidentally, does not at all refer to "empathy" in music, and rather takes up the old theory of *ictus*, in a new psychological version.⁵⁹

It is no coincidence that these discussions remind one, in many respects, of those about aesthetics in the analytic tradition (see below, par. 5). Brentano's intentionality-thesis, variously modified in different ways by the schools that were inspired by it, entails focusing on the musical thing itself, reflecting on the problem of its ontological status. And the ontology of the musical work of art is precisely the problem systematically analysed by Roman Ingarden, in his *The Work of Music and the Problem of Its Identity* (1966). Whilst admitting that the musical work of art does not coincide with its executions, Ingarden also rejects its construal as an ideal object.⁶⁰ Just as with a literary text, what is privileged is the relationship between the work and the music sheet, suggesting a kind of evolution in the work throughout its various executions. Ingarden thus anticipates the aesthetic of reception of the Konstanz school, which had important musicological applications in relation to the idea of a musical hermeneutics. This link allows us to stop and reflect on the substantial absence of music in the work of Martin Heidegger (as was the case in Husserl, after all). This is no mere omission: listening, in Heidegger, is essentially a "poetic-thinking" of Being in language. In the lectures published in *The Principle of Reason,* Heidegger only refers to Beethoven's deafness in order to demonstrate how listening does not need the empir-

---

56 Höfler (1921, p. 59). The example is the third movement of Beethoven's *Ninth symphony*, but Höfler refers also to Wagner, of whom he is a great admirer.
57 Witasek (1906, p. 126).
58 Witasek (1904, p. 133).
59 Cf. Martinelli (1999, p. 187 ff.).
60 Ingarden (1986).

ical dimension ("*we* hear, not the ear") and to cite, on the two-hundredth anniversary of his birth, a famous but unfortunately apocryphal letter by Mozart on creativity.[61]

Vladimir Jankélévitch's ideas in his *Music and the Ineffable* (1961) have great relevance. Jankélévitch moves away from the traditional question of the relationship between music and philosophy, noting that the sensual power of music represents a threat to which philosophy reacts in three ways: trying to discipline its use (Plato), expressing its resentment (Nietzsche), or moving away from ethics towards metaphysics (Schopenhauer).[62] Jankélévitch proceeds to unceremoniously destroying all of these positions and especially the third, focusing on the idea that underpins it: namely that music would be a language that "says what logos says (whether the words are occult or transparent) [...] in the form of sound hieroglyphs". The rhetorical moves used to support this idea are, Jankélévitch claims, nothing but unjustifiable analogies. Music possesses at least three characters that make it irreducible to language: the "absence of any systematic unity", the "insensitivity to repetition" and, mostly, the inability to express something. But how does Jankélévitch substantiate these positions, which are not immediately obvious?

First of all, music is logically incoherent, insofar as it does not aim to recompose contrasting elements into a unity. Therefore, any effort towards a structured listening, typical of "silly people whose brows are furrowed with meditation as they pretend to be 'following' theme A and theme B" is futile. In order to better explain how *not* to listen to music, Jankélévitch jokes about a common situation:

> Everyone knows the type, the cool cerebral people who affect interest in the way the piece is "put together" after the concert. Technical analysis is a means of refusing to abandon oneself spontaneously to grace, which is the request the musical Charm is making. The phobia about consent, the fear of appearing bewitched, the coquetry of refusal, the resolve not to "submit", are the social and sociological forms assumed by alienation, just as the spirit of contradiction is a form of mimicry.[63]

Moreover, music differentiates itself from language through the role played by repetition. Language always proceeds to walk straight, without ever turning back (the move that condemns Eurydice) or coming back—but this is not the case for music. Since music does not "say" anything, music cannot "repeat" anything either: every repetition counts as a novelty. The possibility of iteration dem-

---

61 Heidegger (1991, p. 47 and 67 ff.).
62 Jankélévitch (2003, p. 18, 100 and 102).
63 Jankélévitch (2003, p. 88).

onstrates the distance between music and logic; the former should rather be compared to the sacred, evoked in the repetition of the psalmody. This aspect of Jankélévitch's reflection on time is of particular interest. Time's impregnability to repetition anticipates, in certain ways, Deleuze and Guattari's conclusions about the refrain, meant as a rhythmic repetition of an act. This, they argue, is detectable at the biological, behavioural, and even physiochemical level. The refrain as a "prism" or "block of space-time" is capable of generating "territory" and to lead "from forces of chaos to forces of the earth".[64] Propelled by a blind, animal and mechanical obstinacy, the refrain "fabricates" time, according to procedures that are substantially independent from the phenomenology of consciousness of interior time.

But let us return to Jankélévitch and to his most provocative thesis: music is "incapable of expressing" meanings, ideas, and feelings, or to describe (i.e., represent) landscapes and events. Jankélévitch offers different explanations to support this conception. The central point is doubtlessly his adoption of a Bergsonian perspective. The "duration" of music *in fieri* is a totally different thing compared to the production of meanings attributed to it after listening. Therefore, properly speaking "musical meaning lends itself to the retrospective: music can only signify something in the future perfect tense".[65]

We thus begin to discern the foundation of the ineffable character of music, to which Jankélévitch refers through oxymoronic or allusive expressions like "'inexpressive' espressivo", "almost-nothing" or *je-ne-sais-quoi* as well as the somewhat untranslatable word *charme*, a term echoing the Latin *carmen*, meaning both "chant" and "spell".[66] Jankélévitch's vocabulary is the coherent result of his attempt to avoid assigning retrospective meanings to music. Somehow transcending itself, rather, thought should be able to proceed quietly, in order to prepare the silence that welcomes the musical event.[67] Once explanation and description are abandoned, philosophy transforms itself into music. Music cannot be thought and cannot be talked about. One can only think musically, since music is "an adverb that refers to a way of thinking".[68]

Arguing against the alleged expressive power of music, Jankélévitch finds support in Debussy's impressionism and in those musical experiences that intentionally pursue inexpressiveness. Here lies the theoretical root of Jankélévitch's preference for a musical canon mostly consisting of composers of the

---

64 Deleuze/Guattari (1987, p. 313 and 322).
65 Jankélévitch (2003, p. 61).
66 Cf. Looney (2015, p. 3).
67 Jankélévitch (2003, p. 140).
68 Jankélévitch (2003, p. 101).

French and Russian schools. Musicians like Stravinsky, Ravel, Fauré, Satie, and others all developed rhetorical tools (violence, allusion, humour, litotes, etc.) suited for the destruction of expression in music—a process that culminates in the philhellenism of a certain Fauré, of Satie, or of the late Stravinsky's *Apollon Musagète*. At first sight, this argument might appear counterproductive: if some composers have strived to eliminate expression from music, this demonstrates that expression exists. However, Jankélévitch does not actually dispute this assumption. Music can indeed be expressive, although in that case it fools itself, no less than the listener, who consumes him or herself in the pursuit of some hidden meaning. Music is not "purely and simply inexpressive, since despite all this, the Espressivo is no sin".[69] The inexpressible, the ineffable, therefore allows for a kind of signification to the second power: by refusing expression, music does not express a meaning, but reveals the "meaning of meaning", in an infinite regress.

This ultimately leads us back to the ontological question that Jankélévitch poses in the very first page of his book: what is music, precisely? As ineffable as that which is announced through it, music is revealed to be an almost-nothing:

> Music is a Charm, made of nothing, insisting upon nothing, and perhaps it is nothing—at least for those who expect to discover something, something palpable and unequivocal. Like an iridescent soap bubble that quivers and glows for a few seconds in the sunlight, music collapses the moment you touch it and does not exist, except as a highly dubious, fugitive exaltation in an opportune moment. Music is inconsistent, almost nonexistent [...].[70]

Music, then, "does not exist in itself" but only for that dangerous half hour (and the musician knows this all too well) in which "we bring it into being by playing it". This ontological frailty, however, makes music akin to the most elevated things; like love, poetry, and moral duty music "is not made to be spoken, but for one to do". Jankélévitch reminds us of how rare and precious music, in its authentic meaning, can be—an important reminder indeed. It is not a breach but a tiny fissure: impalpable, music promotes an "escape from immanence".[71]

The unbridgeable gap between logical language and music and the ontological levity of music both focus our attention on the elementary levels of listening: silence and sound. In the numerous *pianissimo* and *perdendosi* that mark the

---

69 Jankélévitch (2003, p. 62).
70 Jankélévitch (2003, p. 120).
71 Jankélévitch (2003, p. 78 and 127).

final moments of several of Jankélévitch's favourite compositions—allergic to perfect and grandiose cadences—it is music itself that summons silence out of its own innermost self. For music silence is like oxygen: it creeps into the music sheet itself—in the form of pauses—in order to give some breathing space. Jankélévitch therefore offers conceptual instruments that are destined for further development. If, for Jean-Luc Nancy, silence is not yet the privation of sound but rather an "arrangement of resonance",[72] the positions we have just explored can be applied, from another perspective, to a wholly different concept, like that of noise. Like silence, noise is an *alter ego* of sound, opposed to it, but also an essential part of it, so that it appears indistinguishable from it both theoretically (as Rousseau already knew) and practically—think of the practice of using noise within music, typical of many contemporary composers from futurism to the present day.

Jankélévitch's abandonment of the idea of expression does not entail naturalist consequences. Sounds and silences are the protagonists of a new kind of (broadly construed) phenomenology of listening, not as material, or physical realities but rather as bearers of a singularity that remains irreducible to the worldly order. Being based on nothingness, music therefore takes the form of a negative theology and of a secular mysticism.

4 Logic and the Symbol: Wittgenstein and Susanne Langer

It is well known that Ludwig Wittgenstein spent his childhood in Vienna surrounded by music: his mother, who was an excellent pianist, was acquainted with famous composers such as Brahms and Mahler. However, perhaps critics haven't yet fully acknowledged the importance of Wittgenstein's observations on music. In his writings after the *Tractatus Logico-philosophicus*—a work which I will come back to when talking about Susanne Langer—Wittgenstein focused on the issue of how to *understand* a piece of music.[73] This question is very illustrative of some typical characters of philosophy of language.

> What we call "understanding a sentence" has, in many cases, a much greater similarity to understanding a musical theme than we might be inclined to think. But I don't mean that understanding a musical theme is more like the picture which one tends to make oneself of understanding a sentence; but rather that this picture is wrong [...]. For understanding a sentence, we say, points to a reality outside the sentence. Whereas one might say, "Under-

---

72 Nancy (2007, p. 21).
73 Cf. Scruton (2009a, p. 33); Voigt (2007, p. 119f.).

standing a sentence means getting hold of its content; and the content of the sentence is *in* the sentence".[74]

The ancient comparison between music and language thus acquires a whole new aspect. Far from applying philosophical notions taken from the analysis of language to the comparatively lesser known field of music, Wittgenstein shows that we need to look at music to understand how language works. In both domains, in any case, posing the problem correctly is more important than any apodictic certainty.

> Understanding a sentence is more akin to understanding a piece of music that one might think. Why must these bars be played just so? [...] Why do I want to produce just this pattern of variation in loudness and tempo? I would like to say "Because I know what it's all about" But what is it all about? I should not be able to say.[75]

The fact that one fails to verbally explain "what it's all about" doesn't mean that Wittgenstein considers ineffability as the (positive) mark of music. On the one hand, music conveys neither meanings nor feelings ("music conveys to us *itself*").[76] On the other hand, as we shall see, it typically brings attention to the *how* of communication rather than the *what*. In music, understanding typically requires a specific approach: one must grasp the given piece according to an appropriate Gestalt order (1) and consequently respond adequately to it (2). The first aspect is related to the *hearing-as*, that is, to perceiving "something new" in music.[77] This process is akin to what happens when, say, a collection of lines on paper is suddenly seen as a cube.[78] Therefore, Wittgenstein doesn't necessarily argue for a "structural" listening informed by historical knowledge or by the analysis of music sheets, even though it is not excluded that knowledge might possibly produce changes in perception.

In any case, "aspect blindness" is similar to the "lack of a musical ear": in both situations it hinders understanding of the meaning emerging from the language game in question.[79] Often this language game has expressive characters akin to those used in music: tone, stress, expression (in the intransitive meaning

---

[74] Wittgenstein (1965, p. 167).
[75] Wittgenstein (1974, p. 41).
[76] Wittgenstein (1965, p. 178); cf. Niro (2008, p. 68).
[77] Cf. Arbo (2009, p. 97 f.).
[78] Wittgenstein (2012, p. 642).
[79] Wittgenstein (1953, p. 214e): in this edition, the added "e" marks to every right page, reporting the English text (with the corresponding German on the left page). Odd and even pages bear the same number.

of expressiveness, not as the expression-of-something) play an important role in verbal understanding—for instance, they define the sense of reading something "with feeling". Also, as mentioned, both in music and language, understanding doesn't amount to "owning" a given content—or emotional character, for that matter—but rather to giving an adequate response. For Wittgenstein it is crucial to abandon introspection:

> Once again: what does it consist in, following a musical phrase with understanding, or, playing it with understanding? Don't look inside yourself. Ask yourself rather, what makes you say that's what *someone* else is doing. And *what* prompts you to say *he* has a particular experience? [...][80]

Provided that the grammar of understanding is related "to that of 'can', 'is able to'", being able to reproduce the piece is certainly a good sign.[81] This holds both for an execution in which—say—one finally finds "the right tempo", and for the simple ability to whistle a tune "correctly". But "innerly experiencing" a piece of music also means connecting the feeling it produces to everything else around it, "e.g. with the existence of the German language & of its intonation, but that means with the whole field of our language games".[82]

Thus far I have only looked at the many implications of the statement "understanding a sentence is more akin to understanding a piece of music that one might think" (see above). Now it might be interesting to address the view Wittgenstein expresses in *Tractatus Logico-philosophicus* (1922). Music notation is a "picture" of music just as "the proposition is a picture of reality". The gramophone record, the musical thought, the score and sound waves share the same "logical structure"; and there is a rule or "projection law" which allows one to easily switch between them.[83] Simplifying, one could say that the early Wittgenstein attempted to explain music through language, whereas after the 1930s he did the opposite and explained language through music. This perfectly symmetrical approach, though, testifies to the continuing importance of the issue of music, which Wittgenstein addressed in different times and different ways.

In the early 1940s, Susanne Langer expressed criticism towards views like that expressed in the *Tractatus*, rejecting the idea that all outside of logical language should be classified as ineffable. In so doing, though, the author embraced a position that is not too far from that of the late Wittgenstein himself

---

80 Wittgenstein (1989, p. 58).
81 Wittgenstein (1953, p. 59e and 206e).
82 Wittgenstein (1989, p. 59).
83 Wittgenstein (1961, par. 4.01–4.0141).

—not surprisingly, critics have noted similarities between the two.[84] Susanne Langer aims for a philosophy that, without giving up a rigorous approach, is able to give an account of the symbols that appear in myth, music and art in general. Looking at her intellectual biography, it is not difficult to identify the sources of this project. Langer was the author of the first textbook of symbolic logic that ever appeared in the United States, and co-founded the society of symbolic logic with Willard van Orman Quine and Alonzo Church. The daughter of Germans emigrated to New York, she knew very well the work of Kant and Cassirer's *Philosophy of Symbolic Forms*, which she read long before the English translation came out. Also, she spent her childhood surrounded by music and played the cello all her life. These are the roots of her very popular book *Philosophy in a New Key*, first published in 1941.

Just as in a piece of music, tuning philosophy "in a new key" changes the meaning of all that has come before. Its "tonic chord", she says, now probably sounds right "a mind essentially preoccupied with logic, scientific language, and empirical fact, although that chord was actually first sounded by thinkers of a very different school".[85] In addition to Wittgenstein and his *Tractatus*, Langer mentions Rudolf Carnap who, in a 1932 essay, had criticised metaphysicians comparing them to "musicians without musical ability".[86] This famous thesis reveals a peculiar aspect in this context, as it contains the essence of a philosophy of music. Carnap, who apparently was a passable cellist in his younger years, believed that music, unlike metaphysics, could express the "feeling of life". In his words:

> Perhaps music is the purest means of expression of the basic attitude because it is entirely free from any reference to objects. The harmonious feeling or attitude, which the metaphysician tries to express in a monistic system, is more clearly expressed in the music of Mozart. And when a metaphysician gives verbal expression to his dualistic-heroic attitude towards life in a dualistic system, is it not perhaps because he lacks the ability of a Beethoven to express this attitude in an adequate medium?[87]

The monism and dualism of metaphysicians are poor versions of a content that Mozart and Beethoven have instead been able to express sublimely. However, if we leave behind those metaphysical systems, Langer wonders, shouldn't we explain how the expressive function works (successfully so, in music)? Despite

---

[84] Cf. for instance Niro (2008, p. 51 f.).
[85] Langer (1954, p. i).
[86] Carnap (1932, p. 29).
[87] Carnap (1932, p. 29).

4 Logic and the Symbol: Wittgenstein and Susanne Langer — 129

drawing on Wittgenstein's *Tractatus*, Russell and Carnap for her conception of logic, Langer feels the need to widen the scope of her investigation. Even things outside of language in the technical sense of logic can have "the character of symbolic expressiveness".[88] The chapter Langer dedicates to music in her book, thus, paves the way to an analytic philosophy of music.

First of all, Langer rejects theories that speak of "self-expression" as the characteristic of music. This widespread trend finds a notable example in Carnap who, for Langer, is able to explain the undeniable relation between music and feelings, enabling an understanding of music in the light of behavioural psychology. However, the thesis of self-expression inevitably entails some philosophical paradoxes.[89] First of all, Langer notes, "sheer self-expression requires no artistic form". Someone in emotional turmoil does not express themselves in music: "the laws of emotional catharsis are natural laws, not artistic". So, music is no "cause or therapy of feelings" but rather their "logical expression". In other words, if music has an emotional content, "it 'has' it in the same sense that language 'has' its conceptual content—*symbolically*". This is a crucial problem: "for to be able to define 'musical meaning' adequately, precisely, but *for an artistic, not a positivistic context and purpose*, is the touchstone of a really powerful philosophy of symbolism". Langer takes cue from a distinction between discursive symbol (language) and representative symbol (myth, etc.). In the case of music, the latter is an "unconsummated" symbol—I shall come back to this expression later.[90]

Analyzing and criticizing the different proposals available, partly drawing on Wolfgang Köhler's Gestalt psychology, Langer sets up a first argument by observing "a certain similarity of logical form" between music and feelings. Music can indeed only reflect the "morphology" of a feeling.[91] Langer's philosophy of music is often identified with this statement,[92] but mistakenly so. In fact, formal homology is for Langer just one feature of meaning in music. The second trait is much more important: music can "articulate feelings without becoming wedded to them". In music "no assignment of meaning is conventional", therefore the association with feeling is only consummated in the musical act itself: contrary to what ancient thinkers believed, it has no permanent effects. Nevertheless, "the brief association was a flash of understanding".[93] In this sense, there is

---

88 Langer (1954, p. 69).
89 Langer (1954, p. 175).
90 Langer (1954, p. 176 f.). On further developments, see Budd (1994, p. 184).
91 Langer (1954, p. 189 and 193).
92 For instance by Levinson (1990, p. 282).
93 Langer (1954, p. 198).

an indirectly lasting effect, akin to what happens in the mind with the first emergence of language. So, music is not communication but insight—non-discursive immediate intuition or intellection—that is, knowledge of "how feelings go". This way, Langer believes, the rather implausible theory proposed, among others, by Carroll C. Pratt acquires a philosophical basis: music produces effects that we "mistake" for feelings.[94]

Musical feeling is the outcome of a sort of self-deceit, which can only sound strange if one doesn't understand music as "implicit symbolism".[95] In fact, "symbolic forms" are mistaken for the things they stand for, before logical abstraction intervenes, and this is not the exception but the rule. This is the "same principle that causes myths to be believed"—a statement that is perhaps the most notable point made by Langer, and yet is often neglected. Herein lies the key of the above-mentioned notion of "unconsummated symbol". Drawing on Cassirer, Langer explains how in myth (and music), the symbol and the object tend to blend in the same undifferentiated thing: it so happens that "names denoting powers to be endowed with power, and sacraments to be taken for efficacious acts". In a way, this is a semi-aware attribution of meaning. Unlike American fundamentalists that actually believe in Jonah and the whale, the Greeks did not take their myths literally. However, Apollo was not for them a merely decorative fiction, but something that worked as a source of inspiration. Today, myth and epos have been overshadowed by art and mostly music, which coincides in the modern age with the division between scientific and mythical knowledge. That is why "music is our myth of the inner life—a young, vital, and meaningful myth, of recent inspiration and still in its 'vegetative' growth".

As for the relationship between music and myth, Langer takes a different position from that later embraced by Claude Lévi-Strauss, even though the general presuppositions are not entirely incompatible. Just as in Langer, Lévi-Strauss focuses on music in the light of a rigorously rational analysis of emotion, rejecting those who proclaim "the intuitive and ineffable character of moral and aesthetic feelings".[96] Music and myth are in very close relationship, determined by that with language. Music is "language minus meaning": as in the cases of phantom limbs, where the subject attributes what he feels to something that is no longer there, the listener tends to overcompensate, attributing music a meaning it doesn't have. The analogy with myth is based on the fact that even in this case, where so to speak the amputation is less radical, the signification still hap-

---

94 Pratt (1968). Cf. Budd (1994, p. 37 ff.).
95 Langer (1954, p. 199).
96 Lévi-Strauss (1990, p. 667).

pens above the level of language. Music is therefore a heir to myth, but Lévi-Strauss introduces here a rather complex framework. The mythical legacy is shared in the first instance with literature, which is replaced by music only in the modern age. The thesis may seem paradoxical, but it is justified in view of the analogy between some typical structures of myth and modern music, such as the fugue. So, Lévi-Strauss outlines a very specific historical junction: only when literature expels the myth, developing innovative forms like the novel, does music intervene to take charge of it. In other words, it was necessary "for myth as such to die for its form to escape from it, like the soul leaving the body, and to seek a means of reincarnation in music".[97]

5 Music and Analytic Philosophy

In recent decades, the reflection on music offered by analytic philosophy has obtained results that have attracted much interest, even outside of the English-speaking world. This brings us to our age, in which the philosophy of music has acquired remarkable importance and faces philosophical problems of various nature related to music, considering musical genres previously neglected by philosophers such as jazz, popular music, rock, non-European traditions, non-artistic forms (like the so-called *mukaz*), etc. This vast universe of ideas, which is constantly evolving, can certainly not be summarized here in these few conclusive pages. I will only highlight some of the main lines of thought that appear in the general discussion.

Two main themes of discussion are the relationship between music and emotions and the ontology of the musical work of art. One of the best-known philosophers is Peter Kivy, who has been systematically working on music for many years. Kivy is among those who like to speak of a "philosophy *of* music"—a choice others find debatable.[98] Kivy first posited that in music there is an interaction between a natural expressivity (based on the likeness between music and the "profile" of human expressive behaviours, which are evolutionarily explainable), and a conventional expressivity.[99] Following a partial retraction of these ideas, Kivy has proceeded to develop the so-called "enhanced formalism": a

---

[97] Lévi-Strauss (1990, p. 652).
[98] Kivy (2002, p. 2ff.). Gracyk and Kania adopt a broader stance in their companion to philosophy *and* music: "We thus take the 'and' in our title quite seriously, due to both the necessity of grounding musical aesthetics in a thorough knowledge of music and the interest of musicologists and other scholars in aesthetic issues". Gracyk/Kania (2011, p. xxiii).
[99] Kivy (1980, p. 71ff.); also in Kivy (1989, p. 83ff.). See also Kivy (2002, p. 58).

theory inspired by Hanslick, but able to include an explanation for the relationship between music and emotions. Kivy rejects the idea that music is able to provoke emotions; rather, emotions are properties of music just like redness is a property of an apple. When it is said that a musical piece is "sad", for example, this does not mean that it can produce sadness, but rather that it has the property of sadness. The core of Kivy's cognitivist solution is that we do not feel emotions because of music, but rather we recognize emotions within the musical piece: "enhanced formalism has [...] moved the garden-variety emotions from the listener into the music. The emotions are not, on this view, felt, but 'cognized'".[100] This thesis requires some explanation: provided that we can indeed describe what it is for someone to be "sad", it is much less clear that we can say of an object such as a musical piece that it is "sad". Moreover, by implying a "recognition" rather than a "feeling" of sadness, the cognitivist approach seems to exclude the possibility that music could affect us emotionally.

Kivy is aware of both these issues, and offers some articulate responses. In order to follow his line of argument we first need to clarify his conception of formalism. In general, the latter is the doctrine according to which music is "a structure of sound events without semantic or representational content".[101] Formalism mostly entails a negative thesis: it defines what music is not. Trying to formulate a positive definition, Kivy indicates two characteristics: the "game of hypothesis" and the "musical game of hide and seek". The act of listening is characterized by a continuous formulation of hypotheses—which may or may not be confirmed—about what is going to happen next in the musical piece. Moreover, the listener is engaged in the search for "hidden" themes, placed by the composer within various musical forms. In both cases, as can be clearly seen, we are dealing with a cognitive activity. In the usual musical forms (a fugue, a sonata, a rondo, or variations on a theme) the formal principle is a way to accomplish "the listener's task". This thesis is principally valid for modern tonal (mostly purely instrumental) music, with the consequent exclusion of styles before and after that, but Kivy doesn't see this as a problem. Like Hanslick, Kivy considers this musical canon as paradigmatic for a definition of musical pleasure: hence his definitions such as the "fine art of repetition" or the "pure abstract art of pattern".[102]

What remains to be explained is how emotions come into play: that is, how can formalism be "enhanced"? From Kivy's perspective, emotional properties

---

[100] Kivy (2002, p. 109).
[101] Kivy (2002, p. 89). As to Hanslick's original formulation of formalism, see above, chap. 3, par. 4.
[102] Kivy (2002, p. 154 and 91).

have never been inner, but are rather the "acoustic properties of music". In this sense, a "tranquil passage of music does not represent tranquillity or mean 'tranquil.' It simply is tranquil". These emotional properties are explained, in the first instance, "in terms of the simplest facts of musical structure": the "patterns" that are repeated and contrasted, or maybe even deeper structures, whose examination, however, is still to come.[103] But, then, why does music move the listener? Kivy distinguishes three factors: the intentional object (the piece), the belief in its beauty, and the feeling of excitement it provokes in us. There are marvellous musical pieces that possess, among their properties, a "deep, funereal melancholy". But no one would be willingly driven to experience a funereal melancholy. Rather, the mark of the aesthetic experience in question is a feeling of joyous excitement. In sum, when we are dealing with music and emotions, we are "not moved to them but by them".[104]

Kivy's insistence on tonal music, and primarily on absolute music, however, causes another problem. What about Opera, *Lied*, and programme music? Kivy holds that the association of music with a text is, in a sense, an impossible task, because a text implies a linear progression, while the fine art of repetition is recursive by definition. Throughout history, various solutions have been advanced to solve this problem, yet all of them have proven unreliable. Kivy's conclusion is that many lovers of music cannot bear the "absurdity" of Wagner's musical theatre, while on the other hand Mozart and Verdi fail to satisfy the "'pure dramatic craving", of those who love theatre.[105] What thus emerges is a radical split between instrumental music—the very paradigm of music—and the poetic and dramaturgic arts: the first cannot provoke emotions in any ordinary sense, only the latter can. When music is joined to a text, or placed in a dramaturgic context, the dominant instance, so to speak, comes to prevail, and ordinary emotions are provoked.

This schematic reconstruction omits Kivy's frequent polemical references to other philosophers. However, his theses need to be contextualized in a debate that is worth reconstructing, at least in its broader outline. Criticizing the claim that music cannot evoke real emotions in the listener, Derek Matravers defends "arousal theory", via a two-pronged strategy. First, we need to distinguish, in an emotion, a cognitive part (oriented towards the intentional object), and a "pure" sentimental one. The intentional object of an emotion is determined by its cognitive element, while the sentimental part borrows its object, so to speak,

---

[103] Kivy (2002, p. 91 ff.).
[104] Kivy (2002, p. 132).
[105] Kivy (2002, p. 181 ff.).

from the cognitive one. Now, and here is the second step, Matravers holds that only this sentimental part is actually evoked within aesthetic experience: "the state which is aroused by an expressive work of art [...] has no object. It is neither 'sadness *about* something' nor 'sadness at the thought *that* something'". This allows him to formalize a proposal regarding music's expressive power:

> a piece of music expresses an emotion *e* if it causes a listener to experience a feeling α, where α is the feeling component of the emotion it would be appropriate to feel (in the central case) when faced with a person expressing *e*.[106]

This disproves the objections of those who, like Kivy, hold that the listener's failure to have an adequate reaction to music (the person angered by music would scream, the saddened cry, etc.) demonstrates that no real emotion is evoked. And it is equally fruitless to object that arousal theory is absurd because no one would listen to melancholy or sad music in order not to experience an unpleasant feeling. Both these objections target an absurdly and unnecessarily strong version of the theory (i.e. the case that $e = α$ in the last quotation)[107]

In relation to negative emotions, Jerrold Levinson elaborates an articulate proposal. Levinson does not share the assumptions of arousal theory; he does not believe that music necessarily evokes analogous emotions in the listener. This can happen, but does not determine or define the role of music.[108] Not even the cognitivist hypothesis, which holds that the listener recognizes the emotion present in music, is able to grasp the essence of the phenomenon. At most, it describes a peculiar and possible attitude—the detached and critical mannerism of the connoisseur—which does not coincide with the ordinary, or even the recommended, instance of fruition: in short, it doesn't correspond to an authentically aesthetic experience of music. According to Levinson, the latter essentially lies in the listener's identification with a hypothetical *persona*, in a complex game of attributions which are not necessarily univocally made explicit. Here certain elements come into play:

> Physiological and affective components of the emotion that is embodied in the music; the thought or idea of this emotion; and the imagination, through identification with the music,

---

106 Matravers (1998, p. 148 ff.). With some differences, the arousal of emotions is also defended by Robinson (1994, *passim*).
107 Kivy (2001, p. 119 ff.) replies that, in a sense, any theory is an arousal theory, including Kivy's. However, Matravers' is closest to its strongest interpretation. Kivy (2001, p. 150).
108 Levinson (2011, p. 333 f. and 318).

of oneself as actually experiencing this emotion, though without the usual determinateness of focus.[109]

According to Levinson this approach has the advantage of being able to explain why, when listening to a sad or melancholic music, we do not experience a generic form of rejoicing, which is the same for every type of music. Rather, we experience precisely those emotions of sadness and melancholy, yet without being totally swept away by them, as happens when their object is given to us as a direct intentional object.[110] In Levinson's theory, on the other hand, this object is given in an oblique manner, so to speak, and remains overall indeterminate. We feel as we would if we were inside the musical piece, yet we are not actually in it. This is how he explains the positive function of "negative emotions" in musical experience. Overall, in a controlled context, one's emotions are put to test in view of their real, future use. One gets to "taste" them, and in so doing one learns to comprehend and share them.

Stephen Davies's position is reminiscent of Levinson's due to its insistence on the indirect character of emotions, but the analogy does not go further than this. For Davies, the terms we use to designate our emotions are acceptable as a secondary use, an orthodox and legitimate one. Someone who "looks sad" is not a sad person: he or she could be sad, but that is not necessarily the case.[111] Real emotions do not enter into music: sad music only "sounds sad" but is not really sad. Davis therefore bypasses any reference to the listener's private (emotive or cognitive) states, without however lending himself to the objection that the listener does not adequately react to music: he or she is not supposed to behave as in the case of ordinary emotions, but will at most be *infected* by the sad tone of music.[112]

The idea that emotive vocabulary can be applied in two different ways—to personal states and to different events, like musical pieces—is, however, far from being universally accepted. Inspired by Wittgenstein's teachings, David Carr asserts that the idea that emotive vocabulary has a representative value, representing something "inner", is misguided. Assuming that this representative function is not realized in ordinary language, it would be pointless to attempt to

---

109 Levinson (2011, p. 322).
110 Kivy responds to this implicit criticism on several occasions: see Kivy (2002, p. 138 ff.; 2001, p. 106 ff).
111 Davies (1994, p. 224).
112 Zangwill presents here a thesis compatible with Davies', but is more radical insofar as it does not exclude only the "literal" uses of emotive descriptions, presented here as "metaphorical descriptions of aesthetic properties". Zangwill (2007, p. 391).

describe music starting from a weakening of this condition. Switching perspectives, we should rather learn to define the feelings of joy or sadness as "precisely the feelings that are appropriately felt on sad or joyful occasions"—occasions, after all, "upon which it is appropriate to play joyful or sad music".[113] Music indeed is played in all those "forms of life" wherein people agree on the emotive character required by that particular occasion of communal life—for example a wedding, a party, or a funeral. Music is not joyous because I project my own joy onto it, nor because it represents joy, but because of "its very nature, and it can be so quite irrespective of my feelings towards it".

The other great topic, the ontology of the musical work of art, can be summarized with this question: what kind of object is a musical work of art? This question is part of the broader context of the ontology of works of art, but has some interesting peculiarities. Unlike a painting, a piece of music needs to be performed, and unlike literature, it employs a very specific kind of writing. I will explore only the better-defined positions on this topic (nominalism, historical definition, extreme Platonism) that represent reference points for the whole debate.

Nelson Goodman's study of the problem of the authenticity of the work of art, as developed in his *Languages of Art* (1968), is an important precedent. Goodman considers music an "allographic" and not "autographic" artform, since the distinction between an original and a forgery does not apply to it. This is so for both stages of musical articulation: composition and execution. A freshly-printed copy of Haydn's *London Symphony* is not a forgery of his original score, nor is a contemporary execution a forgery of its original one.[114] Music is therefore different from other "two-stages" artforms, as for example lithography: the cliché is an original, but can be forged (like a painting); lithographic prints are not forgeries of their cliché, yet it is possible to forge them. The criterion of authenticity is then, so to speak, vertical: linear derivation from the cliché. In the case of music, however, things are different: the only thing that counts in ascertaining that a piece really is the *London Symphony* rather than a forgery (or another work) is the absolute congruence between each execution and its score. Goodman is well aware of the counter-intuitive consequences of this idea. The most flat and uninspired—but correct—execution is indeed the *London Symphony*, while an excellent one, where just one note was misplaced, is—by definition—*not* the *London Symphony*.

---

113 Carr (2004, p. 228 ff.).
114 Goodman (1968, p. 112 ff. and 255).

When we claim that such a slightly misperformed execution is a certain musical work of art we are doing something akin to claiming that the sun rises in the morning: the claim is admissible, but not in a scientific context. To allow for a margin of error of even just one note means, for Goodman, to open a bottomless pit, implicitly allowing for minor tweak upon minor tweak, so that the execution of pretty much anything could become the *London Symphony*. The question of authenticity, in Goodman's sense, must be distinguished from another homonymous one, related to execution. And yet, the two questions appear impossible to decouple, since execution is, for many philosophers, one of the conditions that ontologically realize the musical artwork. This implies that an execution responding to Goodman's criteria—perfect down to the last note—could be still insufficient to realize the work, since it would violate other parameters relative to the mode of execution: from the choice of instruments to a passage played in *crescendo*. It is not surprising that this theme is dear to analytic philosophers, many of whom agree with excommunicating those who defend so-called "period performance" of Baroque music, insisting on the necessity of being faithful to the composer's intention rather than to extrinsic environmental factors.[115] On the one hand, this seems to impose a distinction between the period in which music (which was mostly composed on commission) was linked to specific occasions and the new phase, starting with classicism, of the composer's emancipation, allowing the work of art to acquire full aesthetic autonomy, as if placed in an imaginary museum.[116] On the other hand this is also a problem when it comes to the adherence to those expressive or agogic guidelines often jotted down by the composer on the music sheet, as well as to alternative notational forms. These can come from other cultures, or even from Western culture itself, but they still come before, after, or are anyway different from the classic model of the music sheet, like Goodman's example of the *London Symphony*.[117]

Levinson examines the ontological problem from a historical point of view: a work of art is that which a given person, in a given moment, intends intentionally as a work of art, by ideally placing it in the context of those works which, in the past, have been considered to be art. By applying this general strategy to music, Levinson identifies some specific criteria: the musical work of art does not exist before the composer's activity, it is historically individuated, and it includes the means of its own production. Of these criteria, the first might appear to be the least controversial, but it is not so. Levinson's strategy, in fact, is aimed

---

[115] Davies (1987, *passim*); Levinson (2011, p. 393 ff.); Scruton (1997, p. 448 ff.).
[116] See Goehr (2007, p. 89 ff.).
[117] See Davies (2001, p. 99 ff.); Kivy (2001, p. 3–17).

at defusing one of the main pitfalls awaiting those who try to avoid Goodman's nominalism by defining music as a "structure of sounds" (i.e., in Peirce's terminology, as a "type" as opposed to a "token").[118] Indeed, if the work were a type, it would pre-exist its composition, precisely like a Platonic idea.[119] This view, similarly to the one we have already encountered when examining Höfler's work,[120] is expressed by Kivy's "extreme Platonism": the musical work of art pre-exists its composition, so that the latter would really be an act of discovery rather than creation. Against the objection that the Americas were already there when Columbus first reached them, while Beethoven's *Fifth Symphony* was nowhere before its composition, Kivy observes that the comparison is unfair: one would have to compare Beethoven's Fifth with Newton's laws of motion as "invented" (in the etymological sense: *found*) in his *Principia Mathematica*, thus implying that they were already there before Newton.[121] Therefore, the idea of the "discovery" of a work of art does not devalue the work of the composer, but rather interprets it as a "first exemplification", bearing the mark of its author for its everlasting glory.

Roger Scruton's *The Aesthetics of Music* (1997) deserves to conclude our survey. Taking an ambitious systematic approach, Scruton moves from the basic experience of sound but aims to offer an analysis of the cultural and political value of music in our times. In this project, an important role is played by the so-called Croce-Collingwood hypothesis, which prescribes a clear distinction between representation and expression. Croce's aesthetics, however, is criticized because of its correlation of expression and intuition. On the one hand, Croce refers to the communication of emotional states while, on the other, suggesting that ultimately the work of art is ineffable—even though the two claims are clearly contradictory.[122] Scruton rejects the second part of the dilemma—the ineffability of art—and rather proposes to reconnect the expressivity of music to states of mind (in a sense to be clarified). Music, then, does not have a representative character, but this does not entail any kind of formalism, because it still has an expressive character.

> There is a gesture towards something, in the course of a musical argument: but the music quickly goes on its way, without developing the thought. Call this representation if you like:

---

[118] Levinson (2011, p. 63 ff.).
[119] This assumption is criticized by Scruton (1997, p. 114).
[120] See above, chap. 4, par. 3
[121] Kivy (2002, p. 257). A reply in Levinson (2011, p. 216 ff.).
[122] Scruton (1997, p. 144 and 148).

but acknowledge too that the incompleteness of the thought sets the phenomenon apart from the description or depiction of fictional worlds.[123]

This kind of approach allows Scruton to set up most of the relevant questions: the meaning of music, its relation with the text, its character as a language, the problem of its content, and the emotions associated to it. This happens in the first instance due to a series of tests that a theory should be able to pass: the expression must be an *aesthetic* value, it must be *developed* through a musical structure, and it must be part of that which is *understood* when a piece is musically understood.

But how can music be expressive? We need to step back here and introduce a distinction between sounds and tones. Sounds are pure *events* where the intentional aspect is neutralized: we do not give attention to the object producing the sound, as it is reduced to a mere cause. However, not all aesthetic uses of sound are musical. An architect designing a fountain needs to consider (in a properly aesthetic sense) the acoustic factor, yet this is not music. Here we switch from sounds to tones, which exist in "a musical 'field of force'".[124] Human imagination fills tones with intentional meanings, an operation that is most successful once sounds have eliminated ordinary intentionality. Hence the creation of a "tonal space" in the perceived order, of a "movement", of relations of attraction and repulsion, etc. For this reason, meaning in music never concerns the external world, but has an internal or "acousmatic" character. The listener is not looking for information, but the sounds flow independently from their causes; this is why we can hear the same melody played by an oboe or a violin. In music we do not comprehend the world, but the intentional objects: there is no other reason for listening to music "than the fact that it sounds as it does".[125]

Vibrations in the air are therefore the primary objects, sounds are secondary objects, and tones, with determinate expressive properties, are tertiary ones. To complicate matters, however, there is also the fact that these expressive properties are themselves tertiary properties. They are not primary because music is not sad in the same sense that a person is sad; nor are they secondary, or else any living being (including animals) would perceive them as such. They belong to a third ontological realm.[126] Moreover, the use of terms like "expression" is not always transitive. In many cases, particularly in music, "expressive" does not mean expressive of something, but rather points to a tertiary quality. Similarly,

---

[123] Scruton (1997, p. 129).
[124] Scruton (1997, p. 17).
[125] Scruton (1997, p. 221).
[126] Scruton (1997, p. 161).

we say that a face is "nice" without meaning that it represents or means "niceness".

The attribution of tertiary expressive qualities to music allows us to avoid attributing (as Kivy does) emotive qualities to the musical piece itself. Scruton then offers an "antirealist" solution to the problem, avoiding the rigorous definitions or necessary and sufficient conditions which Levinson (and others) enumerate, and identifying a "state of mind—the 'recognition of expression'—and its place in the aesthetic experience" so that "[t]he description of the work as expressive is an attempt to articulate this state of mind". In this mental state there might be some conceptual perspective, but the intentional order is suspended, and conceptual labour is lost among metaphors.[127] In music we employ concepts to describe appearances rather than the world: "in a mysterious way, this oblique use of our concepts purifies them, and reconciles us with the world that they describe".[128]

A similar cathartic function takes place at the emotive level. The problem of emotions needs to be examined and resolved, Scruton argues, starting with the transitive use of expression. This is an anti-cognitivist approach, since cognitivism, no matter how sophisticated its formulation, is blind to the most important element, that is, the "emotional education" achieved through "the reordering of the sympathies that we acquire through our response to art".[129] There is, then, a deep relation between music and emotions. But Scruton rejects the frequently voiced but wrong hypothesis of an analogy in the formal development of music and emotions: there is no deep similarity between the two processes.[130] On the contrary, it is music that imposes its own order, and it holds an aesthetic value precisely because its order does *not* correspond to the natural order of feelings:

> The great triumphs of music, it seems to me, involve this synthesis, whereby a musical structure, moving according to its own logic, compels our feelings to move along with it, and so leads us to rehearse a feeling at which we would not otherwise arrive.[131]

---

[127] Boghossian criticizes the lack of a distinction between double intentionality (the "seeing as") and metaphor. See Boghossian (2002, p. 51).
[128] Scruton (1997, p. 236).
[129] Scruton (1997, p. 147 fn.).
[130] Scruton (1997, p. 147 fn.).
[131] Scruton (1997, p. 359).

This is not always the case: music can fail, and not accomplish its intent. But when it does reach its desired effect, this represents one of the highest human experiences.

Many classical aesthetic concepts re-emerge in Scruton's perspective: the "aesthetic judgment" is conceived in analogy with morality. What is most striking in moral action is the nobility of the soul's disposition, not its ability to apply a rule. The same can be said for aesthetics: we do not identify laws or rules for the work of art, but rather admire the "taste" as a property allowing a "well-ordered soul" to enter into a relationship with the life that is idealized in the work of art:

> Good taste is not reducible to rules; but we can define it instead through a concept of virtue: it is the sum of those preferences that would emerge in a well-ordered soul, in which human passions are accorded their true significance.[132]

There is clearly some idealism in these appeals to judgment, taste and these analogies with morality; Scruton bends this idealism to an aesthetic choice that is decidedly in favour of tonalism.

Assuming that music is made up of *tones*, in the sense discussed above, Scruton claims that *tonality* as a form of organization is the quintessence of music. Scruton does not promote a naïve return to classical tonal language, but rather asks the question of whether tonal music would not be "the only music that will ever really mean anything to us", while atonal music can be listened to only insofar as "we can elicit within it a latent tonal order". After all, contrary to Adorno's prediction, modernism did not "overthrow the consumer culture" but has had the effect of a vaccine against modernism, "which now floats around the system accompanied by its own friendly antibodies". Although he shares Adorno's concern with the decline of popular taste, Scruton criticizes his idea that mass culture is a bourgeois product, and modernism is the only possible answer to it.[133] What follows, then, is the necessity of a return to tonalism although, so to speak "in inverted commas": that is, with the awareness that it is not music's *natural language,* but one among many possibilities—the object of a precise aesthetic choice endowed with clear conservative political implications.[134] According to Scruton the "great task" faced by music is that of "recov-

---

[132] Scruton (1997, p. 379).
[133] Scruton (1997, p. 159). For the previous citations see Scruton (1997, p. 469, 308 and 504). See also Scruton (2009b, p. 207)
[134] Scruton (1997, p. 308 and 507 f.). On the composers he mentions, see Scruton (1997, p. 508 and 472).

ering" tonality and, with it, the "spiritual community" that constituted its reference point. Once again, the philosophy of music evolves into a reflection on a *certain* kind of music. Once naturalism is jettisoned, will tonality "in inverted commas" really have the final word?

References

Abert, Hermann (1899): *Die Lehre vom Ethos in der griechischen Musik* (1968). Tutzing: Schneider.
Abert, Hermann (1905): *Die Musikanschauung des Mittelalters und ihre Grundlagen* (1968). Tutzing: Schneider.
Adelard of Bath (1998): *Quaestiones naturales*. In: *Conversations with his Nephew. On the Same and the Different, Questions on Natural Science, and On Birds*. Charles Burnett (Ed.). Cambridge: Cambridge University Press, pp. 82–227.
Adorno, Theodor Wiesengrund (1976): *Introduction to the Sociology of Music*. New York: Seabury Press.
Adorno, Theodor Wiesengrund (1978): "Fragment über Musik und Sprache". In: *Musikalische Schriften I–III*. Frankfurt a.M.: Suhrkamp, pp. 251–256.
Adorno, Theodor Wiesengrund (2002a): *Beethoven. The Philosophy of Music*. Rolf Tiedemann (Ed.). Stanford: Stanford University Press.
Adorno, Theodor Wiesengrund (2002b): "Music, Language, and Composition". In: *Essays on Music*. Richard Leppert (Ed.). Berkeley: University of California Press, pp. 113–126.
Adorno, Theodor Wiesengrund (2002c): *Aesthetic Theory*. Gretel Adorno/Rolf Tiedemann (Eds.). London: Continuum.
Adorno, Theodor Wiesengrund (2007): *Philosophy of Modern Music*. London: Continuum.
Affligemensis [Cotto], Johannes (1950): *De musica cum tonario*. Joseph Smits van Waesberghe (Ed.). Roma: American Institute of Musicology.
Alembert, Jean-Baptiste Le Rond [d'] (1752): *Éléments de musique, théorique et pratique, suivant les principes de M. Rameau*. Paris: David.
Alembert, Jean-Baptiste Le Rond [d'] (1766): *Éléments de musique, théorique et pratique, suivant les principes de M. Rameau*. Lyon: Bruyset.
Ammann, Peter J. (1967): "The Musical Theory and Philosophy of Robert Fludd". In: *Journal of the Warburg and Courtauld Institutes* 30, pp. 198–227.
Aquinas, Thomas (1952): *In libros Aristotelis de caelo et mundo expositio*. In: *In Aristotelis libros de caelo et mundo de generatione et corruptione meteorologicorum expositio*. Raymund Spiazzi (Ed.). Torino-Roma: Marietti, pp. 1–311.
Aquinas, Thomas (1972): *Thomae Aquinatis Opuscula theologica*. Vol. 2: *De re spirituali, accedit expositio super Boetium de Trinitate et de hebdomadibus*. Mario Calcaterra (Ed.). Torino-Roma: Marietti.
Arbo, Alessandro (2009): "Some remarks on 'hearing-as' and its role in the aesthetics of music". In: *Topoi* 28, pp. 97–107.
Aristides Quintilian (1984): *De Musica*. In: *Greek Musical Writings*, Vol. 2: *Harmonic and Acoustic Theory*. Anrdew Barker (Ed.). Cambridge: Cambridge University Press, pp. 399–535.
Aristotle (1932): *Politics*. Harris Rackham (Ed.). Loeb Classical Library No. 264. Cambridge MA: Harvard University Press.
Aristotle (1933): *Metaphysics*. Vol. 1: Books 1–9. Hugh Tredennick (Ed.). Loeb Classical Library No. 271. Cambridge MA: Harvard University Press.
Aristotle (1934): *Physics*. Vol. 2: Books 5–8. Philipp Henry Wicksteed/Francis Macdonald Cornford (Eds.). Loeb Classical Library No. 255. Cambridge MA: Harvard University Press.

Aristotle (1935): *Metaphysics*. Vol. 2: Books 10–14. Hugh Tredennick (Ed.). Loeb Classical Library No. 287. Cambridge MA: Harvard University Press.
Aristotle (1938): *On the Heavens*. William Keith Chambers Guthrie (Ed.). Loeb Classical Library No. 338. Cambridge MA: Harvard University Press.
Aristotle (1955): *On interpretation*. In: *The categories. On interpretation. Prior analytics*. Harold P. Cooke/Hugh Tredennick (Eds.). Loeb Classical Library No. 325. Cambridge MA: Harvard University Press, pp. 114–181.
Aristotle (1957): *On the Soul*. In: *On the Soul. Parva Naturalia. On Breath*. Walter Stanley Hett (Ed.). Loeb Classical Library No. 288. Cambridge MA: Harvard University Press.
Aristotle (1965): *History of Animals*. Vol. 2. Arthur Leslie Peck (Ed.). Loeb Classical Library No. 438. Cambridge MA: Harvard University Press.
Aristotle (1995): *Poetics*. In: *Aristotle: Poetics. Longinus: On the Sublime. Demetrius: On Style*. Stephen Halliwell et al. (Eds.). Loeb Classical Library No. 199. Cambridge MA: Harvard University Press.
Aristotle (2011): *Problems*. Vol. 2: Books 20–38. In: *Problems (Vol. 2: Books 20–38). Rhetoric to Alexander*. Robert Mayhew/David C. Mirhady (Eds.). Loeb Classical Library No. 317. Cambridge MA: Harvard University Press.
Aristoxenus of Tarentum (1984): *Elementa Harmonica*. In: *Greek Musical Writings*. Andrew Barker (Ed.). Vol. 2: *Harmonic and Acoustic Theory*. Cambridge: Cambridge University Press, pp. 126–184.
Aristoxenus (1990): *Elementa Rhythmica*. Lionel Pearson (Ed.). Oxford: Clarendon.
Ash, Mitchell Graham (1995): *Gestalt psychology in German Culture, 1890–1967. Holism and the Quest for Objectivity*. Cambridge: Cambridge University Press.
Auger, Léon (1948): "Les apports de J. Sauveur (1653–1716) à la création de l'Acoustique". In: *Revue d'histoire des sciences et de leurs applications* 1, No. 4, pp. 323–336.
Augst, Bertrand (1965): "Descartes's Compendium on Music". In: *Journal of the History of Ideas* 26, pp. 119–132.
Augustine of Hippo (1991): *Confessions*. Henry Chadwick (Ed.). Oxford: Oxford University Press.
Augustine of Hippo (1999): *The Retractations*. Washington: Catholic University of America Press.
Augustine of Hippo (2002a): *On Music*. In: *The Immortality of the Soul; The Magnitude of the Soul; On Music; The Advantage of Believing; On Faith in Things Unseen*. Ludwig Schopp (Ed.). Washington: Catholic University of America Press.
Augustine of Hippo (2002b): *De musica VI. A Critical Edition with a Translation and an Introduction*. Martin Jacobsson (Ed.). Stockholm: Acta Universitatis Stockholmiensis.
Augustine of Hippo (2003): *Exposition of the Psalms [Enarrationes in Psalmos] (99–120)*. Vol. 19. Part 3. Boniface Ramsey (Ed.). New York: New City Press.
Augustine of Hippo (2007): *On Order [De Ordine]*. Silvano Borruso (Ed.). South Bend IN: St. Augustine's Press.
Aurelian of Rêome (1784): *Musica disciplina*. In: *Scriptores ecclesiastici de musica sacra*. Vol. 1. Martin Gerbert (Ed.). St. Blaise: Typis San-Blasianis, pp. 27–63. Repr. Hildesheim: Olms (1963).
Bacon, Francis (1881): *Sylva Sylvarum, or a Natural History in Ten Centuries*. In: *The Works of Francis Bacon*. Vol. 4. Boston: Houghton & Mifflin & Co.
Bacon, Francis (1884): *Wisdom of the Ancients*. Boston: Little, Brown & Co.

Bailhache, Patrice (1993): "Cordes vibrantes et consonances chez Beeckman, Mersenne et Galilée". In: *Musique et mathématiques* 23, pp. 73–91.
Bailhache, Patrice (1999): *La musique, une pratique cachée de l'arithmétique?* In: *L'actualité de Leibniz. Les deux Labyrinthes*. Dominique Berlioz (Ed.). Stuttgart: Steiner, pp. 405–426.
Barbera, André (1984): "Placing Sectio Canonis in Historical and Philosophical Contexts". In: *The Journal of Hellenic Studies* 104, pp. 157–161.
Barker, Andrew (2007): *The Science of Harmonics in Classical Greece*. Cambridge: Cambridge University Press.
Barker Andrew (2014): *Pythagorean Harmonics*. In: *A History of Pythagoreanism*. Carl A. Huffman (Ed.). Cambridge: Cambridge University Press, pp. 185–203.
Barker, Andrew (Ed.) (1984): *Greek Musical Writings*. Cambridge: Cambridge University Press.
Beierwaltes, Werner (1969): "Augustins Interpretation von *Sapientia*, 11.20". In: *Revue des études Augustiniennes* 15, pp. 51–61.
Benjamin, Walter (1998): *The Origin of Germanic Tragic Drama*. London: Verso.
Bernoulli, Daniel (1753): "Réflexions et éclaircissements sur les nouvelles vibrations des cordes exposées dans les Mémoires de l'Académie de 1747 et 1748". In: *Histoire de l'Académie Royale des Sciences et Belles-Lettres* 9. *Année 1753* (Publ. 1755). *Classe de Mathématique*, pp. 147–172.
Besseler, Heinrich (1959): "Das musikalische Hören der Neuzeit". In: *Berichte über die Verhandlungen der Sächsischen Akademie der Wissenschaften zu Leipzig, Philologisch-historische Klasse* 104. No. 6. Berlin: Academie.
Bettetini, Maria (2001): "Musica tra cielo e terra: lettura del *De Musica* di Agostino d'Ippona". In: *La musica nel pensiero medievale*. Letterio Mauro (Ed.). Ravenna: Longo, pp. 103–122.
Bielitz, Mathias (1977): *Musik und Grammatik. Studien zur mittelalterlichen Musiktheorie*. München: Katzbichler.
Bloch, Ernst (1918): *Geist der Utopie*, München: Duncker & Humblot.
Bloch, Ernst (1985a): "The Philosophy of Music". In: *Essays on the Philosophy of Music*. Peter Palmer/David Drew (Eds.). Cambridge: Cambridge University Press, pp. 1–182.
Bloch, Ernst (1985b): "The Exceeding of Limits and the World of Man at its Most Richly Intense in Music". In: *Essays on the Philosophy of Music*. Peter Palmer/David Drew (Eds.). Cambridge: Cambridge University Press, pp. 195–243.
Bloch, Ernst (1995): *The Principle of Hope*. Neville Plaice/Stephen Plaice/Paul Knight (Eds.). Cambridge MA: MIT Press.
Bloch, Ernst (2000): *The Spirit of Utopia*. Anthony A. Nassar (Ed.). Stanford: Stanford University Press.
Boccadoro, Brenno (2010): "Marsilio Ficino: The Soul and the Body of Counterpoint". In: *Number to Sound. The Musical Way to the Scientific Revolution*. Paolo Gozza (Ed.). Dordrecht: Kluwer, pp. 99–134.
Boethius, Anicius Manlius Severinus (1867a): *De institutione arithmetica libri duo*. In: *De institutione arithmetica libri duo. De institutione musica libri quinque*. Gottfried Friedlein (Ed.). Leipzig: Teubner, pp. 1–172.
Boethius, Anicius Manlius Severinus (1867b): *De institutione musica libri quinque*. In: *De institutione arithmetica libri duo. De institutione musica libri quinque*. Gottfried Friedlein (Ed.). Leipzig: Teubner, pp. 177–225.

Boethius, Anicius Manlius Severinus (1968): *The Consolation of Philosophy.* Hugh Fraser Stewart/Edward Kennard Rand (Eds.). Loeb Classical Library No. 317. Cambridge MA: Harvard University Press.

Boethius, Anicius Manlius Severinus (1989): *Fundamentals of music.* Claude Victor Palisca (Ed.). New Haven & London: Yale University Press.

Boghossian, Paul (2002): "On Hearing the Music in the Sound: Scruton on Musical Expression". In: *Journal of Aesthetics and Art Criticism* 60, pp. 49–55.

Brancacci, Aldo (2007): "Democritus' *Mousika*". In: *Democritus: Science, The Arts, And The Care Of The Soul.* Proceedings Of The International Colloquium On Democritus (Paris, 18–20 September 2003). Aldo Brancacci/Pierre-Marie Morel (Eds.). Leiden: Brill, pp. 181–206.

Brancacci, Aldo (2008): *Musica e filosofia da Damone a Filodemo. Sette studi.* Firenze: Olschki.

Brisson, Luc (1974): *Le même et l'autre dans la structure ontologique du Timée de Platon. Un commentaire systématique.* Paris: Klincksieck.

Brüllmann, Philip (2013): "Music Builds Character. Aristotle, 'Politics' VIII 5, 1340a14-b5". In: *Apeiron* 46, pp 345–373.

Budd, Malcolm (1994): *Music and the Emotions. The Philosophical Theories.* London: Routledge.

Burke, Edmund (1757): *A Philosophical Enquiry into the Origin of Our Ideas of the Sublime and Beautiful.* London: R. & J. Dodsley in Pallmall.

Burkert, Walter (1962): *Weisheit und Wissenschaft. Studien zu Pythagoras, Philolaos und Platon.* Nürnberg: Carl.

Cahan, David (Ed.) (1994): *Hermann von Helmholtz and the Foundations of Nineteenth-Century Science.* Berkeley: University of California Press.

Carnap, Rudolf (1932): "The Elimination of Metaphysics Through Logical Analysis of Language". In: Sahotra Sarkar (Ed.): *Logical Empiricism at Its Peak: Schlick, Carnap, and Neurath.* New York: Garland (1996), pp. 10–31.

Carr, David (2004): "Music, Meaning, Emotion". In: *Journal of Aesthetics and Art Criticism* 63, pp. 225–234.

Casini, Paolo (1981): "Newton: gli scolii classici". In: *Giornale critico della filosofia italiana* 60, pp. 7–53.

Cassiodorus, Flavius M.A. (1784): *Institutiones musicae, seu excerpta ex eiusdem libro, de artibus ac disciplinis liberalium litterarum.* In: *Scriptores ecclesiastici de musica sacra potissimum.* Martin Gerbert (Ed.). St. Blaise: Typis San-Blasianis, pp. 15–19. Repr. Hildesheim: Olms (1963).

Cattin, Giulio (1991): *La monodia nel Medioevo.* Torino: EDT.

Cernuschi, Alain (2000): *Penser la musique dans l'Encyclopédie. Étude sur les enjeux de la musicographie des Lumières et sur ses liens avec l'encyclopédisme.* Paris: Champion.

Chadwick, Henry (1981): *Boethius. The Consolations of Music, Logic, Theology, and Philosophy.* Oxford: Oxford University Press.

Chalcidius (2016): *On Plato's Timaeus.* John Magee (Ed.). Dumbarton Oaks Medieval Library. Cambridge MA: Harvard University Press.

Chamberlain, David (1970): "Philosophy of Music in the Consolatio of Boethius". In: *Speculum* 45, pp. 80–97.

Charrak, André (2003): *Raison et perception. Fonder l'harmonie au XVIIIe siècle.* Paris: Vrin.

Chladni, Ernst Florens F. (1787): *Entdeckungen über die Theorie des Klanges*. Leipzig: Wiedmann.
Chladni, Ernst Florens F. (1802): *Die Akustik*. Leipzig: Breitkopf & Härtel.
Chladni, Ernst Florens F. (1809): *Traité d'acoustique*. Paris: Courcier.
Chladni, Ernst Florens F. (1830): *Die Akustik*. Zweite Auflage. Leipzig: Breitkopf & Härtel. Repr. Hildesheim: Olms (2004).
Christensen, Thomas (1993): *Rameau and Musical Thought in the Enlightenment*. Cambridge: Cambridge University Press.
Cicero, Marcus Tullius (2017): *On the Commonwealth. On the Laws*. James E.G. Zetzel (Ed.). Cambridge: Cambridge University Press.
Cohen, H. Floris (1984): *Quantifying Music. The Science of Music at the First Stage of the Scientific Revolution, 1580–1650*. Dordrecht: Kluwer.
Colli, Giorgio (1977): *La sapienza greca*. Milano: Adelphi.
Conrad, Waldemar (1908): "Der ästhetische Gegenstand. Eine phänomenologische Studie". In: *Zeitschrift für Ästhetik und allgemeine Kunstwissenschaft* 3, pp. 71–118.
Coussemaker, Edmond de (Ed.) (1864–1876): *Scriptorum de musica medii aevi*. 3 vols. Paris: Durand. Repr. Hildesheim: Olms (1963).
Cristiani, Marta/Panti, Cecilia/Perillo, Graziano (Eds.) (2007): *"Harmonia mundi". Musica mondana e musica celeste fra Antichità e Medioevo*. Firenze: Edizioni del Galluzzo.
Dahlhaus, Carl (1953): "Zu Kants Musikästhetik". In: *Archiv für Musikwissenschaft* 10, pp. 338–347.
Dahlhaus, Carl (1988): *Klassische und romantische Musikästhetik*. München: Laaber.
Dahlhaus, Carl (1991): *The Idea of Absolute Music*. Chicago: University of Chicago Press.
Davies, Stephen (1987): "Authenticity in Musical Performance". In: *British Journal of Aesthetics* 27, pp. 39–50.
Davies, Stephen (1994): *Musical Meaning and Expression*. Ithaca: Cornell University Press.
Davies, Stephen (2001): *Musical Works and Performances. A Philosophical Exploration*. Oxford: Clarendon Press.
Dear, Peter (1988): *Mersenne and the Learnings of the Schools*. Ithaca: Cornell University Press.
Dear, Peter (2010): "Marin Mersenne: Mechanics, Music and Harmony". In: *Number to Sound. The Musical Way to the Scientific Revolution*. Paolo Gozza (Ed.). Dordrecht: Kluwer, pp. 267–288
Delattre, Daniel (2007): *Introduction*. In: Philodemus of Gadara, *Sur la musique (De musica)*. Daniel Delattre (Ed.). Paris: Les Belles Lettres.
Deleuze Gilles/Guattari, Félix (1987): *A Thousand Plateaus: Capitalism and Schizophrenia*. Minneapolis: University of Minnesota Press.
Descartes, René (1933): "Descartes à Mersenne (4 March 1630, No. 150)". In: *Correspondance du P. Marin Mersenne, Religieux Minime*. Vol. 2. Cornelis de Waard et al. (Eds.). Paris: Editions du Centre National de la Recherche Scientifique, pp. 406–409.
Descartes, René (1961): *Compendium of music*. Rome: American Institute of Musicology.
Descartes, René (1985): *Rules for the Direction of the Mind*. In: *The Philosophical Writings of Descartes*. Vol.1. Cambridge: Cambridge University Press.
Descartes, René (1991): *The Correspondence*. In: *The Philosophical Writings of Descartes*. Vol. 3. Cambridge: Cambridge University Press.
Descartes, René (2003): *Treatise of Man*. New York: Prometheus Books.

Diderot, Denis (1748): *Principes généraux d'acoustique*. In: *Œuvres complètes (1875–1877)*. Vol. 9. Jules Assézat (Ed.). Paris: Garnier, pp. 83–131.

Diderot, Denis (1751): *Lettre sur les sourds et muets a l'usage de ceux qui entendent et qui parlent*. In: *Œuvres complètes (1875–1877)*. Vol. 1. Jules Assézat (Ed.). Paris: Garnier, pp. 343–429.

Diderot, Denis (2000): *Thoughts on the Interpretation of Nature and other Philosophical Works*. Manchester: Clinamen Press.

Diels, Hermann/Kranz, Walther (Eds.) (1952): *Die Fragmente der Vorsokratiker. Griechisch und Deutsch*. Berlin: Weidmann.

Diogenes Laertius (1972a): *Lives of Eminent Philosophers*. Vol. 1. Books 1–5. Robert Drew Hicks (Ed.). Loeb Classical Library No. 184. Cambridge MA: Harvard University Press.

Dostrovsky, Sigalia (1974): "Early Vibration Theory: Physics and Music in the Seventeenth Century". In: *Archive for the History of Exact Sciences* 14, pp. 169–218.

Drake, Stillman (1978): *Galileo at Work. His Scientific Biography*. New York: Dover Publications.

Dyer, Joseph (2007): "The Place of 'Musica' in Medieval Classifications of Knowledge". In: *The Journal of Musicology* 24, pp. 3–71.

Euclid [Ps.] (1984): *The Euclidean Sectio Canonis*. In: *Greek Musical Writings*. Andrew Barker (Ed.). Vol. 2: *Harmonic and Acoustic Theory*. Cambridge: Cambridge University Press, pp. 194–216.

Euler, Leonhard (1802): *Letters to a German Princess*. London: Murray & Highley.

Fabbri, Natacha (2003): *Cosmologia e armonia. Contrappunto a due voci sul tema dell'Harmonice mundi*. Firenze: Olschki.

Fabbri, Natacha (2008): *De l'utilité de l'harmonie. Filosofia, scienza e musica in Mersenne, Descartes e Galileo*. Pisa: Edizioni della Normale.

Ferrara, Lawrence (1996): "Schopenhauer on Music as the Embodiment of Will". In: *Schopenhauer, Philosophy, and the Arts*. Dale Jacquette (Ed.). Cambridge: Cambridge University Press, pp. 183–199.

Ficino, Marsilio (1985): *Commentary on Plato's Symposium*. Sears Raynold Jayne (Ed.). Dallas: Spring.

Fisette, Denis/Martinelli, Riccardo (Eds.) (2015): *Philosophy from an Empirical Standpoint. Essays on Carl Stumpf*. Leiden-Boston: Brill Rodopi.

Folli, Laura (2001): "Canticum cordis: la musica e l'interiorità nelle Enarrationes in Psalmos di Agostino". In: *La musica nel pensiero medievale*. Letterio Mauro (Ed.). Ravenna, Longo, pp 177–184.

Fontenelle, Bernard le Bovier de (1701): "Sur un nouveau système de Musique". In: *Histoire de l'Académie Royale des* Sciences, pp. 121–137.

Fontenelle, Bernard le Bovier de (1702): "Sur l'application des sons harmoniques aux jeux d'orgues". In: *Histoire de l'Académie Royale des* Sciences, pp. 90–93.

Fubini, Enrico (1991a): *The History of Music Aesthetics*. London: Macmillan, 1991.

Fubini, Enrico (1991b): *Gli enciclopedisti e la musica*. Torino: Einaudi, 1991.

Fugate, Joe K. (1966): *The Psychological Basis of Herder's Aesthetics*. The Hague-Paris: Mouton & Co.

Gabriel, Gottfried (2005): "Witz". In: *Historisches Wörterbuch der Philosophie*. Vol. 12. Joachim Ritter et al. (Eds.). Basel: Schwabe, cols. 983–990.

Galilei, Galileo (1914): *Dialogues Concerning Two New Sciences*. New York: MacMillan.

Galilei, Vincenzo (1581): *Dialogo della musica antica et della moderna*. Firenze: Marescotti.
Galilei, Vincenzo (1589): *Discorso intorno all'opere di messer Gioseffo Zarlino da Chioggia, et altri importanti particolari attinenti alla musica*. Firenze: Marescotti.
Galilei, Vincenzo (1989): "A Special Discourse Concerning the Diversity of the Ratios of the Diapason". In: *The Florentine Camerata. Documentary Studies and Translations*. Claude Victor Palisca (Ed.). New Haven: Yale University Press, pp. 180–196.
Gallo, F. Alberto (1991): *La polifonia nel Medioevo*. Torino: EDT.
Geiger, Moritz (1928): *Zugänge zur Ästhetik*. Leipzig: Der neue Geist.
Georgiades, Trasybulos (1958): *Musik und Rhythmus bei den Griechen. Zum Ursprung des abendländischen Musik*. Hamburg: Rowohlt.
Gerbert, Martin (Ed.) (1784): *Scriptores ecclesiastici de musica sacra potissimum*. St. Blaise: Typis San-Blasianis. Repr. Hildesheim: Olms (1963).
Gibson, Sophie (2005): *Aristoxenus of Tarentum and the Birth of Musicology*. London: Routledge.
Giordanetti, Piero (2001): *Kant e la musica*. Milano: Cuem.
Goehr, Lydia (2007): *The Imaginary Museum of Musical Works. An Essay in the Philosophy of Music*. Oxford: Oxford University Press.
Goethe, Johann Wolfgang (1808): "Letter to Zelter (22 June 1808)". In: *Goethe's Letters To Zelter. With Extracts From Those of Zelter to Goethe*. London: George Bell & Sons (1892).
Goethe, Johann Wolfgang (1810): "Zur Tonlehre". In: *Goethes Werke*. Hrsg. im Auftrage der Grossherzogin Sophie von Sachsen (Weimarer-Ausgabe). Sect. 2, vol. 11. Weimar: Böhlau, pp. 285–295.
Goethe, Johann Wolfgang (2014): *Faust. I & II*. Stuart Atkins (Ed.). Princeton: Princeton University Press.
Golden, Leon (1976): "The Clarification Theory of 'Katharsis'". In: *Hermes* 104, pp. 437–452.
Goodman, Nelson (1968): *Languages of Art*. Indianapolis & New York: Bobbs Merrill Company.
Gouk, Penelope (1986): "Newton and Music: From the Microcosm to the Macrocosm". In: *International Studies in the Philosophy of Science* 1, pp. 36–59.
Gouk, Penelope (2010): "Music in Francis Bacon's Natural Philosophy". In: *Number to Sound. The Musical Way to the Scientific Revolution*. Paolo Gozza (Ed.). Dordrecht: Kluwer, pp. 187–196.
Gozza, Paolo (2005): "Fiat sonus! Il Barocco come rappresentazione sonora del mondo". In: *Intersezioni* 25, pp. 237–268.
Gozza, Paolo (Ed.) (2010): *Number to Sound. The Musical Way to the Scientific Revolution*. Dordrecht: Kluwer.
Gracyk, Theodore/Kania, Andrew (2011): "Preface". In: *The Routledge Companion to Philosophy and Music*. London: Routledge, pp. xxii–xxiv.
Gracyk, Theodore/Kania, Andrew (Eds.) (2011): *The Routledge Companion to Philosophy and Music*. London: Routledge.
Greaves, Denise Davidson (1986): "Introduction". In: Sextus Empiricus, *Against the Musicians*. Lincoln: University of Nebraska Press, pp. 1–116.
Grey, Thomas (2011): "Hanslick". In: *The Routledge Companion to Philosophy and Music*. Theodore Gracyk/Andrew Kania (Eds.). London, Routledge, pp. 360–370.
Grocheio, Johannes de (1943): *Der Musiktraktat des Johannes de Grocheo*. Ernst Rohloff (Ed.). Leipzig: Reinecke.

Guicciardini, Niccolò (2013): "The Role of Musical Analogies in Newton's Optical and Cosmological Work". In: *Journal of the History of Ideas* 74, pp. 45–67.
Guido of Arezzo (1985): *Regulae rhythmicae*. In: *Divitiae musicae artis*. Series A, liber 4. Joseph Smits van Waesberghe/Eduard Vetter (Eds.). Buren: Knuf.
Gundisalvi [Gundissalinus], Dominicus (1903): *De divisione philosophiae*. Ludwig Baur (Ed.). Münster: Aschendorff.
Guyer, Paul (1996): *Kant and the Claims of Taste*. Cambridge: Cambridge University Press.
Halm, August (1913): *Von zwei Kulturen der Musik*. München: Müller.
Hanslick, Eduard (1986): *On the Musically Beautiful: A Contribution Towards the Revision of the Aesthetics of Music*. Indianapolis: Hackett Publishing.
Haym, Rudolf (1870): *Die Romantische Schule. Ein Beitrag zur Geschichte des deutschen Geistes*. Berlin: Gaertner.
Hegel, Georg Wilhelm Friedrich (1977): *Phenomenology of Spirit*. John Niemeyer Findlay (Ed.). Oxford: Oxford University Press.
Hegel, Georg Wilhelm Friedrich (1975a): *Aesthetics: Lectures on Fine Art*. Vol. 1. Oxford: Clarendon Press.
Hegel, Georg Wilhelm Friedrich (1975b): *Aesthetics: Lectures on Fine Art*. Vol. 2. Oxford: Clarendon Press.
Hegel, Georg Wilhelm Friedrich (1978): *Hegel's Philosophy of Subjective Spirit*. Vol. 3: *Phenomenology and Psychology*. Michael John Petry (Ed.). Dordrecht: Reidel.
Hegel, Georg Wilhelm Friedrich (2004): *Philosophy of Nature*. In: *Encyclopaedia of the Philosophical Sciences (1830)*. Part 2. Oxford: Oxford University Press.
Heidegger, Martin (1991): *The Principle of Reason*. Bloomington & Indianapolis: Indiana University Press, 1991.
Heimsoeth, Heinz (1967): "Hegels Philosophie der Musik". In: *Hegel-Studien* 2, pp. 161–201.
Heller-Roazen, Daniel (2011): *The Fifth Hammer. Pythagoras and the Disharmony of the World*. Cambridge MA: MIT Press.
Helmholtz, Hermann von (1870): *Die Lehre von den Tonempfindungen, als physiologische Grundlage für die Theorie der Musik*. Dritte Auflage. Braunschweig: Vieweg.
Helmholtz, Hermann von (1877): *Die Lehre von den Tonempfindungen, als physiologische Grundlage für die Theorie der Musik*. Vierte Auflage. Braunschweig: Vieweg.
Helmholtz, Hermann von (1912): *On the Sensations of Tone, as a Physiological Basis for the Theory of Music*. Fourth Edition. Alexander J. Ellis (Ed.). New York: Longmans, Green & Co.
Hentschel, Franz (Ed.) (1989): *Musik und die Geschichte der Philosophie und Naturwissenschaften im Mittelalter*. Leiden: Brill.
Herbart, Johann Friedrich (1811): *Psychologische Bemerkungen zur Tonlehre*. In: *Sämtliche Werke, in chronologischer Reihenfolge*. Vol. 3. Karl Kehrbach/Otto Flügel (Eds.). Langensalza (1887–1915). Repr. Aalen: Scientia, 1989, pp. 9–118.
Herder, Johann Gottfried (1878): *Viertes Wäldchen*. In: *Sämtliche Werke*. Vol. 4. Bernhard Suphan (Ed.). Berlin: Weidmann, pp. 1–198. Repr. Hildesheim: Olms (1994).
Herder, Johann Gottfried (1800): *Kalligone*. In: *Sämtliche Werke*. Vol. 22. Bernhard Suphan (Ed.). Berlin: Weidmann. Repr. Hildesheim: Olms (1994).
Hermann-Sinai, Susanne (2009): "Musik und Zeit bei Kant". In: *Kant-Studien* 4, pp. 427–454.
Hiebert, Erwin (2014): *The Helmholtz Legacy in Physiological Acoustics*. Cham: Springer International Publishing.

Hirtler, Eva (1989): "Die Musica im Übergang von der scientia mathematica zur scientia media". In: *Musik und die Geschichte der Philosophie und Naturwissenschaften im Mittelalter*. Franz Hentschel (Ed.). Leiden: Brill, pp. 19–37.

Hoffmann, Ernst Theodor Amadeus (1810): "Rezension der 5. Symphonie von Ludwig van Beethoven". In: *Allgemeine Musikalische Zeitung* 12. No. 40, cols. 630–642; No. 41, cols. 652–659.

Hoffmann, Ernst Theodor Amadeus (1917): "Beethoven's Instrumental Music". In: *The Musical Quarterly* 3, No. 1, pp. 127–133.

Höfler, Alois (1912): "Gestalt und Beziehung, Gestalt und Anschauung". In: *Zeitschrift für Psychologie* 60, pp. 161–228.

Höfler, Alois (1921): "Tongestalten und lebende Gestalten". In: *Sitzungsberichte der Akademie der Wissenschaften, philosophisch-historische Klasse* (Wien) 196, pp. 3–94.

Horkheimer Max/Adorno, Theodor Wiesengrund (2002): *Dialectic of Enlightenment*. Stanford: Stanford University Press.

Hornby, Emma (2007), "Preliminary Thoughts about Silence in Early Western Chant". In: *Silence, Music, Silent Music*. Nicky Losseff/Jenny Doctor (Eds.). London: Ashgate, pp. 141–154.

Huffman, Carl A. (Ed.) (2014): *A History of Pythagoreanism*. Cambridge: Cambridge University Press.

Hugh of St. Victor, (1961): *Didascalicon; A Medieval Guide to the Arts*. New York: Columbia University Press.

Huhn, Tom (Ed.) (2004): *The Cambridge Companion to Adorno*. Cambridge: Cambridge University Press.

Huygens, Christiaan (1937): *Mécanique théorique et physique de 1666 à 1695. Huygens à l'Académie Royale des Sciences*. In: *Œuvres complètes*. Vol. 19. Den Haag: Nijhoff.

Iamblichus of Chalcis, (1991): *On the Pythagorean Way of Life. Text, Translation, and Notes*. John M. Dillon/Jackson P. Hershbell (Eds.). Atlanta: Scholar Press.

Ingarden, Roman (1986): *The Work of Music and the Problem of Its Identity*. Berkeley, Los Angeles: University of California Press.

Isidore of Seville (2006): *Etymologies*. Cambridge: Cambridge University Press.

Jankélévitch, Vladimir (2003): *Music and the Ineffable*. Princeton: Princeton University Press.

Jay, Martin (1984): *Adorno*. Cambridge MA: Harvard University Press.

Kant, Immanuel (2002): *Critique of the Power of Judgement*. Paul Guyer (Ed.). Cambridge: Cambridge University Press.

Kant, Immanuel (2006): *Anthropology from a Pragmatic Point of View*. Robert B. Louden (Ed.). Cambridge: Cambridge University Press.

Kassler, Jamie (2001): *Music, Science, Philosophy*. Aldershot: Ashgate.

Kepler, Johannes (1940): *Harmonice mundi libri V.* Max Caspar (Ed.). In: *Gesammelte Werke*. Vol. 4. München: Beck.

Kierkegaard, Søren (1992): *Either Or*. London: Penguin.

Kilwardby, Robert (1976): *De ortu scientiarum*. Albert G. Judy (Ed.). London: British Academy.

Kivy, Peter (1980): *The Corded Shell. Reflections on Musical Expression*. Princeton: Princeton University Press.

Kivy, Peter (1989): *Sound Sentiment. An Essay on the Musical Emotions*. Philadelphia: Temple University Press.

Kivy, Peter (1993): "Kant and the '*Affektenlehre*'. What He Said and What I Wish He Had Said". In: *The Fine Art of Repetition. Essays in the Philosophy of Music.* Cambridge: Cambridge University Press, pp. 250–264.
Kivy, Peter (2001): *New Essays in Musical Understanding.* Oxford: Oxford University Press.
Kivy, Peter (2002): *Introduction to a Philosophy of Music.* Oxford: Clarendon Press.
Kulenkampff, Jens (1987): "Musik bei Kant und Hegel". In: *Hegel-Studien* 22, pp. 143–163.
Kursell, Julia (2008). "Hermann von Helmholtz und Carl Stumpf über Konsonanz und Dissonanz". In: *Berichte zur Wissenschaftsgeschichte* 31, pp. 130–143.
Langer, Susanne (1954): *Philosophy in a New Key. A Study in the Symbolism of Reason, Rite and Art.* Sixth edition. New York: New American Library. Repr. Cambridge MA: Harvard University Press (1957).
Laurand, Valery (2014): "Les effets éthiques de la musique: La lecture problématique de Diogène de Babylone par Philodème de Gadara". In: *Méthexis* 27, pp. 197–214.
Lear, Jonathan (1988): "Katharsis". In: *Phronesis* 33, pp. 297–326.
Leibniz, Gottfried Wilhelm (1734): "Ad Christianum Goldbachium (17 January 1714)". In: *Epistolae ad diversos theologici, juridici, medici, philosophici, mathematici, historici et philologici argumenti.* Christian Kortholt (Ed.). Leipzig: Breitkopf, pp. 241–249.
Leibniz Gottfried Wilhelm (1898): *Principles of Nature and Grace Based on Reason.* In: *The Monadology and Other Philosophical Writings.* Robert Latta (Ed.). Oxford: Oxford University Press, pp. 405–424.
Leibniz, Gottfried Wilhelm (1965a): *Scientia Generalis. Characteristica.* In: *Philosophische Schriften.* Vol. 7. Carl Immanuel Gerhardt (Ed.). Berlin: Weidmann (1890). Repr. Hildesheim: Olms, pp. 3–247.
Leibniz, Gottfried Wilhelm (1965b): *Initia et specimina scientiae novae generalis.* In: *Philosophische Schriften.* Vol. 7. Carl Immanuel Gerhardt (Ed.). Berlin: Weidmann (1890). Repr. Hildesheim: Olms, pp. 57–63.
Leodiensis, Jacobus [Jacques de Liège] (1955): *Speculum musicae, Liber primus.* Roger Bragard (Ed.). Roma: American Institute of Musicology.
Leusing, Reinhard (1993): *Die Stimme als Erkenntnisform. Zu Novalis' Roman "Die Lehrlinge zu Sais".* Stuttgart: Verlag für Wissenschaft und Forschung.
Lévi-Strauss, Claude (1990): *The Naked Man.* Chicago: University of Chicago Press.
Levinson, Jerrold (2011): *Music, Art & Metaphysics: Essays in Philosophical Aesthetics.* Oxford: Oxford University Press.
Lichtenberg, Georg Christoph (1958): *Aphorismen.* Max Rychner (Ed.). Zürich: Manesse.
Lippman, Edward A. (1964): *Musical Thought in Ancient Greece.* New York: Columbia University Press.
Lloyd, Geoffrey Ernest Richard (1966): *Polarity and Analogy. Two Types of Argumentation in Early Greek Thought.* Cambridge: Cambridge University Press.
Looney, Aaron T. (2015): *Vladimir Jankélévitch. The Time of Forgiveness.* New York: Fordham University Press.
Lotze, Rudolf Hermann (1868): *Geschichte der Ästhetik in Deutschland.* München: Cotta.
Luppi, Antonio (1988): *Lo specchio dell'armonia universale. Estetica e musica in Leibniz.* Milano: Angeli.
Macrobius, Ambrosius Theodosius (1990): *Commentary on the Dream of Scipio.* New York: Columbia University Press.

Mainoldi, Ernesto (2001): *Ars musica. La concezione della musica nel Medioevo.* Milano: Rugginenti.
Mann, Thomas (1961): *The Story of a Novel. The Genesis of Doctor Faustus.* Richard Winston/ Clara Winston (Eds.). New York: Knopf.
Mann, Thomas (1996): *Doctor Faustus: The Life of the German Composer Adrian Leverkuhn as Told by a Friend.* London: Vintage.
Martianus Capella (1977): *The Marriage of Philology and Mercury.* William Harris Stahl (Ed.). New York: Columbia University Press.
Martinelli, Riccardo (1999): *Musica e natura. Filosofie del suono (1790–1930).* Milano: Unicopli.
Martinelli, Riccardo (2005): "Acustica chimica/acustica trascendentale. Novalis e la filosofia romantica del suono". In: *Intersezioni* 25, pp. 295–317.
Martinelli, Riccardo (2010): "Ehrenfels, Höfler, Witasek. Zur Musikästhetik der Grazer Schule". In: *Meinong and the Aesthetics of the Graz School.* Venanzio Raspa (Ed.). Berlin: De Gruyter, pp. 169–190.
Martinelli, Riccardo (2014): "Melting musics, fusing sounds. Stumpf, Hornbostel and Comparative Musicology in Berlin". In: *The Making of the Humanities.* Vol. 3: *The Modern Humanities.* Rens Bod/Jaap Maat/Thijs Weststeijn (Eds.). Amsterdam: Amsterdam University Press, pp. 391–401.
Mathiesen, Thomas J. (1984): "Harmonia and Ethos in Ancient Greek Music". In: *The Journal of Musicology* 3, pp. 264–279.
Mathieu, Vittorio (1983): *La voce, la musica, il demoniaco. Con un saggio sull'interpretazione musicale.* Milano: Spirali.
Matravers, Derek (1998): *Art and Emotion.* Oxford: Oxford University Press.
Mauro, Letterio (Ed.) (2001): *La musica nel pensiero medievale.* Ravenna: Longo.
McKinnon, James W. (1978): "Jubal vel Pythagoras, quis sit inventor musicae?" In: *The Musical Quarterly* 64, pp. 1–28.
Mei, Girolamo (1960): *Letters on Ancient and Modern Music to Vincenzo Galilei and Giovanni Bardi.* Claude Victor Palisca (Ed.). Roma: American Institute of Musicology.
Meriani, Angelo (2003): *Sulla musica greca antica. Studi e ricerche.* Napoli: Guida.
Mersenne, Marin (1623): *Quaestiones celeberrimae in Genesim.* Paris: Sébastien Cramoisy.
Mersenne, Marin (1636): *Harmonie universelle.* Paris: Sébastien Cramoisy.
Moravia, Jerome [Hieronymus] de (1864), *Tractatus de musica.* In: *Scriptorum de musica medii aevi.* Edmond de Coussemaker (Ed.). Vol. 1. Paris: Durand, pp. 1–89. Repr. Hildesheim: Olms (1963).
Morelli, Anna (2005): "Est autem tonus minima pars musicae. Trasformazioni del suono nell'Alto Medioevo". In: *Intersezioni* 25, pp. 185–208.
Morelli, Anna (2007): *Il "Musica disciplina" di Aureliano di Rêome.* Udine: Forum.
Moretti, Giampiero (1991): *L'estetica di Novalis. Analogia e principio poetico nella profezia romantica.* Torino: Rosenberg & Sellier.
Moro, Nadia (2002): *Der musikalische Herbart: Harmonie und Kontrapunkt als Gegenstände der Psychologie und der Ästhetik.* Würzburg: Königshausen & Neumann.
Most, Glenn (2008): "Die Geburt der Tragödie". In: *Wagner und Nietzsche. Kultur, Werk, Wirkung.* Stefan Lorenz Sorgner/H. James Birk (Eds.) Hamburg: Rowohlt, pp. 420–426
Moutsopoulos, Evanghelos (1989): *La musique dans l'oeuvre de Platon.* Paris: PUF.

Muris, Johannes de (1972): *Notitia artis musicae*. Ulrich Michels (Ed.). Roma: American Institute of Musicology.
Musica et Scolica enchiriadis (1981): Martin Gerbert/Hans Schmid (Eds.). München: Beck.
Nachtsheim, Stephan (1997): *Zu Immanuel Kant Musikästhetik. Texte, Kommentare und Abhandlungen*. Chemnitz: Schröder.
Nancy, Jean-Luc (2007): *Listening*. New York: Fordham University Press.
Neubauer, John (1986): *The Emancipation of Music from Language. Departure from Mimesis in Eighteenth-Century Aesthetics*. New Haven-London: Yale University Press.
Newton, Isaac (1687): *The Principia. Mathematical Principles of Natural Philosophy*. I. Bernard Cohen/Anne Whitman/Julia Budenz (Eds.). Oakland: University of California Press (1999).
Newton, Isaac (1966): *Scholia classica*. English translation in: "Newton and the 'Pipes of Pan'". James E. McGuire/Piyo M. Rattansi. In: *Notes and Records of the Royal Society of London* 21, pp. 108–143.
Nicomachus of Gerasa (1984): *Enchiridion*. In: *Greek Musical Writings*. Andrew Barker (Ed.). Vol. 2: *Harmonic and Acoustic Theory*. Cambridge: Cambridge University Press, pp. 247–269.
Nietzsche, Friedrich (1911a): "The Case Of Wagner: A Musician's Problem". In: *The Case Of Wagner, Nietzsche Contra Wagner, and Selected Aphorisms*. Anthony M. Ludovici (Ed.). Edinburgh & London: Foulis, pp. 1–52.
Nietzsche, Friedrich (1911b): "Nietzsche contra Wagner. The Brief of a Psychologist". In: *The Case Of Wagner, Nietzsche Contra Wagner, and Selected Aphorisms*. Anthony M. Ludovici (Ed.). Edinburgh & London: Foulis, pp. 53–82.
Nietzsche, Friedrich (1979): "On Truth and Lies in a Nonmoral Sense". In: *Philosophy and Truth. Selections From Nietzsche's Notebooks of the Early 1870's*. Daniel Breazeale (Ed.). New Jersey: Humanity Press.
Nietzsche, Friedrich (1992): *Frammenti postumi 1869–1874*. Vol. 3, tomo 1. In: *Opere di Friedrich Nietzsche*. Giorgio Colli/Mazzino Montinari (Eds.). Milano: Adelphi.
Nietzsche, Friedrich (1997): *Richard Wagner in Bayreuth*. In: *Untimely Meditations*. Daniel Breazeale (Ed.). Cambridge: Cambridge University Press.
Nietzsche, Friedrich (1999): *The Birth of Tragedy and Other Writings*. Raymond Geuss/Ronald Speirs (Eds.). Cambridge: Cambridge University Press.
Nietzsche, Friedrich (2001): *The Gay Science. With a Prelude in German Rhymes and an Appendix of Songs*. Bernard Williams (Ed.). Cambridge: Cambridge University Press.
Nietzsche, Friedrich (2002): *Beyond Good and Evil Prelude to a Philosophy of the Future*. Rolf-Peter Horstmann/Judith Norman (Eds.). Cambridge: Cambridge University Press.
Nietzsche, Friedrich (2009): *Writings from the Early Notebooks*. Raymond Geuss/Alexander Nehamas (Eds.). Cambridge: Cambridge University Press.
Niro, Piero (2008): *Ludwig Wittgenstein e la musica*. Napoli: ESI.
Novalis [Hardenberg, Friedrich von] (1968): *Fragmente und Studien 1799–1800*. In: *Schriften. Die Werke Friedrich von Hardenbergs*. Vol 3. Paul Kluckhohn/Richard Samuel (Eds.). Darmstadt: Wissenschaftliche Bichgesellschaft, pp. 556–691.
Novalis [Hardenberg, Friedrich von] (1997): *Philosophical Writings*. Margaret M. Stoljar (Ed.). Albany: SUNY Press.
Novalis [Hardenberg, Friedrich von] (2003): *Fichte Studies*. Jane Kneller (Ed.). Cambridge: Cambridge University Press.

Novalis [Hardenberg, Friedrich von] (2007): *Notes for a Romantic Encyclopaedia. Das Allgemeine Brouillon*. David W. Wood (Ed.). Albany: SUNY Press.
Nowak, Adolf (1971): *Hegels Musikästhetik*. Regensburg: Bosse.
Ovid, Publius Naso (1951a): *Metamorphoses*. Vol. 1: Books 1–14. Frank Justus Miller (Ed.). Loeb Classical Library No. 42. Cambridge MA: Harvard University Press.
Ovid, Publius Naso (1951b): *Metamorphoses*. Vol. 2: Books 9–15. Frank Justus Miller (Ed.). Loeb Classical Library No. 43. Cambridge MA: Harvard University Press.
Paddison, Max (1993): *Adorno's Aesthetics of Music*. Cambridge: Cambridge University Press.
Palisca, Claude Victor (1960): "Introduction". In: G. Mei, *Letters on Ancient and Modern Music to Vincenzo Galilei and Giovanni Bardi*. Claude Victor Palisca (Ed.). Roma: American Institute of Musicology, 1960.
Palisca, Claude Victor (1985): *Humanism in Italian Renaissance Musical Thought*. New Haven & London: Yale University Press.
Palisca, Claude Victor (2001): *Johannes Cotto [Johannes Affligemensis]*. In: *The New Grove Dictionary of Music and Musicians*. Vol. 13. Oxford: Oxford University Press, pp. 137–138.
Palisca, Claude Victor (2006): *Music and Ideas in the Sixteenth and Seventeenth Centuries*. Urbana & Chicago: University of Illinois Press.
Palisca, Claude Victor (Ed.) (1989): *The Florentine Camerata. Documentary Studies and Translations*. New Haven: Yale University Press.
Palmer, Peter (1985): "Translator's Preface". In: Ernst Bloch, *Essays on the Philosophy of Music*. Peter Palmer/David Drew (Eds.). Cambridge: Cambridge University Press, pp. vii–ix.
Panaiotidi, Elvira (2014): "'The Same Thing in Another Medium': Plotinus' Notion of Music". In: *Ancient Philosophy* 34, pp. 393–413.
Pangrazi, Tiziana (2009): *La "Musurgia universalis" di Athanasius Kircher: contenuti, fonti, terminologia*. Firenze: Olschki.
Panti, Cecilia (1989): "Robert Grosseteste's Theory of Sound". In: *Musik und die Geschichte der Philosophie und Naturwissenschaften im Mittelalter*. Franz Hentschel (Ed.). Leiden: Brill, pp. 3–17.
Panti, Cecilia (2008): *Filosofia della musica. Tarda Antichità e Medioevo*. Roma: Carocci.
Pelosi, Francesco (2010): *Plato on Music, Soul and Body*. Cambridge: Cambridge University Press.
Philodemus of Gadara (2007): *Sur la musique (De musica)*. Daniel Delattre (Ed.). Paris: Les Belles Lettres.
Pirrotta, Nino (1984): *Musica tra Medioevo e Rinascimento*. Torino: Einaudi.
Plato (1921): *Sophist*. In: *Theaetetus. Sophist*. Harold North Fowler (Ed.). Loeb Classical Library No. 123. Cambridge MA: Harvard University Press, pp. 264–459.
Plato (1924a): *Laches*. In: *Laches. Protagoras. Meno. Euthydemus*. Walter Rangeley Maitland Lamb (Ed.). Loeb Classical Library No. 165. Cambridge MA: Harvard University Press, pp. 3–83.
Plato (1924b): *Euthydemus*. In: *Laches. Protagoras. Meno. Euthydemus*. Walter Rangeley Maitland Lamb (Ed.). Loeb Classical Library No. 165. Cambridge MA: Harvard University Press, pp. 378–505.
Plato (1925): *Philebus*. In: *Statesman. Philebus. Ion*. Harold North Fowler (Ed.). Loeb Classical Library No. 164. Cambridge MA: Harvard University Press, pp. 202–399.

Plato (1926a): *Laws*. Vol. 1: Books 1–6. Robert Gregg Bury (Ed.). Loeb Classical Library No. 187. Cambridge MA: Harvard University Press.
Plato (1926b): *Laws*. Vol. 2: Books 7–12. Robert Gregg Bury (Ed.). Loeb Classical Library No. 192. Cambridge MA: Harvard University Press.
Plato (1929a): *Timaeus*. In: *Timaeus. Critias. Cleitophon. Menexenus. Epistles*. Robert Gregg Bury (Ed.). Loeb Classical Library No. 234. Cambridge MA: Harvard University Press, pp. 16–253.
Plato (1929b): *Menexenus*. In: *Timaeus. Critias. Cleitophon. Menexenus. Epistles*. Robert Gregg Bury (Ed.). Loeb Classical Library No. 234. Cambridge MA: Harvard University Press, pp. 332–381.
Plato (1937a): *Republic*. Vol. 1: Books 1–5. Chris Emlyn-Jones/William Preddy (Eds.). Loeb Classical Library No. 237. Cambridge MA: Harvard University Press.
Plato (1937b): *Republic*. Vol. 2: Books 6–10. Chris Emlyn-Jones/William Preddy (Eds.). Loeb Classical Library No. 276. Cambridge MA: Harvard University Press.
Plato (1938a): *Phaedo*. In: *Euthyphro. Apology. Crito. Phaedo. Phaedrus*. Chris Emlyn-Jones/William Preddy (Eds.). Loeb Classical Library No. 36. Cambridge MA: Harvard University Press, pp. 200–403.
Plato (1938b): *Phaedrus*. In: *Euthyphro. Apology. Crito. Phaedo. Phaedrus*. Chris Emlyn-Jones/William Preddy (Eds.). Loeb Classical Library No. 36. Cambridge MA: Harvard University Press, pp. 413–579.
Plato (1953): *Symposium*. In: *Lysis, Symposium, Gorgias*. Walter Rangeley Maitland Lamb (Ed.). Loeb Classical Library No. 166. Cambridge MA: Harvard University Press, pp. 80–245.
Plotinus (2014a): *Enneads*. Arthur Hilary Armstrong (Ed.). Vol. 2. Cambridge MA: Harvard University Press.
Plotinus (2014b): *Enneads*. Arthur Hilary Armstrong (Ed.). Vol. 5. Cambridge MA: Harvard University Press.
Plotinus (2014c): *Enneads*. Arthur Hilary Armstrong (Ed.). Vol. 6. Cambridge MA: Harvard University Press.
Poirier, John C. (2010): *The Tongues of Angels. The Concept of Angelic Languages in Classical Jewish and Christian Texts*. Tübingen: Mohr.
Pratt, Carroll C. (1968): *The Meaning of Music. A Study in Psychological Aesthetics*. New York: Johnson.
Ptolemy, Claudius (1984): *Harmonics*. In: *Greek Musical Writings*. Andrew Barker (Ed.). Vol. 2: *Harmonic and Acoustic Theory*. Cambridge: Cambridge University Press, pp. 275–391.
Rameau, Jean-Philippe (1722): *Traité de l'harmonie réduite à ses principes naturels*. Paris: Ballard.
Rameau, Jean-Philippe (1726): *Nouveau système de musique théorique*. Paris: Ballard.
Rameau, Jean-Philippe (1737): *Génération harmonique, ou traité de musique théorique et pratique*. Paris: Prault.
Rameau, Jean-Philippe (1750): *Démonstration du principe de l'harmonie*. Paris: Durand & Fissot.
Rameau, Jean-Philippe (1760): *Code de musique pratique*. Paris: Imprimerie Royale.
Rispoli, Gioia Maria (1974): "Filodemo sulla musica". In: *Cronache Ercolanesi* 4, pp. 57–87.
Ritter, Johann Wilhelm (2010): *Key Texts of Johann Wilhelm Ritter (1776–1810) on the Science and Art of Nature*. Jocelyn Holland (Ed.). Boston: Leiden.

Robinson, Jenefer (1994): "The Expression and Arousal of Emotion in Music". In: *Journal of Aesthetics and Art Criticism* 52, pp. 180–189.
Rocconi, Eleonora (2003): *Le parole delle muse. La formazione del lessico tecnico musicale nella Grecia antica*. Roma: Quasar.
Rousseau, Jean-Jacques (1753): *Lettre sur la Musique Françoise*. In: *Œuvres complètes*. Vol. 5: *Écrits sur la musique, la langue et le théâtre*. Bernard Gagnebin/Marcel Raimond/Samuel Baud-Bovy (Eds.). Paris: Gallimard (1995), pp. 289–328.
Rousseau, Jean-Jacques (1966): *On the Origin of Language*. Chicago: University of Chicago Press.
Rousseau, Jean-Jacques (2002). *On the Inequality among Mankind: Reply to a topic set by the Academy of Dijon in 1751: "What is the Origin of Inequality among Mankind and is it justified by Natural Law?"* G.D.H. Cole (Ed.). https://ocw.mit.edu/courses/literature/21 l-449-end-of-nature-spring-2002/readings/lecture10.pdf, visited on 13 June 2019.
Rousseau, Jean-Jacques (2008): *Dictionnaire de musique. Une édition critique*. Claude Dauphin (Ed.). Bern: Lang.
Sachs, Klaus-Jürgen (1989): "Zur Funktion der Berufungen auf das achte Buch von Aristoteles' Politik im Musiktraktaten des 15. Jahrhunderts". In: *Musik und die Geschichte der Philosophie und Naturwissenschaften im Mittelalter*. Franz Hentschel (Ed.). Leiden: Brill, pp. 269–290.
Sauveur, Joseph (1701): "Système general des intervalles des sons, & son application à tous les systèmes & à tous les instrumens de musique". In: *Mémoires de l'Academie Royale des Sciences*, pp. 390–482.
Schelling, Freidrich Wilhelm Joseph (1989): *The Philosophy of Art*. Douglas W. Scott (Ed.). Minneapolis: University of Minnesota Press.
Schlegel, Friedrich (1967): *Athenäum-Fragmente*. In: *Kritische Friedrich-Schlegel-Ausgabe*. Vol. 2: *Charakteristiken und Kritiken I (1796–1801)*. Ernst Behler et al. (Eds.). München: Schöningh.
Schlegel, Friedrich (1981): *Fragmente zur Poesie und Litteratur II. Und Ideen zu Gedichten* [*Literary Notebooks*]. In: *Kritische Friedrich-Schlegel-Ausgabe*. Vol. 16: *Fragmente zur Poesie und Litteratur*. Ernst Behler et al. (Eds.). München: Schöningh, pp. 253–338.
Schmidt, James (2004): "Mephistopheles in Hollywood. Adorno, Mann, and Schoenberg". In: *The Cambridge Companion to Adorno*. Tom Huhn (Ed.). Cambridge: Cambridge University Press, pp. 148–221.
Schopenhauer, Arthur (1969a): *The World as Will and Representation*. Vol. 1. New York: Dover.
Schopenhauer, Arthur (1969b): *The World as Will and Representation*. Vol. 2. New York: Dover.
Schopenhauer, Arthur (2014): "Fragments for the History of Philosophy". In: *Parerga and Paralipomena. Short Philosophical Essays*. Vol. 1. Sabine Roehr/Christopher Janaway (Eds.). Cambridge: Cambridge University Press, pp. 35–148.
Schubert, Mary Hurst (1970): *Wilhelm Heinrich Wackenroder's Confessions and Fantasies: Translated and Annotated with a Critical Introduction*. Ph.D. Diss.: Stanford University.
Scotus Eriugena, Johannes (1939): *Annotationes in Marcianum*. Cora Lutz (Ed.). Cambridge MA: Medieval Academy Books.
Scruton, Roger (1997): *The Aesthetics of Music*. Oxford: Oxford University Press.
Scruton, Roger (2009a): "Wittgenstein on Music". In: *Understanding Music*. London: Continuum, pp. 33–42.

Scruton, Roger (2009b): "Why Read Adorno?". In: *Understanding Music*. London: Continuum, pp. 204–227.
Sextus Empiricus (1986): *Against the Musicians*. Denise Davidson Greaves (Ed.). Lincoln: University of Nebraska Press.
Simon, Artur (Ed.) (2000): *Das Berliner Phonogramm-Archiv 1900–2000. Sammlungen der traditionellen Musik der Welt*. Berlin: Verlag für Wissenschaft und Bildung.
Sörbom, Göran (1994): "Aristotle on Music as Representation". In: *Journal of Aesthetics and Art Criticism* 52, pp. 37–46.
Sorgner, Stefan Lorenz (Ed.) (2011): *Music in German Philosophy. An Introduction*. Chicago: University of Chicago Press.
Sorgner, Stefan Lorenz/Birk, H. James (Eds.) (2008): *Wagner und Nietzsche. Kultur, Werk, Wirkung*. Hamburg: Rowohlt.
Sorgner, Stefan Lorenz/Schramm, Michael (Eds.) (2010): *Musik in der antiken Philosophie. Eine Einführung*. Würzburg: Königshausen & Neumann.
Spitzer, Leo (1963): *Classical and Christian Ideas of World Harmony. Prolegomena to an Interpretation of the Word "Stimmung"*. Baltimore: Johns Hopkins Press.
Starobinski, Jean (1971): *Jean-Jacques Rousseau. Transaprency and Obstruction*. Arthur Goldhammer (Ed.). Chicago: University of Chicago Press.
Stumpf, Carl (1890): *Tonpsychologie*. Vol. 2. Leipzig: Hirzel.
Stumpf, Carl (1896): "Geschichte des Consonanzbegriffs. Erster Teil: Die Definition der Consonanz im Altertum". In: *Abhandlungen der philosophisch-philologischen Classe der Königlich Bayerischen Akademie der Wissenschaften*, pp. 1–85.
Stumpf, Carl (2012): *The Origins of Music*. David Trippett (Ed.). Oxford: Oxford University Press.
Sulzer, Johann Georg (1771): *Allgemeine Theorie der schönen Künste*. 2 Bände. Leipzig: Weidmann & Reich.
Szabó, István (1977): *Geschichte der mechanischen Prinzipien und ihrer wichtigsten Anwendungen*. Basel-Stuttgart: Birkhäuser.
Tatarkiewicz, Władysław (1980): *A History Of Six Ideas. An Essay In Aesthetics*. The Hague: Nijhoff.
Tedeschini Lalli, Marta (1993): *"Vom Musikalisch-Schönen" di Eduard Hanslick dalla prima alla nona edizione*. Firenze: Passigli.
Thaler, Naly (2015): "Plato on the Philosophical Benefits of Musical Education". In: *Phronesis* 60, pp. 410–435.
Thesaurus Musicarum Latinarum (1990): http://www.chmtl.indiana.edu/tml/, visited on 13 June 2019.
Truesdell, Clifford Ambrose (1960): "The Rational Mechanics of Flexible or Elastic Bodies: 1638–1788". In: *Leonhardi Euleri Opera Omnia*. Series tertia, vol. 9. Andreas Speiser (Ed.). Zürich: Füssli, pp. 7–428.
Turner, Steven R. (1977): "The Ohm-Seebeck Dispute, Hermann von Helmholtz, and the Origins of Physiological Acoustics". In: *The British Journal for the History of Science* 10, pp. 1–24.
Ullmann, Dietrich (1996): *Chladni und die Entwicklung der Akustik von 1750–1860*. Basel: Birkhäuser.
Vogel, Stephan (1994): "Sensation of Tone, Perception of Sound, and Empiricism. Helmholtz's Physiological Acoustics". In: *Hermann von Helmholtz and the Foundations of Nineteenth-*

Century Science. David Cahan (Ed.). Berkeley: University of California Press, pp. 258–287.

Voigt, Boris (2007): "Musik und Musikverstehen bei Ludwig Wittgenstein". In: *Zeitschrift für Ästhetik und allgemeine Kunstwissenschaft* 52, pp. 119–131.

Wackenroder, Wilhelm Heinrich (1970a): *Confessions from the Heart of an Art-Loving Friar*. In: *Wilhelm Heinrich Wackenroder's Confessions and Fantasies: Translated and Annotated with a Critical Introduction*. Mary Hurst Schubert (Ed.). Ph.D. Diss.: Stanford University, pp. 145–303.

Wackenroder, Wilhelm Heinrich (1970b), *Phantasies on Art for Friends of Art*. In: *Wilhelm Heinrich Wackenroder's Confessions and Fantasies: Translated and Annotated with a Critical Introduction*. Mary Hurst Schubert (Ed.). Ph.D. Diss.: Stanford University, pp. 304–378.

Walker, Daniel Pickering (1978): *Studies in Musical Science in the Late Renaissance*. Leiden: Brill.

Wallace, Robert W./MacLachlan, Bonnie (Eds.) (1991): *Harmonia mundi. Musica e filosofia nell'antichità*. Roma: Edizioni dell'Ateneo.

Werner, Eric (1942): "The Psalmodic Formula Neannoe and Its Origin", *The Musical Quarterly* 28, No. 1, pp. 93–99.

Wilkinson, Lancelot Patrick (1938): "Philodemus on Ethos in Music". In: *The Classical Quarterly* 32, pp. 174–181.

Wiora, Walter (1965): "Die Musik im Weltbild der deutschen Romantik". In: Walter Salmen, *Beiträge zur Geschichte der Musikanschauung im 19. Jahrhundert*. Regensburg: Bosse, pp. 11–60.

Witasek, Stephan (1904): *Grundzüge der allgemeinen Ästhetik*. Leipzig: Barth.

Witasek, Stephan (1906): "Zur allgemeinen psychologischen Analyse des musikalischen Genusses". In: *Bericht über den zweiten Kongress der internationalen Musikgesellschaft*. Leipzig: Breitkopf & Härtel, pp. 111–128.

Witkin, Robert W. (1998): *Adorno on Music*. London: Routledge.

Wittgenstein, Ludwig (1953): *Philosophical Investigations*. Oxford: Basil Blackwell.

Wittgenstein, Ludwig (1961): *Tractatus logico-philosophicus* and *Notebooks 1914–1916*. New York: Harper.

Wittgenstein, Ludwig (1965): *The Blue and Brown Books*. New York: Harper.

Wittgenstein, Ludwig (1974): *Philosophical Grammar: Part I, The Proposition, and Its Sense, Part II, On Logic and Mathematics, Parts 1–2*. Berkeley: University of California Press.

Wittgenstein, Ludwig (1989): *Culture and Value. A Selection from Posthumous Remains*. Georg Henrik von Wright (Ed.). Oxford: Basil Blackwell.

Wittgenstein, Ludwig (2012): *Big Typescript TS 213*. Hoboken: Wiley-Blackwell.

Zangwill, Nick (2007): "Music, Metaphor, and Emotion". In: *Journal of Aesthetics and Art Criticism* 65, pp. 391–400.

Zanoncelli, Luisa (1977): "La filosofia musicale di Aristide Quintiliano". In: *Quaderni Urbinati di Cultura Classica* 24, pp. 51–93.

Zarlino, Gioseffo (1558): *Istitutioni harmoniche*. Venezia: de' Franceschi.

Zarlino, Gioseffo (1588): *Soppliменti musicali*. Venezia: de' Franceschi.

Zoltai, Dénes (1970): *Ethos und Affekt. Geschichte der philosophischen Musikästhetik von den Anfängen bis zu Hegel*. Berlin: Akademie.

Index of Names

Abert, Hermann   12, 25
Adelard of Bath   36
Adorno, Theodor Wiesengrund   2f., 6, 70, 99, 108, 110–118, 141
Adrastus   35
Al-Farabi   36
Albert the Great [Albertus Magnus]   37
Alembert, Jean-Baptiste Le Rond [d']   58, 72f.
Alexander the Great   101
Ambrose [Ambrosius, Aurelius]   32
Ammann, Peter J.   48
Aquinas, Thomas   37
Arbo, Alessandro   126
Archytas Aristarchus
Aristides Quintilian   26, 28
Aristophanes   11
Aristotle   6–8, 10, 15–22, 33, 36–38, 49, 56, 119
Aristoxenus
Ash, Mitchell Graham   94
Auger, Léon   56
Augst, Bertrand   50
Augustine [Aurelius Augustinus]   29
Aurelian of Rêome   34f.

Bach, Johann Sebastian   101, 108, 112
Bacon, Francis   41f.
Bailhache, Patrice   49, 55
Barbera, André   27
Bardi, Giovanni de'   42
Barker, Andrew   5, 7, 20–22, 27, 35
Baumgarten, Alexander Gottlieb   55
Beeckman, Issac   45, 48, 50
Beethoven, Ludwig van   82f., 97, 100–102, 108, 110–114, 116, 118, 121, 128, 138
Beierwaltes, Werner   30
Benedetti, Giovanni Battista   45
Benjamin, Walter   76
Bergson, Henri   119
Berlioz, Hector   71
Bernoulli, Daniel   73
Besseler, Heinrich   50

Bettetini, Maria   30
Bielitz, Mathias   35
Bizet, Georges   103f.
Bloch, Ernst   38, 106–110, 116
Boccadoro, Brenno   41
Boethius, Anicius Manlius Severinus   9, 27–29, 33–36, 38–40
Boghossian, Paul   140
Bonaventure [Giovanni di Fidanza]   34
Brahms, Johannes   125
Brancacci, Aldo   11f., 14, 20, 25
Brentano, Franz   93f., 96, 119–121
Brisson, Luc   10, 13
Bruckner, Anton   108
Brüllmann, Philip   19
Budd, Malcolm   94, 129f.
Burke, Edmund   68f.
Burkert, Walter   6

Caccini, Giulio   41
Campanella, Tommaso   44
Cardano, Girolamo   41
Carnap, Rudolf   128f.
Carr, David   135f.
Carré, Louis   72
Casini, Paolo   45
Cassiodorus, Flavius Magnus Aurelius   34
Cassirer, Ernst   128, 130
Cattin, Giulio   32
Cernuschi, Alain   58
Chadwick, Henry   28
Chalcidius   13, 33
Chamberlain, David   29
Charrak, André   59
Chladni, Ernst Florens Friedrich   4, 72–77, 93
Christensen, Thomas   56f.
Church, Alonzo   32, 128
Cicero, Marcus Tullius   25–27
Cohen, H. Floris   42, 45f., 50
Colli, Giorgio   8
Columbus, Cristopher   138
Connus   11

Conrad, Waldemar   120
Coussemaker, Edmond de   34
Cristiani, Marta   29
Croce, Benedetto   138

Dahlhaus, Carl   66, 71, 98, 102
Damon of Athens   8, 12
Dante
Davies, Stephen   135, 137
Dear, Peter   49
Debussy, Claude   123
Delattre, Daniel   25
Deleuze, Gilles   123
Democritus   25
Descartes, René   45, 49–52, 57, 68, 73
Diderot, Denis   58f., 72f.
Didymus
Diels, Hermann   5, 7f.
Diogenes Laertius   10
Diogenes of Babylon   25
Doctor, Jenny   75
Dostrovsky, Sigalia   43, 56, 73
Drake, Stillman   43
Dyer, Joseph   36

Ehrenfels, Christian von   94
Empedocles   8
Euclid   27, 33, 36, 40
Euler, Leonhard   55f., 64, 69, 73
Euripides   62

Fabbri, Natacha   44, 48, 52
Fauré, Gabriel   124
Fechner, Gustav Theodor   92
Ferrara, Lawrence   85
Fichte, Johann Gottlieb   76
Ficino, Marsilio   41, 44
Fisette, Denis   119
Fludd, Robert   48
Folli, Laura   32
Fontenelle, Bernard le Bovier de   57
Franklin, Benjamin   75
Freud, Sigmund   70
Fubini, Enrico   58, 60, 95
Fugate, Joe K.   65

Gabriel, Gottfried   70

Gaffurius, Franchinus   41
Galilei, Galileo   42–44, 46f., 49
Galilei, Vincenzo   41–45, 73
Gallo, F. Alberto   35, 38
Gaudentius   9
Geiger, Moritz   120
Georgiades, Trasybulos   22
Gerard of Cremona   36
Gibson, Sophie   21
Giordanetti, Piero   64
Glaucus of Rhegium   7
Goehr, Lydia   137
Goethe, Johann Wolfgang   76, 117
Golden, Leon   19
Goodman, Nelson   136–138
Görres, Johann Joseph   76
Gouk, Penelope   42, 45
Gozza, Paolo   40, 42, 47
Gracyk, Theodore   131
Greaves, Denise Davidson   25
Gregory the Great [Gregorius I]   34
Grey, Thomas   95
Grocheio, Johannes de   38
Grosseteste, Robert   36
Guattari, Félix   123
Guicciardini, Niccolò   45
Guido of Arezzo   35, 38
Gundisalvi [Gundissalinus], Dominicus   36
Gurney, Edmund   94
Guyer, Paul   63

Halm, August   108
Hanslick, Eduard   92, 95–99, 132
Haydn, Joseph   79, 83, 136
Haym, Rudolf   81
Hegel, Georg Wilhelm Friedrich   65, 72, 75f.,
   87–93, 96, 108, 112, 114–118
Heidegger, Martin   121f.
Heimsoeth, Heinz   90f.
Heller-Roazen, Daniel   9
Hellwag, Christoph Friedrich   64
Helmholtz, Hermann von   8, 75, 92–95, 105,
   119
Heraclitus   5
Herbart, Johann Friedrich   85, 92–94, 96
Herder, Johann Gottfried   65, 71f., 74, 76,
   89, 91

Hering, Ewald 94
Hermann-Sinai, Susanne 69
Hiebert, Erwin 93
Hildegard of Bingen 34
Hippasus
Hire, Philippe de la 72
Hirtler, Eva 37
Hoffmann, Ernst Theodor Amadeus 82 f.
Höfler, Alois 120 f., 138
Homer 62
Horkheimer, Max 117
Hornbostel, Erich Moritz von 119
Hornby, Emma 32
Huffman, Carl A. 6
Hugh of St. Victor 36
Husserl, Edmund 119–121
Huygens, Christiaan 43, 45

Iamblichus
Ingarden, Roman 121
Isidore of Seville 34

Jankélévitch, Vladimir 3, 119, 122–125
Jay, Martin 113
Jean Paul
Johannes Affligemensis [Johannes Cotto] 37
Josquin des Prez 116
Julian [the Apostate] 62

Kania, Andrew 131
Kant, Immanuel 9, 63–70, 72, 76 f., 79, 83, 90 f., 93, 95, 99, 101, 105, 113, 128
Kassler, Jamie 55
Kepler, Johannes 44 f., 48
Kierkegaard, Søren 86 f.
Kilwardby, Robert 36 f.
Kircher, Athanasius 47 f., 55
Kivy, Peter 68, 131–135, 137 f., 140
Klemperer, Otto 106
Köhler, Wolfgang 129
Körner, Christian G. 102
Kranz, Walther 5, 7 f.
Kulenkampff, Jens 90
Kursell, Julia 119

Lagrange, Joseph-Louis 73
Lange, Friedrich Albert 105

Langer, Susanne 125, 127–130
Lasus of Hermione 7
Laurand, Valery 24
Lear, Jonathan 18
Leibniz, Gottfried Wilhelm 8, 50, 53–55, 67, 84, 94
Leodiensis, Jacobus [Jacques de Liège]
Leusing, Reinhard 77
Lévi-Strauss, Claude 130 f.
Levinson, Jerrold 129, 134 f., 137 f., 140
Lichtenberg, Georg Christoph 69 f., 75
Lippman, Edward A. 5
Lipps, Theodor 92, 121
Liszt, Franz 71
Lloyd, Geoffrey Ernest Richard 6
Looney, Aaron T. 123
Lotze, Rudolf Hermann 92, 98 f., 119
Luppi, Antonio 53
Luther, Martin 116

Mach, Ernst 94
MacLachlan, Bonnie 5
Macrobius, Ambrosius Theodosius 26 f., 33, 45
Mahler, Gustav 125
Mainoldi, Ernesto 34
Malebranche, Nicholas 59
Mann, Thomas 70, 75 f., 110 f.
Martianus Capella 28, 35
Martinelli, Riccardo 76, 92, 119–121
Mathiesen, Thomas J. 26
Mathieu, Vittorio 87
Matravers, Derek 133 f.
McKinnon, James W. 47
Mei, Girolamo 41
Meinong, Alexius 119 f.
Meriani, Angelo 24
Mersenne, Marin 8, 45, 48 f., 52, 55
Moravia, Jerome [Hieronymus] de 38
Moravia, Jerome of 37
Morelli, Anna 35
Moretti, Giampiero 77
Moro, Nadia 93
Most, Glenn 17, 33, 70, 93, 99 f.
Moutsopoulos, Evanghelos 12 f.
Mozart, Wolfgang Amadeus 79, 83, 86, 108, 112, 122, 128, 133

Müller, Johannes 93
Muris, Johannes de 38

Nachtsheim, Stephan 63
Nancy, Jean-Luc 125
Neubauer, John 57
Newton, Isaac 44f., 57, 73, 93f., 138
Nicomachus of Gerasa 9, 26f., 43
Nietzsche, Friedrich 3, 62, 70, 76, 99–105, 107, 111f., 122
Niro, Piero 126, 128
Novalis
Nowak, Adolf 89

Ohm, Georg Simon 93
Ørsted, Hans Christian 75f.
Overbeck, Franz 102
Ovid, Publius Naso 8, 107

Paddison, Max 115
Palisca, Claude Victor 37, 40f.
Palmer, Peter 106
Panaiotidi, Elvira 26
Pangrazi, Tiziana 48
Panti, Cecilia 29, 36
Peirce, Charles Sanders 138
Pelosi, Francesco 12
Pergolesi, Giovanni Battista 60
Peri, Jacopo 40
Perillo, Graziano 29
Philodemus 24
Philolaus 7
Pico
Pirrotta, Nino 35, 37
Plato 5–7, 10–16, 18f., 21, 23f., 26, 28, 41, 61f., 99, 118, 122
Plotinus 26
Plutarch 40
Poirier, John C. 32
Porphyry 20
Pratt, Carroll C. 130
Proclus 44
Ptolemy, Claudius 27f., 33
Pythagoras 3, 5–10, 37f., 43–45, 47, 58, 84, 94

Quine, Willard van Orman 128

Rameau, Jean-Philippe 57–59, 72, 75
Ravel, Maurice 124
Regino of Prüm 34f.
Reichardt, Johann Friedrich 80
Remigius of Auxerre 35
Riccati, Giordano 73
Rispoli, Gioia Maria 24
Ritter, Johann Wilhelm 76
Robartes, Francis 56
Robinson, Jenefer 134
Rocconi, Eleonora 5, 24
Rousseau, Jean-Jacques 3, 56, 58–63, 72, 78, 99, 125
Russell, Bertrand 129

Sachs, Curt 119
Sachs, Klaus-Jürgen 36
Satie, Erik [Éric Alfred Leslie] 124
Sauveur, Joseph 53, 56f., 72
Schelling, Friedrich Wilhelm Joseph 78f., 107
Schlegel, Friedrich 80
Schmidt, James 110
Schoenberg, Arnold 111, 118
Schopenhauer, Arthur 75, 79, 83–86, 96, 100–102, 104, 107, 110, 122
Schramm, Michael 19
Schubert, Franz 71, 79, 108, 114
Schütz, Heinrich 112
Scotus Eriugena, Johannes 35
Scruton, Roger 125, 137–141
Seebeck, August 93
Sextus
Simon, Artur 119
Simplicius
Socrates 10f., 15
Sörbom, Göran 18
Sorgner, Stefan Lorenz 19, 99
Spitzer, Leo 5, 65
Starobinski, Jean 59
Stravinsky, Igor 111, 124
Stumpf, Carl 17, 92, 94, 119
Sulzer, Johann Georg 63
Szabó, István 74

Tartini, Giuseppe 58
Tatarkiewicz, Władysław 25

Index of Names

Tedeschini Lalli, Marta 96
Thaler, Naly 13
Theon of Smyrna 7, 35
Tieck, Ludwig 71, 79, 81
Tiedemann, Rolf 111
Truesdell, Clifford Ambrose 73
Turner, Steven R. 93

Ullmann, Dietrich 75

Varro, Marcus Terentius 28
Verdi, Giuseppe 133
Vincent of Beauvais 37
Vogel, Stephan 93
Voigt, Boris 125

Wackenroder, Wilhelm Heinrich 71, 79–83
Wagner, Richard 97, 99–105, 108, 121, 133
Walker, Daniel Pickering 42, 46
Wallace, Robert W. 5

Wallis, John 56
Weber, Wilhelm 93
Webern, Anton 112
Werner, Eric 32
Wertheimer, Max 119
Wilkinson, Lancelot Patrick 25
William of Moerbeke 37
Wiora, Walter 71
Witasek, Stephan 121
Witkin, Robert W. 111, 115
Wittgenstein, Ludwig 125–129, 135
Wolff, Christian 55, 70
Wundt, Wilhlem 92

Zangwill, Nick 135
Zanoncelli, Luisa 26
Zarlino, Gioseffo 42f., 47, 57
Zelter, Carl Friedrich 76, 79
Zimmermann, Robert 96
Zoltai, Dénes 66

Subject Index

absolute music   86, 97 f., 116, 133
academies   41, 56
acoustics   2, 56, 59, 63, 71–76, 79, 93
acute and grave   5, 12, 17, 22 f., 30, 60, 81, 110
aeolian harp   77 f.
aesthetic idea   66–68
aesthetics of music   138
affects   6, 12, 14, 19, 27 f., 54, 65–70, 80, 95, 122, 132
air   7, 16, 29, 36, 41 f., 45–49, 52, 54, 64, 73, 77, 139
Amphion, myth of   8
analytic philosophy   118, 129, 131
ancient and modern music   2, 5 f., 22, 29, 40 f., 57, 60–62, 78 f., 86, 100, 106 f., 130
angelic choir   34, 108
anthropology   1 f., 6, 40, 47 f., 59, 60 f., 68 f., 91, 105, 113, 115–118, 120
anti-naturalism   109
antirealism   140
Apollo   11, 14, 100, 107, 124, 130
apperception   94
Arion   8
Aristotelianism   6
arousal theory   133 f.
ars   33, 36–38
ars combinatoria   55
ars nova   38
atonal music   141
aulos   14, 16, 18, 100

Berlin school of comparative musicology   120
Bible   8, 30, 47, 58

Cartesianism   73
catharsis   7, 18 f., 129, 140
charm   15, 53, 63–66, 79, 87, 122–124
charme   123
chord   9, 16, 44, 56 f., 59, 91, 113, 128
choreutics   12

chromatic tuning   5, 7, 24
cicadas, myth of   10
classicism   78 f., 137
classification of the arts   2, 20, 37, 47, 49, 64, 67, 77 f., 87 f.
cognitivism   132, 134, 140
consonance   6–9, 17, 23 f., 27, 29, 35, 42 f., 46 f., 49, 51–53, 55 f., 68, 84 f., 92 f., 119
continental philosophy   118
cosmic music   6, 12 f., 16 f., 20, 25, 28 f., 34–37, 39 f., 44 f., 48, 108
counterpoint   38, 41, 108 f.
Croce-Collingwood hypothesis   138
crying   117
cultural value of music   63, 65

dance   2, 5, 12, 26, 30 f., 54, 77, 82, 104, 108
Demiurge, myth of   12, 26
demonic in music   6, 82, 87, 110
diatonic tuning   5, 7, 24
dissonance   41, 47, 49, 51, 54, 56, 84, 93, 106
dorian harmony   5, 14
dualism   79, 128
duration of sounds
Dyonisos

ecclesiastical modes   35
Echo, myth of   1, 48, 78, 114
education   13 f., 17–20, 24 f., 80, 105, 140
Egyptians, music of the   11, 106
emotions   2, 15, 51, 62 f., 82, 102, 130–135, 139 f.
empathy   121
empiricism   7 f.
encyclopedists   58–60
enhanced formalism   131 f.
enharmonic tuning   5, 7, 24, 62, 103
entertainment   17 f., 25, 103
Epicureans   24
Er, myth of   11, 13

Subject Index

ethics 1, 5–8, 11, 13, 15, 17f., 24f., 28f., 32, 48f., 55, 62, 77, 96, 99, 103, 110, 122, 141
ethnomusicology 119
ethos 5–8, 12, 17–20, 22, 24f., 28, 42, 75, 81, 85, 87, 102, 108, 112, 115, 121–123, 125–127, 129f., 135f., 138f.
Eurydice, myth of 7f., 117, 122
experimentation 7, 9, 40, 42f., 45, 49, 56, 63, 73–76, 93
expert listening 12, 14, 18, 87, 90, 103, 109, 122
expression in music 62, 66, 77, 90, 110, 121, 123f., 126, 128, 131, 134, 137–140
expressionism 106
extreme Platonism 136, 138

fantasy 78, 82, 92
feelings 2, 14, 19, 31f., 53f., 56, 60, 64, 67, 69, 71f., 80–83, 88, 90f., 95–99, 102, 104, 108f., 114, 121, 123, 126–130, 132–134, 136, 140
fifth 6f., 9, 23, 27f., 34, 46f., 51, 60, 82, 138
formalism 95f., 114, 132, 138
fourth 6f., 9, 23, 27, 71, 94, 106
Frankfurt School 111
frequency 8, 29, 45–48, 56, 94
fugue 77, 108, 131f.
fundamental bass 57, 84

games 55, 68
German music 101, 104f., 111f., 118
German philosophy 101, 118
Gestalt psychology 94, 129
Glasharmonika 75
Glaucus, myth of 7, 61
grammar 3, 28, 35, 38, 80, 127
gramophone 106, 119, 127

harmonics 5, 21, 34, 57, 75
harmonikoi 21
harmony 5–9, 12–14, 20, 23, 25–28, 30, 34, 36–38, 40, 42, 44–46, 48, 54, 56–60, 62, 66, 72, 75, 79, 83f., 91, 100, 104, 108f.

hearing 2, 13, 16, 20–22, 29, 31, 34, 37, 42, 54, 64, 86, 97, 107, 109
hearing-as 126
heliocentrism 48
hermeneutics 121
history of music 24, 103
humanism 40f.
humanity 112f., 115f., 118

ictus, theory of 42, 45–49, 52–54, 56
ideal objects 120f.
idealism 92, 103, 141
imaginary museum of musical works 137
imagination 51, 55, 65, 67, 80–82, 86, 95, 97, 100, 114, 134, 139
imitation 13, 18–20, 25f., 34, 40, 57, 60, 62, 77, 109
impressionism
ineffability 80, 122–124, 126f., 130, 138
inexpressiveness 123f.
instrumental music 1, 14, 28, 33, 35, 40, 71, 77, 80–83, 90, 97f., 112, 133
intellectualism 54, 114
intentionality 2, 8, 96, 99, 119, 121, 123, 133, 135, 137, 139f.

jazz 115, 131
je-ne-sais-quoi 123
joke 63, 68–70, 122
jubilus 32

language games 127
Lied 71, 133
listening 2, 28, 32, 80, 87, 90, 96, 100, 115, 118f., 121, 123–126, 132, 135, 139
lyre 5, 8, 14, 16, 22f., 100
lyrics 5, 14, 90f., 98, 100

madness 41, 103
magic 12, 14, 20, 40, 79, 82f., 103, 105, 123
marxism 106
master-slave dialectic 89
mathematical ratios 7, 13, 17, 27, 84, 91
mathematics 2f., 6f., 9, 16, 27–29, 36–38, 41–43, 58, 64, 66–68, 73, 79f., 92–94, 97, 107, 109, 115, 119

Subject Index — 167

meaning of music   1, 12, 49, 70, 98, 106, 108, 139
medicine   13 f., 19 f., 40 f., 69, 103, 129
melody   5, 12, 14, 17 f., 21–24, 26, 57, 60, 66, 72, 78 f., 91, 100, 104, 112, 120 f., 139
memory   16, 31, 34
metaphysics   1, 3, 6–8, 29, 37 f., 40, 44, 53 f., 58, 83 f., 87, 98, 110, 114, 122, 128
metrics   5, 21, 28, 30, 34
mixis   17, 119
modulation   9, 16, 29–31, 34, 44, 54, 61, 64, 66, 69, 78
monism   128
monochord   6, 9 f., 27, 76, 93
movement   6 f., 12, 17 f., 20–23, 31, 36 f., 59, 65 f., 68–70, 72, 80, 88, 91 f., 98, 109, 111, 114, 121, 139
movie soundtracks   115
music and history   2, 92, 109, 118
music and language   1 f., 4, 7, 9, 16, 22, 33, 35, 60–63, 65 f., 77, 80–82, 86, 91, 95, 98, 102, 106, 108, 110, 112 f., 118, 121 f., 125–131, 135 f., 139, 141
music and logic   38, 113 f., 122–124, 127
music and philosophy   1, 6, 10 f., 15, 20, 38, 40, 59, 62, 80, 83, 106, 109 f., 112 f., 118, 122 f.
music theory   3, 20, 29, 37, 41, 49, 57, 93
music writing   34, 58 f.
music, definition of   1–3, 5–21, 23–26, 28–45, 48, 50–74, 76–92, 94–142
musical aesthetics   1, 50, 52, 59, 71, 95, 97, 120, 131
musical instruments   5, 14, 16–18, 27, 35, 41 f., 44, 58, 75 f., 93, 103, 107, 125, 137
musical persona, theory of   134
musical space   22 f.
musical subconscious   54
musical temperament   3, 85
musicology   71, 95, 111, 118, 120 f.
mysticism   34, 107, 125

naturalism
neo-Kantianism   93
neo-Pythagoreanism   6, 26 f.
Neoplatonism   15

neue Musik   62, 78, 104–106, 108, 111, 116 f., 131
Newtonian prism   76
Newtonianism   73
nominalism   136, 138
non-filiform bodies   7, 43, 73, 75, 119
nothingness   70, 114, 125
numbers   7, 44

octave   6 f., 9, 23 f., 27, 42–44, 46 f., 49, 52, 85, 120
oneiric character of music   10 f., 25–27, 33, 73, 78, 82, 105, 110, 114
ontology   2, 120 f., 124, 131, 136 f., 139
Opera   40, 83, 97, 103, 108, 133
order   5, 7 f., 10–13, 15–17, 23, 28–31, 34, 40, 42, 47–49, 54, 62, 79, 108, 111, 113, 118, 120–123, 125 f., 132, 134, 139–141
organ   37, 43, 76
origin of music   25, 34, 47, 58, 61, 94, 107
Orpheus, myth of   7 f., 11, 25, 45
Orphism   6

Pan, myth of   41 f., 107
pantomime   56, 82
partial tones   56 f., 59, 73, 75, 93, 120
passions   19, 42, 60, 69, 72, 81, 83, 89, 102 f., 141
pathos   102 f.
perception of sound   36, 46, 53, 64, 68, 92
period performance   137
Peripatetic School   17, 26
phenomenology   7 f., 44, 89, 112, 119 f., 123, 125
philosophy of music   1, 5, 7–9, 20, 78, 83, 92, 102, 110 f., 116–118, 128 f., 131, 142
phonograph   106, 119
Phonographic Archive
phrygian harmony   5, 14
phthongos
physics of sounds   7, 15, 21, 29, 36, 45, 47, 52, 60, 71, 73
physiology of hearing   2, 16, 46 f., 52, 65, 68, 70, 73, 93–95, 97, 99, 103–105, 134
piano   76, 94, 96, 110, 120
pitch   7, 9, 22 f., 27, 29, 46, 50–53, 94

Platonism 26
pleasure 13–15, 18 f., 31, 50, 52–56, 58 f., 68 f., 81–83, 97, 101, 117, 121, 132
poetics 18, 38
politics 14 f., 17, 19, 36, 99
polyphonic music 5, 33, 35, 38, 44
pop music 115
profane music 1, 33
programme music 71, 133
proportion 6 f., 9 f., 16, 26, 38, 45, 50–52, 55–58, 65–67, 79, 97, 107
psychology of music 1 f., 15, 17, 40, 46, 91–95, 97, 113, 115, 118 f., 129
Ptolemaic system 45
Pythagoras's hammers 5, 9, 27, 30, 42 f.
Pythagoreanism 6–8, 12, 16, 20 f., 24, 27 f., 94, 108

quadrivium 28 f., 33 f., 48
querelle des bouffons 60

radio 106, 115
rationalism 73, 112
ratios 6, 8 f., 27, 43 f., 46 f., 51 f., 59, 70, 72, 92 f.
rattle
refrain 31, 96, 123
Renaissance 2, 39 f., 44, 47, 111
repetition 84, 122 f., 132 f.
representation 2, 19, 22, 60, 65, 68, 83 f., 88, 92 f., 95 f., 113–115, 138
resonance 54, 94, 98, 125
resonators 93
resurrection 81
rhythm 2, 5, 12–14, 26, 28, 30 f., 51, 69, 78 f., 91, 108 f.
rhythmic 5, 17, 21, 31, 34, 55, 78 f., 123
rhythms 17 f., 31–33, 53, 104
rock music 131
Romanticism 71, 78, 90
rondo 132
rotating siren 93

savages 58 f., 61 f.
scales 3, 5, 9, 18, 20, 22 f., 35
scepticism 6 f., 25
semiotics 64 f., 67

senario, numero 42
sensation 21 f., 24 f., 47, 60, 63–68, 70, 72, 91–94, 97, 113, 117, 119
sentimentalism 78, 95, 99, 117
silence 22, 37, 115, 119, 123–125
sirens, myth of 117
sonata 77, 108, 110, 132
sound machines 48
sound numbers 36, 40, 42, 45
sound patterns 4, 74–76
sound tremors 72 f., 89
specific energy 94
speech 2, 15, 18, 22, 35, 46, 62, 64–66, 71, 77, 84, 98, 104, 118, 121, 123, 131
Stoics 24 f.
subjectivity 77, 90 f., 106, 110, 116 f.
symbol
symbolism 103, 113, 129 f.
sympathetic resonance 27, 46, 52, 57
synaesthesia 86, 106
Syrinx, myth of 14, 107

temporality 17, 88–90, 92, 120
tertiary properties 139
tetraktys 6
theatrocracy 14, 104
theodicy 54
thing-in-itself 83, 109
third sound 58
timbre 93
tonal fusion 119 f.
tonal music 106, 113, 120, 133, 141
tonal space 139
tonality 141 f.
tone 9, 23, 27, 35, 41, 46 f., 56, 63–66, 69 f., 72 f., 75, 78 f., 81, 84 f., 92 f., 96 f., 119, 126, 135, 139, 141
tragedy 7, 11, 18 f., 60 f., 100 f.
transcendental philosophy 76 f., 108
trembling 81, 87, 89
trivium 28, 33, 38
tunings 5

unison 47, 49
utopia 2, 106, 108, 110

variety 42, 50, 52–54, 132

vibrating string 6, 9, 22, 27, 42–46, 48, 52, 56, 59, 72f., 75–79, 94
virtuosity 18, 116
vocal music 1, 12, 16, 21, 33, 58, 81, 98, 112, 116
voice 7, 12, 15, 21
voice, articulated 15–17, 20, 35, 41
voice, continuous and discontinuous 22, 27

Wagnerism 103f., 120
wisdom 12, 45, 101
Witz 70